NO PLACE TO HIDE

ALSO BY GLENN GREENWALD

How Would a Patriot Act?

A Tragic Legacy

Great American Hypocrites

With Liberty and Justice for Some

NO PLACE TO HIDE

EDWARD SNOWDEN, THE NSA AND THE SURVEILLANCE STATE

GLENN GREENWALD

HAMISH HAMILTON
an imprint of
PENGUIN BOOKS

HAMISH HAMILTON

Published by the Penguin Group
Penguin Books Ltd, 80 Strand, London WC2R ORL, England
Penguin Group (USA) Inc., 375 Hudson Street, New York, New York 10014, USA
Penguin Group (Canada), 90 Eglinton Avenue East, Suite 700, Toronto, Ontario, Canada M4P 2Y3
(a division of Pearson Penguin Canada Inc.)
Penguin Ireland, 25 St Stephen's Green, Dublin 2, Ireland (a division of Penguin Books Ltd)
Penguin Group (Australia), 707 Collins Street, Melbourne, Victoria 3008, Australia
(a division of Pearson Australia Group Pty Ltd)
Penguin Books India Pvt Ltd, 11 Community Centre,
Panchsheel Park, New Delhi – 110 017, India
Penguin Group (NZ), 67 Apollo Drive, Rosedale, North Shore 0632, New Zealand
(a division of Pearson New Zealand Ltd)
Penguin Books (South Africa) (Pty) Ltd, Block D, Rosebank Office Park,
181 Jan Smuts Avenue, Parktown North, Gauteng 2193, South Africa

Penguin Books Ltd, Registered Offices: 80 Strand, London WC2R ORL, England

www.penguin.com

First published in the United States of America by Metropolitan Books,
Henry Holt and Company LLC 2014
First published in Great Britain by Hamish Hamilton 2014
002

Copyright © Glenn Greenwald, 2014

The moral right of the author has been asserted

Printed in Great Britain by Clays Ltd, St Ives plc

A CIP catalogue record for this book is available from the British Library

HARDBACK ISBN: 978-0-241-14669-9
TRADE PAPERBACK ISBN: 978-0-241-14670-5

www.greenpenguin.co.uk

Penguin Books is committed to a sustainable
future for our business, our readers and our planet.
This book is made from Forest Stewardship
Council™ certified paper.

This book is dedicated to all those who have sought
to shine a light on the US government's secret
mass surveillance systems, particularly the courageous
whistle-blowers who have risked their liberty to do so.

The United States government has perfected a technological capability that enables us to monitor the messages that go through the air. . . . That capability at any time could be turned around on the American people, and no American would have any privacy left, such is the capability to monitor everything—telephone conversations, telegrams, it doesn't matter. There would be no place to hide.

—Senator Frank Church, Chair, Senate Select Committee to Study
Governmental Operations with Respect to Intelligence Activities, 1975

CONTENTS

INTRODUCTION

In the fall of 2005, without much in the way of grandiose expectations, I decided to create a political blog. I had little idea at the time how much this decision would eventually change my life. My principal motive was that I was becoming increasingly alarmed by the radical and extremist theories of power the US government had adopted in the wake of 9/11, and I hoped that writing about such issues might allow me to make a broader impact than I could in my then-career as a constitutional and civil rights lawyer.

Just seven weeks after I began blogging, the *New York Times* dropped a bombshell: in 2001, it reported, the Bush administration had secretly ordered the National Security Agency (NSA) to eavesdrop on the electronic communications of Americans without obtaining the warrants required by relevant criminal law. At the time that it was revealed, this warrantless eavesdropping had been going on for four years and had targeted at least several thousand Americans.

The subject was a perfect convergence of my passions and my expertise. The government tried to justify the secret NSA program by invoking exactly the kind of extreme theory of executive power that had motivated me to begin writing: the notion that the threat of terrorism vested the president with virtually unlimited authority to do anything to "keep the nation safe," including the authority to break the law. The ensuing debate entailed complex questions of constitutional law and statutory interpretation, which my legal background rendered me well suited to address.

I spent the next two years covering every aspect of the NSA warrantless wiretapping scandal, on my blog and in a bestselling 2006 book. My position was straightforward: by ordering illegal eavesdropping, the president had committed crimes and should be held accountable for them. In America's increasingly jingoistic and oppressive political climate, this proved to be an intensely controversial stance.

It was this background that prompted Edward Snowden, several years later, to choose me as his first contact person for revealing NSA wrongdoing on an even more massive scale. He said he believed I could be counted on to understand the dangers of mass surveillance and extreme state secrecy, and not to back down in the face of pressure from the government and its many allies in the media and elsewhere.

The remarkable volume of top secret documents that Snowden passed on to me, along with the high drama surrounding Snowden himself, have generated unprecedented worldwide interest in the menace of mass electronic surveillance and the value of privacy in the digital age. But the underlying problems have been festering for years, largely in the dark.

There are, to be sure, many unique aspects to the current NSA controversy. Technology has now enabled a type of ubiquitous surveillance that had previously been the province of only the most imaginative science fiction writers. Moreover, the post-9/11 American veneration of security above all else has created a climate particularly conducive to abuses of power. And thanks to Snowden's bravery and the relative ease of copying digital information, we have an unparalleled firsthand look at the details of how the surveillance system actually operates.

Still, in many respects the issues raised by the NSA story resonate with numerous episodes from the past, stretching back across the centuries. Indeed, opposition to government invasion of privacy was a major factor in the establishment of the United States itself, as American colonists protested laws that let British officials ransack at will any home they wished. It was legitimate, the colonists agreed, for the state to obtain specific, targeted warrants to search individuals when there was evidence

to establish probable cause of their wrongdoing. But general warrants—
the practice of making the entire citizenry subject to indiscriminate
searches—were inherently illegitimate.

The Fourth Amendment enshrined this idea in American law. Its
language is clear and succinct: "The right of the people to be secure in
their persons, houses, papers, and effects, against unreasonable searches
and seizures, shall not be violated, and no warrants shall issue, but upon
probable cause, supported by oath or affirmation, and particularly describing the place to be searched, and the persons or things to be seized."
It was intended, above all, to abolish forever in America the power of the
government to subject its citizens to generalized, suspicionless surveillance.

The clash over surveillance in the eighteenth century focused on
house searches, but as technology evolved, surveillance evolved with it.
In the mid-nineteenth century, as the spread of railways began to allow
for cheap and rapid mail delivery, the British government's surreptitious
opening of mail caused a major scandal in the UK. By the early decades
of the twentieth century, the US Bureau of Investigation—the precur-
sor of today's FBI—was using wiretaps, along with mail monitoring and
informants, to clamp down on those opposed to American government
policies.

No matter the specific techniques involved, historically mass surveillance has had several constant attributes. Initially, it is always the country's dissidents and marginalized who bear the brunt of the surveillance,
leading those who support the government or are merely apathetic to
mistakenly believe they are immune. And history shows that the mere
existence of a mass surveillance apparatus, regardless of how it is used, is
in itself sufficient to stifle dissent. A citizenry that is aware of always being watched quickly becomes a compliant and fearful one.

Frank Church's mid-1970s investigation into the FBI's spying shockingly found that the agency had labeled half a million US citizens as potential "subversives," routinely spying on people based purely on their
political beliefs. (The FBI's list of targets ranged from Martin Luther King
to John Lennon, from the women's liberation movement to the anti-
Communist John Birch Society.) But the plague of surveillance abuse is

hardly unique to American history. On the contrary, mass surveillance is a universal temptation for any unscrupulous power. And in every instance, the motive is the same: suppressing dissent and mandating compliance.

Surveillance thus unites governments of otherwise remarkably divergent political creeds. At the turn of the twentieth century, the British and French empires both created specialized monitoring departments to deal with the threat of anticolonialist movements. After World War II, the East German Ministry of State Security, popularly known as the Stasi, became synonymous with government intrusion into personal lives. And more recently, as popular protests during the Arab Spring challenged dictators' grasp on power, the regimes in Syria, Egypt, and Libya all sought to spy on the Internet use of domestic dissenters.

Investigations by Bloomberg News and the *Wall Street Journal* have shown that as these dictatorships were overwhelmed by protestors, they literally went shopping for surveillance tools from Western technology companies. Syria's Assad regime flew in employees from the Italian surveillance company Area SpA, who were told that the Syrians "urgently needed to track people." In Egypt, Mubarak's secret police bought tools to penetrate Skype encryption and eavesdrop on activists' calls. And in Libya, the *Journal* reported, journalists and rebels who entered a government monitoring center in 2011 found "a wall of black refrigerator-size devices" from the French surveillance company Amesys. The equipment "inspected the Internet traffic" of Libya's main Internet service provider, "opening emails, divining passwords, snooping on online chats and mapping connections among various suspects."

The ability to eavesdrop on people's communications vests immense power in those who do it. And unless such power is held in check by rigorous oversight and accountability, it is almost certain to be abused. Expecting the US government to operate a massive surveillance machine in complete secrecy without falling prey to its temptations runs counter to every historical example and all available evidence about human nature.

Indeed, even before Snowden's revelations, it was already becoming clear that treating the United States as somehow exceptional on the issue of surveillance is a highly naive stance. In 2006, at a congressional hearing titled "The Internet in China: A Tool for Freedom or Suppression?," speakers lined up to condemn American technology companies for helping China suppress dissent on the Internet. Christopher Smith (R-NJ), the congressman presiding over the hearing, likened Yahoo!'s cooperation with Chinese secret police to handing Anne Frank over to the Nazis. It was a full-throated harangue, a typical performance when American officials speak about a regime not aligned with the United States.

But even the congressional attendees couldn't help noting that the hearing happened to take place just two months after the *New York Times* revealed the vast warrantless domestic wiretapping carried out by the Bush administration. In light of those revelations, denouncing other countries for carrying out their own domestic surveillance rang rather hollow. Representative Brad Sherman (D-CA), speaking after Representative Smith, noted that the technology companies being told to resist the Chinese regime should also be careful regarding their own government. "Otherwise," he warned prophetically, "while those in China may see their privacy violated in the most heinous ways, we here in the United States may also find that perhaps some future president asserting these very broad interpretations of the Constitution is reading our e-mail, and I would prefer that not happen without a court order."

Over the past decades, the fear of terrorism—stoked by consistent exaggerations of the actual threat—has been exploited by US leaders to justify a wide array of extremist policies. It has led to wars of aggression, a worldwide torture regime, and the detention (and even assassination) of both foreign nationals and American citizens without any charges. But the ubiquitous, secretive system of suspicionless surveillance that it has spawned may very well turn out to be its most enduring legacy. This is so because, despite all the historical parallels, there is also a genuinely new dimension to the current NSA surveillance scandal: the role now played by the Internet in daily life.

Especially for the younger generation, the Internet is not some standalone, separate domain where a few of life's functions are carried out. It is not merely our post office and our telephone. Rather, it is the epicenter of our world, the place where virtually everything is done. It is where friends are made, where books and films are chosen, where political activism is organized, where the most private data is created and stored. It is where we develop and express our very personality and sense of self.

To turn *that* network into a system of mass surveillance has implications unlike those of any previous state surveillance programs. All the prior spying systems were by necessity more limited and capable of being evaded. To permit surveillance to take root on the Internet would mean subjecting virtually all forms of human interaction, planning, and even thought itself to comprehensive state examination.

From the time that it first began to be widely used, the Internet has been seen by many as possessing an extraordinary potential: the ability to liberate hundreds of millions of people by democratizing political discourse and leveling the playing field between the powerful and the powerless. Internet freedom—the ability to use the network without institutional constraints, social or state control, and pervasive fear—is central to the fulfillment of that promise. Converting the Internet into a system of surveillance thus guts it of its core potential. Worse, it turns the Internet into a tool of repression, threatening to produce the most extreme and oppressive weapon of state intrusion human history has ever seen.

That's what makes Snowden's revelations so stunning and so vitally important. By daring to expose the NSA's astonishing surveillance capabilities and its even more astounding ambitions, he has made it clear, with these disclosures, that we stand at a historic crossroads. Will the digital age usher in the individual liberation and political freedoms that the Internet is uniquely capable of unleashing? Or will it bring about a system of omnipresent monitoring and control, beyond the dreams of even the greatest tyrants of the past? Right now, either path is possible. Our actions will determine where we end up.

1

CONTACT

On December 1, 2012, I received my first communication from Edward Snowden, although I had no idea at the time that it was from him.

The contact came in the form of an email from someone calling himself Cincinnatus, a reference to Lucius Quinctius Cincinnatus, the Roman farmer who, in the fifth century BC, was appointed dictator of Rome to defend the city against attack. He is most remembered for what he did after vanquishing Rome's enemies: he immediately and voluntarily gave up political power and returned to farming life. Hailed as a "model of civic virtue," Cincinnatus has become a symbol of the use of political power in the public interest and the worth of limiting or even relinquishing individual power for the greater good.

The email began: "The security of people's communications is very important to me," and its stated purpose was to urge me to begin using PGP encryption so that "Cincinnatus" could communicate things in which, he said, he was certain I would be interested. Invented in 1991, PGP stands for "pretty good privacy." It has been developed into a sophisticated tool to shield email and other forms of online communications from surveillance and hacking.

The program essentially wraps every email in a protective shield, which is a code composed of hundreds, or even thousands, of random

numbers and case-sensitive letters. The most advanced intelligence agencies around the world—a class that certainly includes the National Security Agency—possess password-cracking software capable of one billion
guesses per second. But so lengthy and random are these PGP encryption codes that even the most sophisticated software requires many years
to break them. People who most fear having their communications monitored, such as intelligence operatives, spies, human rights activists, and
hackers, trust this form of encryption to protect their messages.

In this email, "Cincinnatus" said he had searched everywhere for my
PGP "public key," a unique code set that allows people to receive encrypted email, but could not find it. From this, he concluded that I was
not using the program and told me, "That puts anyone who communicates with you at risk. I'm not arguing that every communication you are
involved in be encrypted, but you should at least provide communicants
with that option."

"Cincinnatus" then referenced the sex scandal of General David Petraeus, whose career-ending extramarital affair with journalist Paula
Broadwell was discovered when investigators found Google emails between the two. Had Petraeus encrypted his messages before handing
them over to Gmail or storing them in his drafts folder, he wrote, investigators would not have been able to read them. "Encryption matters, and
it is not just for spies and philanderers." Installing encrypted email, he
said, "is a critically-necessary security measure for anyone who wishes to
communicate with you."

To motivate me to follow his advice, he added, "There are people out
there you would like to hear from who will never be able to contact you
without knowing their messages cannot be read in transit."

Then he offered to help me install the program: "If you need any help
at all with this, please let me know, or alternately request help on Twitter.
You have many technically-proficient followers who are willing to offer
immediate assistance." He signed off: "Thank you. C."

Using encryption software was something I had long intended to
do. I had been writing for years about WikiLeaks, whistle-blowers, the
hacktivist collective known as Anonymous, and related topics, and had
also communicated from time to time with people inside the US national

security establishment. Most of them are very concerned about the security of their communications and preventing unwanted monitoring. But the program is complicated, especially for someone who had very little skill in programming and computers, like me. So it was one of those things I had never gotten around to doing.

C.'s email did not move me to action. Because I had become known for covering stories the rest of the media often ignores, I frequently hear from all sorts of people offering me a "huge story," and it usually turns out to be nothing. And at any given moment I am usually working on more stories than I can handle. So I need something concrete to make me drop what I'm doing in order to pursue a new lead. Despite the vague allusion to "people out there" I "would like to hear from," there was nothing in C.'s email that I found sufficiently enticing. I read it but did not reply.

Three days later, I heard from C. again, asking me to confirm receipt of the first email. This time I replied quickly. "I got this and am going to work on it. I don't have a PGP code, and don't know how to do that, but I will try to find someone who can help me."

C. replied later that day with a clear, step-by-step guide to the PGP system: Encryption for Dummies, in essence. At the end of the instructions, which I found complex and confusing, mostly due to my own ignorance, he said these were just "the barest basics. If you can't find anyone to walk you through installation, generation, and use," he added, "please let me know. I can facilitate contact with people who understand crypto almost anywhere in the world."

This email ended with more a pointed sign-off: "Cryptographically yours, Cincinnatus."

Despite my intentions, I never created the time to work on encryption. Seven weeks went by, and my failure to do this weighed a bit on my mind. What if this person really did have an important story, one I would miss just because I failed to install a computer program? Apart from anything else, I knew encryption might be valuable in the future, even if Cincinnatus turned out to have nothing of interest.

On January 28, 2013, I emailed C. to say that I would get someone to help me with encryption and hopefully would have it done within the next day or so.

C. replied the next day: "That's great news! If you need any further help or have questions in the future, you will always be welcome to reach out. Please accept my sincerest thanks for your support of communications privacy! Cincinnatus."

But yet again, I did nothing, consumed as I was at the time with other stories, and still unconvinced that C. had anything worthwhile to say. There was no conscious decision to do nothing. It was simply that on my always too-long list of things to take care of, installing encryption technology at the behest of this unknown person never became pressing enough for me to stop other things and focus on it.

C. and I thus found ourselves in a Catch-22. He was unwilling to tell me anything specific about what he had, or even who he was and where he worked, unless I installed encryption. But without the enticement of specifics, it was not a priority to respond to his request and take the time to install the program.

In the face of my inaction, C. stepped up his efforts. He produced a ten-minute video entitled *PGP for Journalists*. Using software that generates a computer voice, the video instructed me in an easy, step-by-step fashion how to install encryption software, complete with charts and visuals.

Still I did nothing. It was at that point that C., as he later told me, become frustrated. "Here am I," he thought, "ready to risk my liberty, perhaps even my life, to hand this guy thousands of Top Secret documents from the nation's most secretive agency—a leak that will produce dozens if not hundreds of huge journalistic scoops. And he can't even be bothered to install an encryption program."

That's how close I came to blowing off one of the largest and most consequential national security leaks in US history.

The next I heard of any of this was ten weeks later. On April 18, I flew from my home in Rio de Janeiro to New York, where I was scheduled to give some talks on the dangers of government secrecy and civil liberties abuses done in the name of the War on Terror.

On landing at JFK Airport, I saw that I had an email message from

Laura Poitras, the documentary filmmaker, which read: "Any chance you'll be in the US this coming week? I'd love to touch base about something, though best to do in person."

I take seriously any message from Laura Poitras. One of the most focused, fearless, and independent individuals I've ever known, she has made film after film in the riskiest of circumstances, with no crew or the support of a news organization, just a modest budget, one camera, and her determination. At the height of the worst violence of the Iraq War, she ventured into the Sunni Triangle to make *My Country, My Country*, an unflinching look at life under US occupation that was nominated for an Academy award.

For her next film, *The Oath*, Poitras traveled to Yemen, where she spent months following two Yemeni men—Osama bin Laden's bodyguard as well as his driver. Since then, Poitras has been working on a documentary about NSA surveillance. The three films, conceived as a trilogy about US conduct during the War on Terror, made her a constant target of harassment by government authorities every time she entered or left the country.

Through Laura, I learned a valuable lesson. By the time we first met, in 2010, she had been detained in airports by the Department of Homeland Security more than three dozen times as she entered the United States—interrogated, threatened, her materials seized, including her laptop, cameras, and notebooks. Yet she repeatedly decided not to go public with the relentless harassment, fearing that the repercussions would make her work impossible. That changed after an unusually abusive interrogation at Newark Liberty International Airport. Laura had had enough. "It's getting worse, not better, from my being silent." She was ready for me to write about it.

The article I published in the online political magazine *Salon* detailing the constant interrogations to which Poitras had been subjected received substantial attention, drawing statements of support and denunciations of the harassment. The next time Poitras flew out of the United States after the article ran, there was no interrogation and she did not have her materials seized. Over the next couple of months, there was no harassment. For the first time in years, Laura was able to travel freely.

The lesson for me was clear: national security officials do not like the light. They act abusively and thuggishly only when they believe they are safe, in the dark. Secrecy is the linchpin of abuse of power, we discovered, its enabling force. Transparency is the only real antidote.

At JFK, reading Laura's email, I replied immediately: "Actually, just got to the US this morning. . . . Where are you?" We arranged a meeting for the next day, in the lobby at my hotel in Yonkers, a Marriott, and found seats in the restaurant, At Laura's insistence, we moved tables twice before beginning our conversation to be sure that nobody could hear us. Laura then got down to business. She had an "extremely important and sensitive matter" to discuss, she said, and security was critical.

Since I had my cell phone with me, Laura asked that I either remove the battery or leave it in my hotel room. "It sounds paranoid," she said, but the government has the capability to activate cell phones and laptops remotely as eavesdropping devices. Powering off the phone or laptop does not defeat the capability: only removing the battery does. I'd heard this before from transparency activists and hackers but tended to write it off as excess caution, but this time I took it seriously because it came from Laura. After discovering that the battery on my cell phone could not be removed, I took it back to my room, then returned to the restaurant.

Now Laura began to talk. She had received a series of anonymous emails from someone who seemed both honest and serious. He claimed to have access to some extremely secret and incriminating documents about the US government spying on its own citizens and on the rest of the world. He was determined to leak these documents to her and had specifically requested that she work with me on releasing and reporting on them. I made no connection at the time to the long-since-forgotten emails I had received from Cincinnatus months earlier. They had been parked at the back of my mind, out of view.

Laura then pulled several pages out of her purse from two of the emails sent by the anonymous leaker, and I read them at the table from start to finish. They were riveting.

The second of the emails, sent weeks after the first, began: "Still here."

With regard to the question at the forefront of my mind—when would he be ready to furnish documents?—he had written, "All I can say is 'soon.'"

After urging her to always remove batteries from cell phones before talking about sensitive matters—or, at least, to put the phones in the freezer, where their eavesdropping capability would be impeded—the leaker told Laura that she should work with me on these documents. He then got to the crux of what he viewed as his mission:

> The shock of this initial period [after the first revelations] will provide the support needed to build a more equal internet, but this will not work to the advantage of the average person unless science outpaces law. By understanding the mechanisms through which our privacy is violated, we can win here. We can guarantee for all people equal protection against unreasonable search through universal laws, but only if the technical community is willing to face the threat and commit to implementing over-engineered solutions. In the end, we must enforce a principle whereby the only way the powerful may enjoy privacy is when it is the same kind shared by the ordinary: one enforced by the laws of nature, rather than the policies of man.

"He's real," I said when I finished reading. "I can't explain exactly why, but I just feel intuitively that this is serious, that he's exactly who he says he is."

"So do I," Laura replied. "I have very little doubt."

Reasonably and rationally, Laura and I knew that our faith in the leaker's veracity might have been misplaced. We had no idea who was writing to her. He could have been anyone. He could have been inventing the entire tale. This also could have been some sort of plot by the government to entrap us into collaborating with a criminal leak. Or perhaps it had come from someone who sought to damage our credibility by passing on fraudulent documents to publish.

We discussed all these possibilities. We knew that a 2008 secret report by the US Army had declared WikiLeaks an enemy of the state and proposed ways to "damage and potentially destroy" the organization. The report (ironically leaked to WikiLeaks) discussed the possibility of passing on fraudulent documents. If WikiLeaks published them as authentic, it would suffer a serious blow to its credibility.

Laura and I were aware of all the pitfalls but we discounted them, relying instead on our intuition. Something intangible yet powerful about those emails convinced us that their author was genuine. He wrote out of a belief in the dangers of government secrecy and pervasive spying; I instinctively recognized his political passion. I felt a kinship with our correspondent, with his worldview, and with the sense of urgency that was clearly consuming him.

Over the past seven years, I had been driven by the same conviction, writing almost on a daily basis about the dangerous trends in US state secrecy, radical executive power theories, detention and surveillance abuses, militarism, and the assault on civil liberties. There is a particular tone and attitude that unites journalists, activists, and readers of mine, people who are equally alarmed by these trends. It would be difficult, I reasoned, for someone who did not truly believe and feel this alarm to replicate it so accurately, with such authenticity.

In one of the last passages of Laura's emails, her correspondent wrote that he was completing the final steps necessary to provide us with the documents. He needed another four to six weeks, and we should wait to hear from him. He assured us that we would.

Three days later, Laura and I met again, this time in Manhattan, and with another email from the anonymous leaker, in which he explained why he was willing to risk his liberty, to subject himself to the high likelihood of a very lengthy prison term, in order to disclose these documents. Now I was even more convinced: our source was for real, but as I told my partner, David Miranda, on the flight home to Brazil, I was determined to put the whole thing out of my mind. "It may not happen. He could change his mind. He could get caught." David is a person of powerful intuition, and he was weirdly certain. "It's real. He's real. It's going to happen," he declared. "And it's going to be huge."

After returning to Rio, I heard nothing for three weeks. I spent almost no time thinking about the source because all I could do was wait. Then, on May 11, I received an email from a tech expert with whom Laura and I had worked in the past. His words were cryptic but his meaning clear: "Hey Glenn, I'm following up with learning to use PGP. Do you have an address I can mail you something to help you get started next week?"

I was sure that the something he wanted to send was what I needed to begin working on the leaker's documents. That, in turn, meant Laura had heard from our anonymous emailer and received what we had been waiting for.

The tech person then sent a package via Federal Express, scheduled to arrive in two days. I did not know what to expect: a program, or the documents themselves? For the next forty-eight hours, it was impossible to focus on anything else. But on the day of scheduled delivery, 5:30 p.m. came and went and nothing arrived. I called FedEx and was told that the package was being held in customs for "unknown reasons." Two days went by. Then five. Then a full week. Every day FedEx said the same thing—that the package was being held in customs, for reasons unknown.

I briefly entertained the suspicion that some government authority—American, Brazilian, or otherwise—was responsible for this delay because they knew something, but I held on to the far likelier explanation that it was just one of those coincidental bureaucratic annoyances.

By this point, Laura was very reluctant to discuss any of this by phone or online, so I didn't know what exactly was in the package.

Finally, roughly ten days after the package had been sent to me, FedEx delivered it. I tore open the envelope and found two USB thumb drives, along with a typewritten note containing detailed instructions for using various computer programs designed to provide maximum security, as well as numerous passphrases to encrypted email accounts and other programs I had never heard of.

I had no idea what all this meant. I had never heard of these specific programs before, although I knew about passphrases, basically long passwords containing randomly arranged case-sensitive letters and punctuation, designed to make them difficult to crack. With Poitras deeply reluctant to talk by phone or online, I was still frustrated: finally in possession of what I was waiting for, but with no clue where it would lead me.

I was about to find out, from the best possible guide.

The day after the package arrived, during the week of May 20, Laura told me we needed to speak urgently, but only through OTR (off-the-record) chat, an encrypted instrument for talking online securely. I had used OTR previously, and managed to install the chat program, signed up for an account, and added Laura's user name to my "buddy list." She showed up instantly.

I asked about whether I now had access to the secret documents. They would only come to me from the source, she told me, not from her. Laura then added some startling new information, that we might have to travel to Hong Kong immediately, to meet our source. Now I was baffled. What was someone with access to top secret US government documents doing in Hong Kong? I had assumed that our anonymous source was in Maryland or northern Virginia. What did Hong Kong have to do with any of this? I was willing to travel anywhere, of course, but I wanted more information about why I was going. But Laura's inability to speak freely forced us to postpone that discussion.

She asked whether I'd be willing to travel to Hong Kong within the next few days. I wanted to be certain that this would be worthwhile, meaning: Had she obtained verification that this source was real? She cryptically replied, "Of course, I wouldn't ask you to go to Hong Kong if I hadn't." I assumed this meant she had received some serious documents from the source.

But she also told me about a brewing problem. The source was upset by how things had gone thus far, particularly about a new turn: the possible involvement of the *Washington Post*. Laura said it was critical that I speak to him directly, to assure him and placate his growing concerns.

Within an hour, the source himself emailed me.

This email came from Verax@▓▓▓▓▓▓▓▓▓. *Verax* means "truth teller" in Latin. The subject line read, "Need to talk."

"I've been working on a major project with a mutual friend of ours," the email began, letting me know that it was he, the anonymous source, clearly referring to his contacts with Laura.

"You recently had to decline short-term travel to meet with me. You need to be involved in this story," he wrote. "Is there any way we can talk on short notice? I understand you don't have much in the way of secure infrastructure, but I'll work around what you have." He suggested that we speak via OTR and provided his user name.

I was uncertain what he had meant about "declining short-term travel": I had expressed confusion about why he was in Hong Kong but certainly hadn't refused to go. I chalked that up to miscommunication and replied immediately. "I want to do everything possible to be involved in this," I told him, suggesting that we talk right away on OTR. I added his user name to my OTR buddy list and waited.

Within fifteen minutes, my computer sounded a bell-like chime, signaling that he had signed on. Slightly nervous, I clicked on his name and typed "hello." He answered, and I found myself speaking directly to someone who I assumed had, at that point, revealed a number of secret documents about US surveillance programs and who wanted to reveal more.

Right off the bat, I told him I was absolutely committed to the story. "I'm willing to do what I have to do to report this," I said. The source—whose name, place of employment, age, and all other attributes were still unknown to me—asked if I would come to Hong Kong to meet him. I did not ask why he was in Hong Kong; I wanted to avoid appearing to be fishing for information.

Indeed, from the start I decided I would let him take the lead. If he wanted me to know why he was in Hong Kong, he would tell me. And if he wanted me to know what documents he had and planned to provide me, he would tell me that, too. This passive posture was difficult for me. As a former litigator and current journalist, I'm accustomed to aggressive questioning when I want answers, and I had hundreds of things I wanted to ask.

But I assumed his situation was delicate. Whatever else was true, I knew that this person had resolved to carry out what the US government would consider a very serious crime. It was clear from how concerned he was with secure communications that discretion was vital. And, I reasoned,—since I had so little information about whom I was talking to, about his thinking, his motives and fears—that caution and restraint on my part were imperative. I did not want to scare him off, so I forced myself to let the information come to me rather than trying to grab it.

"Of course I'll come to Hong Kong," I said, still having no idea why he was there, of all places, or why he wanted me to go there.

We spoke online that day for two hours. His first concern was what was happening with some of the NSA documents that, with his consent, Poitras had talked about to a *Washington Post* reporter, Barton Gellman. The documents pertained to one specific story about a program called PRISM, which allowed the NSA to collect private communications from the world's largest Internet companies, including Facebook, Google, Yahoo!, and Skype.

Rather than report the story quickly and aggressively, the *Washington Post* had assembled a large team of lawyers who were making all kinds of demands and issuing all sorts of dire warnings. To the source, this signaled that the *Post*, handed what he believed was an unprecedented journalistic opportunity, was being driven by fear rather than conviction and determination. He was also livid that the *Post* had involved so many people, afraid that these discussions might jeopardize his security.

"I don't like how this is developing," he told me. "I had wanted someone else to do this one story abut PRISM so you could focus on the broader archive, especially the mass domestic spying, but now I really want you to be the one to report this. I've been reading you a long time," he said, "and I know you'll be aggressive and fearless in how you do this."

"I'm ready and eager," I told him. "Let's decide now what I need to do."

"The first order of business is for you to get to Hong Kong," he said. He returned to that again and again: *come to Hong Kong immediately.*

The other significant topic we discussed in that first online conversation was his goal. I knew from the emails Laura had shown me that he felt compelled to tell the world about the massive spying apparatus the US government was secretly building. But what did he hope to achieve?

"I want to spark a worldwide debate about privacy, Internet freedom, and the dangers of state surveillance," he said. "I'm not afraid of what will happen to me. I've accepted that my life will likely be over from my doing this. I'm at peace with that. I know it's the right thing to do."

He then said something startling: "I want to identify myself as the person behind these disclosures. I believe I have an obligation to explain why I'm doing this and what I hope to achieve." He told me he had written a document that he wanted to post on the Internet when he outed himself as the source, a pro-privacy, anti-surveillance manifesto for people around the world to sign, showing that there was global support for protecting privacy.

Despite the near-certain costs of outing himself—a lengthy prison term if not worse—he was, the source said again and again, "at peace" with those consequences. "I only have one fear in doing all of this," he said, which is "that people will see these documents and shrug, that they'll say, 'we assumed this was happening and don't care.' The only thing I'm worried about is that I'll do all this to my life for nothing."

"I seriously doubt that will happen," I assured him, but I wasn't convinced I really believed that. I knew from my years of writing about NSA abuses that it can be hard to generate serious concern about secret state surveillance: invasion of privacy and abuse of power can be viewed as abstractions, ones that are difficult to get people to care about viscerally. What's more, the issue of surveillance is invariably complex, making it even harder to engage the public in a widespread way.

But this felt different. The media pays attention when top secret documents are leaked. And the fact that the warning was coming from someone on the inside of the national security apparatus—rather than an American Civil Liberties Union lawyer or a civil liberties advocate—surely meant that it would have added weight.

That night, I talked to David about going to Hong Kong. I was still reluctant to drop all of my work to fly to the other side of the world to meet someone I knew nothing about, not even his name, particularly since I had no real evidence that he was who he said he was. It could be a complete waste of time—or entrapment or some other weird plot.

"You should tell him that you want to see a few documents first to know that he's serious and that this is worth it for you," David suggested.

As usual, I took his advice. When I signed on to OTR the next morning, I said I was planning to leave for Hong Kong within days but first wanted to see some documents so that I understood the types of disclosures he was prepared to make.

To do that, he told me again to install various programs. I then spent a couple of days online as the source walked me through, step by step, how to install and use each program, including, finally, PGP encryption. Knowing that I was a beginner, he exhibited great patience, literally on the level of "Click the blue button, now press OK, now go to the next screen."

I kept apologizing for my lack of proficiency, for having to take hours of his time to teach me the most basic aspects of secure communication. "No worries," he said, "most of this makes little sense. And I have a lot of free time right now."

Once the programs were all in place, I received a file containing roughly twenty-five documents: "Just a very small taste: the tip of the tip of the iceberg," he tantalizingly explained.

I un-zipped the file, saw the list of documents, and randomly clicked on one of them. At the top of the page in red letters, a code appeared: "TOP SECRET//COMINT/NOFORN/."

This meant the document had been legally designated top secret, pertained to communications intelligence (COMINT), and was not for distribution to foreign nationals, including international organizations or coalition partners (NOFORN). There it was with incontrovertible clarity: a highly confidential communication from the NSA, one of the most secretive agencies in the world's most powerful government. Nothing of this significance had ever been leaked from the NSA, not in all the six-decade history of the agency. I now had a couple dozen such items in my possession. And the person I had spent hours chatting with over the last two days had many, many more to give me.

That first document was a training manual for NSA officials to teach analysts about new surveillance capabilities. It discussed in broad terms the type of information the analysts could query (email addresses, IP [Internet protocol] locator data, telephone numbers) and the type of data they would receive in response (email content, telephone "metadata," chat logs). Basically, I was eavesdropping on NSA officials as they instructed their analysts on how to listen in on their targets.

My heart was racing. I had to stop reading and walk around my house a few times to take in what I had just seen and calm myself enough to focus on reading the files. I went back to my laptop and randomly clicked on the next document, a top secret PowerPoint presentation, entitled "PRISM/US-984XN Overview." Each page bore the logos of nine of the largest Internet companies, including Google, Facebook, Skype, and Yahoo!.

The first slides laid out a program under which the NSA had what it called "collection directly from the servers of these U.S. Service Providers: Microsoft, Yahoo, Google, Facebook, Paltalk, AOL, Skype, YouTube, Apple." A graph displayed the dates on which each of these companies had joined the program.

Again I became so excited, I had to stop reading.

The source also said he was sending me a large file that I would be unable to access until the time was right. I decided to set aside that cryptic though significant statement for the moment, in line with my approach of letting him decide when I got information but also because I was so excited by what I had in front of me.

From the first glimpse I'd had of just these few documents, I knew two things: I needed to get to Hong Kong right away, and I would have to have substantial institutional support to do this reporting. This meant involving the *Guardian*, the newspaper and online news website that I had joined as a daily columnist only nine months earlier. Now I was about to bring them in to what I knew already would be a major explosive story.

Using Skype, I called Janine Gibson, the British editor in chief of the US edition of the *Guardian*. My agreement with the *Guardian* was that I had full editorial independence, which meant that nobody could edit or even review my articles before they ran. I wrote my pieces, and then published them directly to the Internet myself. The only exceptions to this arrangement were that I would alert them if my writing could have legal consequences for the newspaper or posed an unusual journalistic quandary. That had happened very few times in the previous nine months, only once or twice, which meant that I had had very little interaction with the *Guardian* editors.

Obviously, if any story warranted a heads-up, it was this one. Also, I knew I would need the paper's resources and support.

"Janine, I have a huge story," I plunged in. "I have a source who has access to what seems to be a large amount of top secret documents from the NSA. He's given me a few already, and they're shocking. But he says he has many, many more. For some reason, he's in Hong Kong, I have no idea why yet, and he wants me to go there to meet him and get the rest. What he's given me, what I just looked at, show some pretty shocking—"

Gibson interrupted. "How are you calling me?"

"By Skype."

"I don't think we should talk about this on the phone, and definitely not by Skype," she wisely said, and she proposed that I get on a plane to New York immediately so that we could discuss the story in person.

My plan, which I told Laura, was to fly to New York, show the documents to the *Guardian*, get them excited about the story, and then have them send me to Hong Kong to see the source. Laura agreed to meet me in New York, and then we intended to travel together to Hong Kong.

The next day, I flew from Rio to JFK on the overnight flight, and by 9:00 a.m. the following day, Friday, May 31, I had checked in to my Manhattan hotel and then met Laura. The first thing we did was go to a store to buy a laptop that would serve as my "air gapped machine," a computer that never connected to the Internet. It is much more difficult to subject an Internet-free computer to surveillance. To monitor an air gapped computer, an intelligence service such as the NSA would have to engage in far more difficult methods, such as obtaining physical access to the computer and placing a surveillance device on the hard drive. Keeping the computer close at all times helps prevent that type of invasion. I would use this new laptop to work with materials that I didn't want monitored, like secret NSA documents, without fear of detection.

I shoved my new computer into my backpack and walked the five Manhattan blocks with Laura to the *Guardian*'s Soho office.

Gibson was waiting for us when we arrived. She and I went directly into her office, where we were joined by Stuart Millar, Gibson's deputy. Laura sat outside. Gibson didn't know Laura, and I wanted us to be able to talk freely. I had no idea how the *Guardian* editors would react to what I had. I hadn't worked with them before, certainly not on anything remotely approaching this level of gravity and importance.

After I pulled up the source's files on my laptop, Gibson and Millar sat together at a table and read the documents, periodically muttering "wow" and "holy shit" and similar exclamations. I sat on a sofa and watched them read, observing the shock registering on their faces when the reality of what I possessed began to sink in. Each time they finished with one document, I popped up to show them the next one. Their amazement only intensified.

In addition to the two dozen or so NSA documents the source had sent, he had included the manifesto he intended to post, calling for signatures as a show of solidarity with the pro-privacy, anti-surveillance cause. The manifesto was dramatic and severe, but that was to be expected, given the dramatic and severe choices he had made, choices that would upend his life forever. It made sense to me that someone who had witnessed the shadowy construction of a ubiquitous system of state surveillance, with no oversight or checks, would be gravely alarmed by what he had seen and the dangers it posed. Of course his tone was extreme; he had been so alarmed that he had made an extraordinary decision to do something brave and far-reaching. I understood the reason for his tone, although I worried about how Gibson and Millar would react to reading the manifesto. I didn't want them to think we were dealing with someone unstable, particularly since, having spent many hours talking to him, I knew that he was exceptionally rational and deliberative.

My fear was quickly validated. "This is going to sound crazy to some people," Gibson pronounced.

"Some people and pro-NSA media types will say it's a bit Ted Kaczynski–ish," I agreed. "But ultimately, the documents are what matters, not him or his motives for giving them to us. And besides, anyone who does something this extreme is going to have extreme thoughts. That's inevitable."

Along with that manifesto, Snowden had written a missive to the journalists to whom he gave his archive of documents. It sought to explain his purpose and goals and predicted how he would likely be demonized:

My sole motive is to inform the public as to that which is done in their name and that which is done against them. The U.S. government, in conspiracy with client states, chiefest among them the Five Eyes—the United Kingdom, Canada, Australia, and New Zealand—have inflicted upon the world a system of secret, pervasive surveillance from which there is no refuge. They protect their domestic systems from the oversight of citizenry through classification and lies, and shield themselves from outrage in the event of leaks by overemphasizing limited protections they choose to grant the governed. . . .

The enclosed documents are real and original, and are offered to provide an understanding of how the global, passive surveillance system works so that protections against it may be developed. On the day of this writing, all new communications records that can be ingested and catalogued by this system are intended to be held for [] years, and new "Massive Data Repositories" (or euphemistically "Mission" Data Repositories) are being built and deployed worldwide, with the largest at the new data center in Utah. While I pray that public awareness and debate will lead to reform, bear in mind that the policies of men change in time, and even the Constitution is subverted when the appetites of power demand it. In words from history: Let us speak no more of faith in man, but bind him down from mischief by the chains of cryptography.

I instantly recognized the last sentence as a play on a Thomas Jefferson quote from 1798 that I often cited in my writing: "In questions of power, then, let no more be heard of confidence in man, but bind him down from mischief by the chains of the Constitution."

After reviewing all of the documents, including Snowden's missive, Gibson and Millar were persuaded. "Basically," Gibson concluded within two hours of my arrival that morning, "you need to go to Hong Kong as soon as possible, like tomorrow, right?"

The *Guardian* was on board. My mission in New York had been accomplished. Now I knew that Gibson was committed to pursuing the story aggressively, at least for the moment. That afternoon, Laura and I worked with the *Guardian*'s travel person to get to Hong Kong as quickly as possible. The best option was a sixteen-hour non-stop flight on Cathay Pacific that left from JFK the next morning. But just as we began to celebrate our imminent meeting with the source, we ran into a complication.

At the end of the day, Gibson declared that she wanted to involve a longtime *Guardian* reporter, Ewen MacAskill, who had been at the paper for twenty years. "He's a great journalist," she said. Given the magnitude of what I was embarking on, I knew that I'd need other *Guardian* reporters on the story and had no objection in theory. "I'd like Ewen to go with you to Hong Kong," she added.

I didn't know MacAskill. More important, neither did the source, and as far as he knew, only Laura and I were coming to Hong Kong. And Laura, who plans everything meticulously, was also bound to be furious at this sudden change in our plans.

I was right. "No way. Absolutely not," she responded. "We can't just add some new person at the last minute. And I don't know him at all. Who has vetted him?"

I tried to explain what I thought was Gibson's motive. I didn't really know or trust the *Guardian* yet, not when it came to such a huge story, and I assumed they felt the same way about me. Given how much the *Guardian* had at stake, I reasoned that they likely wanted someone they knew very well—a longtime company man—to tell them what was going on with the source and to assure them that this story was something they should do. Besides, Gibson would need the full support and approval of the *Guardian* editors in London, who knew me even less well than she did. She probably wanted to bring in someone who could make London feel safe, and Ewen fit that bill perfectly.

"I don't care," Laura said. "Traveling with some third person, some stranger, could attract surveillance or scare the source." As a compromise, Laura suggested that they send Ewen after a few days, once we had established contact with the source in Hong Kong and built trust. "You have all the leverage. Tell them they can't send Ewen until we're ready."

I went back to Gibson with what seemed like a smart compromise, but she was determined. "Ewen can travel with you to Hong Kong, but he won't meet the source until you and Laura both say you're ready."

Clearly, Ewen coming with us to Hong Kong was crucial to the *Guardian*. Gibson would need assurances about what was happening there and a way to assuage any worries her bosses in London might have. But Laura was just as adamant that we would travel alone. "If the source surveils us at the airport and sees this unexpected third person he doesn't know, he'll freak out and terminate contact. No way." Like a State Department diplomat shuttling between Middle East adversaries in the futile hope of brokering a deal, I went back to Gibson, who gave a vague reply designed to signal that Ewen would follow a couple of days later. Or maybe that's what I wanted to hear.

Either way, I learned from the travel person late that night that Ewen's ticket had been bought—for the next day, on the same flight. And they were sending him on that plane no matter what.

In the car on the way to the airport, Laura and I had our first and only argument. I gave her the news as soon as the car pulled out of the hotel and she exploded with anger. I was jeopardizing the entire arrangement, she insisted. It was unconscionable to bring some stranger in at this late stage. She didn't trust someone who hadn't been vetted for work on something so sensitive and she blamed me for letting the *Guardian* risk our plan.

I couldn't tell Laura that her concerns were invalid, but I did try to convince her that the *Guardian* was insistent, there was no choice. And Ewen would only meet the source when we were ready.

Laura didn't care. To placate her anger, I even offered not to go, a suggestion she instantly rejected. We sat in miserable, angry silence for ten minutes as the car was stuck in traffic on the way to JFK.

I knew Laura was right: it shouldn't have happened this way, and I broke the silence by telling her so. I then proposed that we ignore Ewen and freeze him out, pretend that he's not with us. "We're on the same side," I appealed to Laura. "Let's not fight. Given what's at stake, this won't be the last time that things happen beyond our control." I tried to persuade Laura that we should keep our focus on working together to overcome obstacles. In a short time, we returned to a state of calm.

As we arrived in the vicinity of JFK Airport, Laura pulled a thumb drive out of her backpack. "Guess what this is?" she asked with a look of intense seriousness.

"What?"

"The documents," she said. "All of them."

Ewen was already at our gate when we arrived. Laura and I were cordial but cold, ensuring that he felt excluded, that he had no role until we were ready to give him one. He was the only present target for our irritation, so we treated him like extra baggage with which we had been saddled. It was unfair, but I was too distracted by the prospect of the treasures on Laura's thumb drive and the significance of what we were doing to give much more thought to Ewen.

Laura had given me a five-minute tutorial on the secure computer system in the car and said she intended to sleep on the plane. She handed over the thumb drive and suggested that I start looking at her set of documents. Once we arrived in Hong Kong, she said, the source would ensure I had full access to my own complete set.

After the plane took off, I pulled out my new air gapped computer, inserted Laura's thumb drive, and followed her instructions for loading the files.

For the next sixteen hours, despite my exhaustion, I did nothing but read, feverishly taking notes on document after document. Many of the files were as powerful and shocking as that initial PRISM PowerPoint presentation I had seen back in Rio. A lot of them were worse.

One of the first I read was an order from the secret Foreign Intelligence Surveillance Act (FISA) court, which had been created by Congress in 1978, after the Church Committee discovered decades of abusive government eavesdropping. The idea behind its formation was that the government could continue to engage in electronic surveillance, but to prevent similar abuse, it had to obtain permission from the FISA court before doing so. I had never seen a FISA court order before. Almost nobody had. The court is one of the most secretive institutions in the government. All of its rulings are automatically designated top secret, and only a small handful of people are authorized to access its decisions.

The ruling I read on the plane to Hong Kong was amazing for several reasons. It ordered Verizon Business to turn over to the NSA "all call detail records" for "communications (i) between the United States and abroad; and (ii) wholly within the United States, including local telephone calls." That meant the NSA was secretly and indiscriminately collecting the telephone records of tens of millions of Americans, at least. Virtually nobody had any idea that the Obama administration was doing any such thing. Now, with this ruling, I not only knew about it but had the secret court order as proof.

Moreover, the court order specified that the bulk collection of American telephone records was authorized by Section 215 of the Patriot Act. Almost more than the ruling itself, this radical interpretation of the Patriot Act was especially shocking.

What made the Patriot Act so controversial when it was enacted in the wake of the 9/11 attack was that Section 215 lowered the standard the government needed to meet in order to obtain "business records," from "probable cause" to "relevance." This meant that the Federal Bureau of Investigation, in order to obtain highly sensitive and invasive documents—such as medical histories, banking transactions, or phone records—needed to demonstrate only that those documents were "relevant" to a pending investigation.

But nobody—not even the hawkish Republican House members who authored the Patriot Act back in 2001 or the most devoted civil liberties advocates who depicted the bill in the most menacing light—thought that the law empowered the US government to collect records on *everyone*, in bulk and indiscriminately. Yet that's exactly what this secret FISA court order, open on my laptop as I flew to Hong Kong, had concluded when instructing Verizon to turn over to the NSA all phone records for all of its American customers.

For two years Democratic senators Ron Wyden of Oregon and Mark Udall of New Mexico had been going around the country warning that Americans would be "stunned to learn" of the "secret interpretations of law" the Obama administration was using to vest itself with vast, unknown spying powers. But because these spying activities and "secret interpretations" were classified, the two senators, who were members of the Senate Intelligence Committee, had stopped short of disclosing to the public what they found so menacing, despite the legal shield of immunity granted to members of Congress by the Constitution to make such disclosures had they chosen to.

I knew as soon as I saw the FISA court order that this was at least part of the abusive and radical surveillance programs Wyden and Udall had tried to warn the country about. I instantly recognized the order's significance. I could barely wait to publish it, sure that its exposure would trigger an earthquake, and that calls for transparency and accountability were sure to follow. And this was just one of hundreds of top secret documents I read on my way to Hong Kong.

Yet again, I felt my perspective shift on the significance of the source's actions. This had already happened three times before: when I first saw the emails Laura had received, then again when I began speaking to the source, and yet again when I'd read the two dozen documents he sent by email. Only now did I feel that I was truly beginning to process the true magnitude of the leak.

On several occasions on the flight, Laura came over to the row where I was sitting, which faced the bulkhead of the plane. As soon as I saw her, I would pop up out of my seat and we'd stand in the open space of the bulkhead, speechless, overwhelmed, stunned by what we had.

Laura had been working for years on the subject of NSA surveillance, herself repeatedly subjected to its abuses. I had been writing about the threat posed by unconstrained domestic surveillance going back to 2006, when I published my first book, warning of the lawlessness and radicalism of the NSA. With this work, both of us had struggled against the great wall of secrecy shielding government spying: How do you document the actions of an agency so completely shrouded in multiple layers of official secrecy? At this moment, we had breached that wall. We had in our possession, on the plane, thousands of documents that the government had desperately tried to hide. We had evidence that would indisputably prove all that the government had done to destroy the privacy of Americans and people around the world.

As I continued reading, two things struck me about the archive. The first was how extraordinarily well organized it was. The source had created countless folders and then sub-folders and sub-sub-folders. Every last document had been placed exactly where it belonged. I never found a single misplaced or misfiled document.

I had spent years defending what I view as the heroic acts of Chelsea (then Bradley) Manning, the army private and whistle-blower who became so horrified at the behavior of the US government—its war crimes and other systematic deceit—that she risked her liberty to disclose classified documents to the world through WikiLeaks. But Manning was criticized (unfairly and inaccurately, I believe) for supposedly leaking documents that she had not first reviewed—in contrast to Daniel Ells-berg, the critics speculated. This argument, baseless though it was (Ells-berg was one of Manning's most devoted defenders, and it seemed clear that Manning had at least surveyed the documents), was frequently used to undermine the notion that Manning's actions were heroic.

It was clear that nothing of the sort could be said about our NSA source. There was no question that he had carefully reviewed every docu-ment he had given us, that he had understood their meaning, then me-ticulously placed each one in an elegantly organized structure.

The other striking facet of the archive was the extent of government lying it revealed, evidence of which the source had prominently flagged. He had titled one of his first folders "BOUNDLESS INFORMANT (NSA lied to Congress)." This folder contained dozens of documents showing elaborate statistics maintained by the NSA on how many calls and emails the agency intercepts. It also contained proof that the NSA had been col-lecting telephone and email data about millions of Americans every day. BOUNDLESS INFORMANT was the name of the NSA program designed to quantify the agency's daily surveillance activities with mathematical ex-actitude. One map in the file showed that for a thirty-day period ending in February 2013, one unit of the NSA collected more than *three billion* pieces of communication data from US communication systems alone.

The source had given us clear proof that NSA officials had lied to Congress, directly and repeatedly, about the agency's activities. For years, various senators had asked the NSA for a rough estimate of how many Americans were having their calls and emails intercepted. The officials insisted they were unable to answer because they did not and could not maintain such data: the very data extensively reflected in the "BOUND-LESS INFORMANT" documents.

Even more significant, the files—along with the Verizon document—suggested that the Obama administration's senior national security official, Director of National Intelligence James Clapper, lied to Congress when, on March 12, 2013, he was asked by Senator Ron Wyden: "Does the NSA collect any type of data at all on millions or hundreds of mil-lions of Americans?"

Clapper's reply was as succinct as it was dishonest: "No, sir."

In sixteen hours of barely interrupted reading, I managed to get through only a small fraction of the archive. But as the plane landed in Hong Kong, I knew two things for certain. First, the source was highly sophisticated and politically astute, evident in his recognition of the significance of most of the documents. He was also highly rational. The way he chose, analyzed, and described the thousands of documents I now had in my possession proved that. Second, it would be very difficult to deny his status as a classic whistle-blower. If disclosing proof that top-level national security officials lied outright to Congress about domestic spying programs doesn't make one indisputably a whistle-blower, then what does?

I knew that the harder it would be for the government and its allies to demonize the source, the more powerful the effect of the source's disclosures would be. The two most favored lines of whistle-blower demonization—"he's unstable" and "he's naive"—were not going to work here.

Shortly before landing, I read one final file. Although it was entitled "README_FIRST," I saw it for the first time only at the very end of the flight. This document was another explanation from the source for why he had chosen to do what he did and what he expected to happen as a result, and it was similar in tone and content to the manifesto I had shown the *Guardian* editors.

But this document had facts the others did not. It included the source's name—the first time I learned it—along with clear predictions for what would likely be done to him once he identified himself. Referring to events that proceeded from the 2005 NSA scandal, the note ended this way:

Many will malign me for failing to engage in national relativism, to look away from [my] society's problems toward distant, external evils for which we hold neither authority nor responsibility, but citizenship carries with it a duty to first police one's own government before seeking to correct others. Here, now, at home, we suffer a government that only grudgingly allows limited oversight, and refuses accountability when crimes are committed. When marginalized youths commit minor infractions, we as a society turn a blind eye as they suffer insufferable consequences in the world's largest prison system, yet when the richest and most powerful telecommunications providers in the country knowingly commit tens of millions of felonies, Congress passes our nation's first law providing their elite friends with full retroactive immunity—civil and criminal—for crimes that would have merited the longest sentences in [] history.

These companies . . . have the best lawyers in the country on their staff and they do not suffer even the slightest consequences. When officials at the highest levels of power, to specifically include the Vice President, are found on investigation to have personally directed such a criminal enterprise, what should happen? If you believe that investigation should be stopped, its results classified above-top-secret in a special "Exceptionally Controlled Information" compartment called STLW (STELLARWIND), any future investigations ruled out on the principle that holding those who abuse power to account is against the national interest, that we must "look forward, not backward," and rather than closing the illegal program you would expand it with even more authorities, you will be welcome in the halls of America's power, for that is what came to be, and I am releasing the documents that prove it.

I understand that I will be made to suffer for my actions, and that the return of this information to the public marks my end. I will be satisfied if the federation of secret law, unequal pardon, and irresistible executive powers that rule the world that I love are revealed for even an instant. If you seek to help, join the open source community and fight to keep the spirit of the press alive and the internet free. I have been to the darkest corners of government, and what they fear is light.

Edward Joseph Snowden, SSN: ███████

CIA Alias "███████"

Agency Identification Number: ████████

Former Senior Advisor | United States National Security Agency, under corporate cover

Former Field Officer | United States Central Intelligence Agency, under diplomatic cover

Former Lecturer | United States Defense Intelligence Agency, under corporate cover

2

TEN DAYS IN HONG KONG

We arrived in Hong Kong on Sunday night, June 2. The plan was that we would meet Snowden immediately after we arrived in our hotel. As soon I got to my room, at the W Hotel in the upscale Kowloon District, I turned on the computer and looked for him on the encrypted chat program we used. As was almost always the case, he was there, waiting.

After exchanging a few pleasantries about the flight, we got down to the logistics of our meeting. "You can come to my hotel," he said.

That was my first surprise, to learn that he was staying in a hotel. I still didn't know why he was in Hong Kong but assumed by this point that he had gone there to hide. I'd pictured him in some hovel, a cheap apartment where he could afford to go underground without a regular paycheck coming in, not comfortably installed in a hotel, out in the open, running up daily charges.

Changing our plans, we decided it would be best to wait until the morning to meet. It was Snowden who made the decision, setting the hyper-cautious, cloak-and-dagger mood of the next few days.

"You'll be more likely to draw attention to yourselves if you move around at night," he said. "It's strange behavior for two Americans to check into their hotel at night and then immediately go out. It'll be more natural if you come here in the morning."

Snowden was worried as much about surveillance by Hong Kong and Chinese authorities as by the Americans. He was very concerned that we would be followed by local intelligence agents. Assuming he had some deep involvement with US spying agencies and knew what he was talking about, I deferred to his judgment but was disappointed that we wouldn't be meeting that night.

With Hong Kong being exactly twelve hours ahead of New York, night and day were now reversed, so I hardly slept at all that night, nor at any other time during the trip. Jet lag was only partly to blame; in a state of barely controllable excitement, I was able to doze off for only ninety minutes or so, two hours at the most, and that remained my normal sleep pattern for the entire stay.

The next morning, Laura and I met in the lobby and entered a waiting cab to go to Snowden's hotel. Laura was the one who had arranged the details of the meeting with him. She was very reluctant to speak in the taxi, fearing that the driver might be an undercover agent. I was no longer quite as quick as I might have been to dismiss such fears as paranoia. Despite the constraints, I pried enough out of Laura to understand the plan.

We were to go to the third floor of Snowden's hotel, which was where the conference rooms were located. He had chosen a specific conference room for what he thought was its perfect balance: sufficiently isolated to discourage substantial "human traffic," as he called it, but not so obscure and hidden that we would attract attention while waiting there.

Laura told me that once we got to the third floor, we were supposed to ask the first hotel employee we ran into near the designated room whether there was a restaurant open. The question would signal to Snowden, who would be hovering nearby, that we had not been followed. Inside the designated room, we were to wait on a couch near "a giant alligator," which, Laura confirmed, was some kind of room decoration rather than a live animal.

We had two different meeting times: 10:00 and then 10:20. If Snowden failed to arrive within two minutes of the first time, we were to leave the room and come back later at the second time, when he would find us.

"How will we know it's him?" I asked Laura. We still knew virtually nothing about him, not his age, race, physical appearance, or anything else.

"He'll be carrying a Rubik's Cube," she said.

I laughed out loud: the situation seemed so bizarre, so extreme and improbable. This is a surreal international thriller set in Hong Kong, I thought.

Our taxi dropped us at the entrance to the Mira Hotel, which, I noted, was also located in the Kowloon District, a highly commercial neighborhood filled with sleek high-rises and chic stores: as visible as it gets. Entering the lobby, I was taken aback all over again: Snowden wasn't staying in just any hotel, but in a sprawling high-priced one, which I knew must cost several hundred dollars a night. Why, I wondered, would someone who intended to blow the whistle on the NSA, and who needed great secrecy, go to Hong Kong to hide in a five-star hotel in one of the most visible neighborhoods in the city? There was no point at that moment in dwelling on the mystery—I'd be meeting the source within a matter of minutes and presumably would have all the answers.

Like many Hong Kong buildings, the Mira Hotel was the size of a village. Laura and I spent at least fifteen minutes searching the cavernous hallways for our designated meeting spot. We had to take multiple elevators, cross internal bridges, and repeatedly ask for directions. When we thought we were close to the room, we saw a hotel employee. Somewhat awkwardly, I asked the coded question, and we listened to instructions about various restaurant options.

Turning a corner, we saw an open door and a huge, green, plastic alligator lying across the floor. As instructed, we sat on the couch that was stranded in the middle of this otherwise empty room, waiting nervously and in silence. The small room appeared to have no real function, no reason for anybody to enter it, as there was nothing in it but the couch and the alligator. After five very long minutes of sitting in silence, nobody came, so we left and found another room nearby where we waited another fifteen minutes.

At 10:20, we returned and again took our place near the alligator, on the couch, which faced the back wall of the room and a large mirror. After two minutes, I heard someone come into the room.

Rather than turn around to see who had entered, I continued to stare at the back wall mirror, which showed a man's reflection walking toward us. Only when he was within a few feet of the couch did I turn around.

The first thing I saw was the unsolved Rubik's Cube, twirling in the man's left hand. Edward Snowden said hello but did not extend his hand to shake, as the point of the arrangement was to make this encounter appear to be random. As they had planned, Laura asked him about the food in the hotel and he replied that it was bad. Of all the surprising turns in this entire story, the moment of our meeting proved to be the biggest surprise of all.

Snowden was twenty-nine years old at the time, but he appeared at least several years younger, dressed in a white T-shirt with some faded lettering, jeans, and chic-nerd glasses. He had a weak goatee of stubble but looked like he had only recently started shaving. He was basically clean-cut and his posture military-firm, but he was quite thin and pale, and—like all three of us at that moment—clearly somewhat guarded and cautious. He could have been any mildly geeky guy in his early to mid-twenties working in a computer lab on a college campus.

In the moment, I simply couldn't put the pieces together. Without having consciously thought about it, I had assumed for a number of reasons that Snowden was older, probably in his fifties or sixties. First, given the fact that he had access to so many sensitive documents, I had presumed he held a senior position within the national security system. Beyond that, his insights and strategies were invariably sophisticated and informed, leading me to believe he was a veteran of the political scene. Last, I knew he was prepared to throw his life away, probably spending the rest of it in prison, to disclose what he felt the world must know, so I imagined he was near the end of his career. For someone to arrive at so extreme and self-sacrificing a decision, I figured, he must have experienced many years, even decades, of profound disillusionment.

To see that the source of the astonishing cache of NSA material was a man so young was one of the most disorienting experiences I have ever had. My mind began racing to consider the possibilities: Was this some sort of fraud? Had I wasted my time flying across the world? How could someone this young possibly have access to the type of information we

had seen? How could this person be as savvy and experienced in intelligence and spycraft as our source clearly was? Maybe, I thought, this was
the source's son, or assistant, or lover, who was now going to take us to
the source himself. Every conceivable possibility flooded my mind, and
none of them made any real sense.

"So, come with me," he said, obviously tense. Laura and I followed
him. We all muttered a few incoherent words of pleasantries as we
walked. I was too stunned and confused to speak much, and I could see
that Laura felt the same way. Snowden seemed very vigilant, as though
he were searching for potential watchers or other signs of trouble. So we
followed him, mostly in silence.

With no idea where he was taking us, we entered the elevator, got off
on the tenth floor, and then made our way to his room. Snowden pulled
out a card key from his wallet and opened the door. "Welcome," he said.
"Sorry it's a bit messy, but I basically haven't left the room in a couple of
weeks."

The room was indeed messy, with plates of half-eaten room-service
food piled up on the table and dirty clothes strewn about. Snowden
cleared off a chair and invited me to sit down. He then sat on his bed.
Because the room was small, we were sitting less than five feet apart. Our
conversation was tense, awkward, and stilted.

Snowden immediately raised issues of security, asking whether I had
a cell phone. My phone only worked in Brazil, but Snowden nonetheless insisted that I remove the battery or place it in the refrigerator of his
minibar, which would at least muffle conversations, making them more
difficult to overhear.

Just as Laura had told me back in April, Snowden said the US government has the capability to remotely activate cell phones and convert
them into listening devices. So I knew that the technology existed but
still chalked up their concerns to borderline paranoia. As it turned out, I
was the one who was misguided. The government has used this tactic in
criminal investigations for years. In 2006, a federal judge presiding over
the criminal prosecution of alleged New York mobsters had ruled that
the FBI's use of so-called roving bugs—turning a person's own cell phone
into a listening device through remote activation—was legal.

Once my cell phone was safely sealed in the refrigerator, Snowden took the pillows from his bed and placed them at the bottom of the door. "That's for passersby in the hallway," he explained. "There may be room audio and cameras, but what we're about to discuss is all going on the news anyway," he said, only half joking.

My ability to assess any of this was very limited. I still had very little idea of who Snowden was, where he worked, what truly motivated him, or what he had done, so I couldn't be sure what threats might be lurking, of surveillance or any other kind. My one consistent feeling was uncertainty.

Without bothering to sit down or say anything, Laura, perhaps to relieve her own tension, began unpacking her camera and tripod and setting them up. She then came over and put microphones on both Snowden and me.

We had discussed her plan to film us while in Hong Kong: she was, after all, a documentarian working on a film about the NSA. Inevitably, what we were doing would become a huge part of her project. I knew that, but I hadn't been prepared for the recording to begin quite so soon. There was great cognitive dissonance between, on one hand, meeting so covertly with a source who, to the US government, had committed serious crimes and, on the other, filming it all.

Laura was ready in a matter of minutes. "So I'm going to begin filming now," she announced, as though it was the most natural thing in the world. The realization that we were about to be taped heightened the tension even more.

That initial interaction between Snowden and myself was already awkward, but as soon as the camera began rolling, we both became instantly more formal and less friendly; our posture stiffened and our speech slowed down. Over the years, I've given many speeches about how surveillance changes human behavior, highlighting studies showing that people who know they are being watched are more confined, more cautious about what they say, less free. Now I saw and felt a vivid illustration of that dynamic.

Given the futility of our attempts at exchanging pleasantries, there was nothing to do but plunge right in. "I have a lot of questions for you, and I'm just going to start asking them, one by one, and, if that's OK with you, we can go from there," I began.

"That's fine," Snowden said, clearly as relieved as I was to get down to business.

I had two primary goals at that point. Because we all knew there was a serious risk that he could be arrested at anytime, my urgent priority was to learn everything I could about Snowden: his life, his jobs, what led him to the extraordinary choice he had made, what he had done specifi- cally to take those documents and why, and what he was doing in Hong Kong. Second, I was determined to figure out whether he was honest and fully forthcoming or whether he was hiding important things about who he was and what he had done.

Although I had been a political writer for almost eight years, the more relevant experience for what I was about to do was my prior career as a litigator, which included taking depositions of witnesses. In a deposition, the lawyer sits across a table with a witness for hours, sometimes days. The witness is forced by law to be there and required to answer every one of your questions honestly. A key goal is to expose lies, find inconsisten- cies in the witness's story, and break through any fiction the witness has created in order to let the concealed truth emerge. Taking depositions was one of the few things I really liked about being a lawyer, and I had developed all sorts of tactics for breaking down a witness. They always involved a relentless barrage of questions, often the same questions asked repeatedly but in different contexts, from different directions and angles, to test the solidity of the story.

Shifting from my stance with Snowden online, where I had been will- ing to be passive and deferential, these were the aggressive tactics I used that day. Without so much as a bathroom break or a snack, I spent five straight hours questioning him. I started with his early childhood, his grade school experiences, his pre-government work history. I demanded every detail he could recall. Snowden, I learned, had been born in North Carolina and grew up in Maryland, the son of lower-middle-class federal government employees (his father had been in the Coast Guard for thirty years). Snowden felt deeply unchallenged in high school and never finished, far more interested in the Internet than in classes.

Almost instantly, I could see in person what I had observed from our online chats: Snowden was highly intelligent and rational, and his thought processes methodical. His answers were crisp, clear, and cogent. In virtually every case, they were directly responsive to what I had asked, thoughtful, and deliberative. There were no strange detours or wildly improbable stories of the type that are the hallmark of emotionally unstable people or those suffering from psychological afflictions. His stability and focus instilled confidence.

Although we readily form impressions of people from online interactions, we still need to meet in person to develop a reliable sense of who they are. I quickly felt better about the situation, recovering from my initial doubts and disorientation about whom I was dealing with. But I still remained intensely skeptical because I knew the credibility of everything we were about to do depended on the reliability of Snowden's claims about who he was.

We spent several hours on his work history and intellectual evolution. As with so many Americans, Snowden's political views had changed significantly after the 9/11 attack: he became much more "patriotic." In 2004, at twenty, he had enlisted in the US Army intending to fight in the Iraq War, which he thought at the time was a noble effort to free the Iraqi people from oppression. After only a few weeks in basic training, however, he saw that there was more talk of killing Arabs than liberating anyone. By the time both of his legs were broken in a training accident and he was forced to leave the military, he had become highly disillusioned about the real purpose of the war.

But Snowden still believed in the core goodness of the United States government, so he decided to follow the example of many of his family members and went to work for a federal agency. With no high school degree, he had nonetheless managed in early adulthood to create opportunities for himself, including paid technical work at thirty dollars an hour before he turned eighteen, and he had been a Microsoft Certified Systems Engineer since 2002. But he viewed a career in the federal government as something both noble and professionally promising, so he started as a security guard at the Center for Advanced Study of Language at the University of Maryland, a building secretly managed and used by the NSA. The intention, he said, was to get top secret clearance and thus get his foot in the door to then do technical work.

Although Snowden was a high school dropout, he had a natural talent for technology that became evident in his early adolescence. Combined with his obvious intelligence, those attributes, despite his young age and lack of formal education, enabled him to advance quickly in his jobs, moving rapidly from security guard to a position in 2005 as a technical expert for the CIA.

He explained that the entire intelligence community was desperate for tech-savvy employees. It had transformed itself into such a large and sprawling system that finding enough people capable of operating it was hard. Thus the national security agencies had to turn to nontraditional talent pools to recruit. People with sufficiently advanced computer skills tended to be young and sometimes alienated, and had often failed to shine in mainstream education. They often found Internet culture far more stimulating than formal educational institutions and personal interactions. Snowden became a valued member of his IT team at the agency, clearly more knowledgeable and proficient than most of his older, college-educated colleagues. Snowden felt that he had found exactly the right environment in which his skills would be rewarded and his lack of academic credentials ignored.

In 2006, he transitioned from being a contractor with the CIA to full-time staff, which increased his opportunities further. In 2007, he learned of a CIA job posting that entailed working on computer systems while being stationed overseas. Boasting glowing recommendations from his managers, he got the job and eventually ended up working for the CIA in Switzerland. He was stationed in Geneva for three years, through 2010, deployed there undercover with diplomatic credentials.

As Snowden described his work in Geneva, he was far more than a mere "systems administrator." He was considered the top technical and cybersecurity expert in Switzerland, ordered to travel throughout the region to fix problems nobody else could. He was hand-picked by the CIA to support the president at the 2008 NATO summit in Romania. Despite this success, it was during his stint with the CIA that Snowden began to feel seriously troubled by his government's actions.

"Because of the access technical experts have to computer systems, I saw a lot of secret things," Snowden told me, "and many of them were quite bad. I began to understand that what my government really does in the world is very different from what I'd always been taught. That recognition in turn leads you to start reevaluating how you look at things, to question things more."

One example he recounted was an attempt by CIA case officers to recruit a Swiss banker to provide confidential information. They wanted to know about the financial transactions of people of interest to the United States. Snowden recounted how one of the undercover officers befriended the banker, got him drunk one night, and encouraged him to drive home. When the banker was stopped by the police and arrested for DUI, the CIA agent offered to help him personally in a variety of ways, provided that the banker cooperated with the agency. The recruitment effort ultimately failed. "They destroyed the target's life for something that didn't even work out, and simply walked away," he said. Beyond the scheme itself, Snowden was disturbed by how the agent bragged about the methods used to reel in his catch.

An added element of frustration came from Snowden's efforts to make his superiors aware of problems in computer security or systems he thought skirted ethical lines. Those efforts, he said, were almost always rebuffed.

"They would say this isn't your job, or you'd be told you don't have enough information to make those kinds of judgments. You'd basically be instructed not to worry about it," he said. He developed a reputation among colleagues as someone who raised too many concerns, a trait that did not endear him to superiors. "This was when I really started seeing how easy it is to divorce power from accountability, and how the higher the levels of power, the less oversight and accountability there was."

Near the end of 2009, Snowden, now disillusioned, decided he was ready to leave the CIA. It was at this stage, at the end of his stint in Geneva, that he first began to contemplate becoming a whistle-blower and leaking secrets that he believed revealed wrongdoing.

"Why didn't you do it then?" I asked.

At the time he thought or at least hoped that the election of Barack Obama as president would reform some of the worst abuses he had seen. Obama entered office vowing to change the excessive abuses of national security that had been justified by the War on Terror. Snowden expected that at least some of the roughest edges of the intelligence and military world would be smoothed over.

"But then it became clear that Obama was not just continuing, but in many cases expanding these abuses," he said. "I realized then that I couldn't wait for a leader to fix these things. Leadership is about acting first and serving as an example for others, not waiting for others to act."

He was also concerned about the damage that would result from disclosing what he had learned at the CIA. "When you leak the CIA's secrets, you can harm people," he said, referring to covert agents and informants. "I wasn't willing to do that. But when you leak the NSA's secrets, you only harm abusive systems. I was much more comfortable with that."

So Snowden returned to the NSA, this time working for the Dell Corporation, which contracted with the agency. In 2010, he was stationed in Japan and given a much higher degree of access to surveillance secrets than he previously had.

"The stuff I saw really began to disturb me," Snowden said. "I could watch drones in real time as they surveilled the people they might kill. You could watch entire villages and see what everyone was doing. I watched NSA tracking people's Internet activities as they typed. I became aware of just how invasive US surveillance capabilities had become. I realized the true breadth of this system. And almost nobody knew it was happening."

The perceived need, the *obligation*, to leak what he was seeing felt increasingly urgent to him. "The more time I spent at the NSA in Japan, the more I knew that I couldn't keep it all to myself. I felt it would be wrong to, in effect, help conceal all of this from the public."

Later, once Snowden's identity was revealed, reporters tried to depict him as some sort of simple-minded, low-level IT guy who happened to stumble into classified information. But the reality was far different.

Throughout his work at both the CIA and NSA, Snowden told me, he was progressively trained to become a high-level cyber operative, someone who hacks into the military and civilian systems of other countries, to steal information or prepare attacks without leaving a trace. In Japan, that training intensified. He became adept at the most sophisticated methods for safeguarding electronic data from other intelligence agencies and was formally certified as a high-level cyber operative. He was ultimately chosen by the Defense Intelligence Agency's Joint Counterintelligence Training Academy to teach cyber counterintelligence at their Chinese counterintelligence course.

The operational security methods he insisted we follow were ones he learned and even helped design at the CIA and especially the NSA.

In July 2013 the *New York Times* confirmed what Snowden had told me, reporting that "while working for a National Security Agency contractor, Edward J. Snowden learned to be a hacker" and that "he had transformed himself into the kind of cybersecurity expert the N.S.A. is desperate to recruit." The training he received there, said the *New York Times*, was "pivotal in his shift toward more sophisticated cybersecurity." The article added that the files Snowden accessed showed that he had "shifted to the offensive side of electronic spying or cyberwarfare, in which the N.S.A. examines other nations' computer systems to steal information or to prepare attacks."

Although I tried to adhere to the chronology in my questioning, I often couldn't resist jumping ahead, mostly out of eagerness. I particularly wanted to get to the heart of what, for me, had been the most amazing mystery since I began speaking to him: What had really driven Snowden to throw away his career, turn himself into a potential felon, and breach the demands of secrecy and loyalty that had been drummed into his head for years?

I asked this same question in many different ways, and Snowden thus answered in many different ways, but the explanations felt either too superficial, too abstract, or too devoid of passion and conviction. He was very comfortable talking about NSA systems and technology, but clearly less so when he himself was the subject, particularly in response to the suggestion that he had done something courageous and extraordinary that warranted a psychological explanation. His answers seemed more abstract than visceral, and so I found them unconvincing. The world had a right to know what was being done to its privacy, he said; he felt a moral obligation to take a stand against wrongdoing; he could not in good conscience remain silent about the hidden threat to the values he cherished.

I believed those political values were real to him, but I wanted to know what had driven him personally to sacrifice his life and liberty in defense of those values, and I felt I wasn't getting the true answer. Maybe he didn't have the answer, or maybe, like many American men, especially when immersed in a national security culture, he was reluctant to dig too deep into his own psyche, but I had to know.

Apart from anything else, I wanted to be sure he had made his choice with a genuine and rational understanding of the consequences: I was unwilling to help him take so great a risk unless I was convinced he was doing so with full autonomy and agency, with a real grasp of his purpose.

Finally, Snowden gave me an answer that felt vibrant and real. "The true measurement of a person's worth isn't what they say they believe in, but what they do in defense of those beliefs," he said. "If you're not acting on your beliefs, then they probably aren't real."

How had he developed this measure for assessing his worth? Where did he derive this belief that he could only be acting morally if he was willing to sacrifice his own interests for the sake of the greater good?

"From a lot of different places, a lot of experiences," Snowden said. He had grown up reading large amounts of Greek mythology and was influenced by Joseph Campbell's *The Hero with a Thousand Faces*, which, he noted, "finds common threads among the stories we all share." The primary lesson he took away from that the book was that "it is we who infuse life with meaning through our actions and the stories we create with them." People are only that which their actions define them as being. "I don't want to be a person who remains afraid to act in defense of my principles."

This theme, this moral construct for evaluating one's identity and worth, was one he repeatedly encountered on his intellectual path, including, he explained with a hint of embarrassment, from video games. The lesson Snowden had learned from immersion in video games, he said, was that just one person, even the most powerless, can confront great injustice. "The protagonist is often an ordinary person, who finds himself faced with grave injustices from powerful forces and has the choice to flee in fear or to fight for his beliefs. And history also shows that seemingly ordinary people who are sufficiently resolute about justice can triumph over the most formidable adversaries."

He wasn't the first person I'd heard claiming video games had been instrumental in shaping their worldview. Years earlier, I might have scoffed, but I'd come to accept that, for Snowden's generation, they played no less serious a role in molding political consciousness, moral reasoning, and an understanding of one's place in the world than literature, television, and film. They, too, often present complex moral dilemmas and provoke contemplation, especially for people beginning to question what they've been taught.

Snowden's early moral reasoning—drawn from work that formed, as he said, "a model for who we want to become, and why"—had evolved into serious adult introspection about ethical obligations and psychological limits. "What keeps a person passive and compliant," he explained, "is fear of repercussions, but once you let go of your attachment to things that don't ultimately matter—money, career, physical safety—you can overcome that fear."

Equally central to his worldview was the unprecedented value of the Internet. As for many of his generation, "the Internet" for him wasn't some isolated tool to use for discrete tasks. It was the world in which his mind and personality developed, a place unto itself that offered freedom, exploration, and the potential for intellectual growth and understanding.

To Snowden, the unique qualities of the Internet were incomparably valuable, to be preserved at all costs. He had used the Internet as a teenager to explore ideas and speak with people in faraway places and from radically different backgrounds whom he'd never otherwise have encountered. "Basically, the Internet allowed me to experience freedom and explore my full capacity as a human being." Clearly animated, even passionate, when talking about the value of the Internet, Snowden added, "For many kids, the Internet is a means of self-actualization. It allows them to explore who they are and who they want to be, but that works only if we're able to be private and anonymous, to make mistakes without them following us. I worry that mine was the last generation to enjoy that freedom."

The role this played in his decision became clear to me. "I do not want to live in a world where we have no privacy and no freedom, where the unique value of the Internet is snuffed out," Snowden told me. He felt compelled to do what he could to stop that from happening or, more accurately, to enable others to make the choice whether to act or not in defense of those values.

Along those lines, Snowden repeatedly emphasized that his goal was not to destroy the NSA's capability to eliminate privacy. "It's not my role to make that choice," he said. Instead, he wanted American citizens and people around the world to know about what was being done to their privacy, to give them the information. "I don't intend to destroy these systems," he insisted, "but to allow the public to decide whether they should go on."

Often, whistle-blowers like Snowden are demonized as loners or losers, acting not out of conscience but alienation and frustration at a failed life. Snowden was the opposite: he had a life filled with the things people view as most valuable. His decision to leak the documents meant giving up a long-term girlfriend whom he loved, a life in the paradise of Hawaii, a supportive family, a stable career, a lucrative paycheck, a life ahead full of possibilities of every type.

After Snowden's NSA stint in Japan ended in 2011, he went to work again for the Dell Corporation, this time deployed to a CIA office in Maryland. With bonuses, he was on track to make in the range of $200,000 that year, working with Microsoft and other tech companies to build secure systems for the CIA and other agencies to store documents and data. "The world was getting worse," said Snowden of that time. "In that position, I saw firsthand that the state, especially the NSA, was working hand in hand with the private tech industry to get full access to people's communications."

Throughout the five hours of questioning that day—indeed, for the entire time I spoke with him in Hong Kong—Snowden's tone was almost always stoic, calm, matter-of-fact. But as he explained what he had discovered that finally moved him to action, he became impassioned, even slightly agitated. "I realized," he said, "that they were building a system whose goal was the elimination of all privacy, globally. To make it so that no one could communicate electronically without the NSA being able to collect, store, and analyze the communication."

It was that realization that fixed Snowden's determination to become a whistle-blower. In 2012, he was transferred by Dell from Maryland to Hawaii. He spent parts of 2012 downloading the documents he thought the world should see. He took certain other documents not for publication, but so that journalists would be able to understand the context of the systems on which they were reporting.

In early 2013, he realized that there was one set of documents he needed to complete the picture he wanted to present to the world that he could not access while at Dell. They would be accessible only if he obtained a different position, one where he would be formally assigned as an infrastructure analyst, allowing him to go all the way into the raw surveillance repositories of the NSA.

With this goal in mind, Snowden applied for a job opening in Hawaii with Booz Allen Hamilton, one of the nation's largest and most powerful private defense contractors, filled with former government officials. He took a pay cut to get that job, as it gave him access to download the final set of files he felt he needed to complete the picture of NSA spying. Most important, that access allowed him to collect information on the NSA's secret monitoring of the entire telecommunications infrastructure inside the United States.

In mid-May of 2013, Snowden requested a couple of weeks off to receive treatment for epilepsy, a condition he learned that he had the year before. He packed his bags, including several thumb drives full of NSA documents, along with four empty laptops to use for different purposes. He did not tell his girlfriend where he was going; it was, in fact, common for him to travel for work without being able to tell her his destination. He wanted to keep her unaware of his plans, in order to avoid exposing her to government harassment once his identity was revealed.

He arrived in Hong Kong from Hawaii on May 20, checking into the Mira Hotel under his own name, and he had been there ever since.

Snowden was staying at the hotel quite openly, paying with his credit card because, he explained, he knew that his movements would ultimately be scrutinized by the government, the media, and virtually everyone else. He wanted to prevent any claim that he was some type of a foreign agent, which would be easier to make had he spent this period in hiding. He had set out to demonstrate, he said, that his movements could be accounted for, there was no conspiracy, and he was acting alone. To the Hong Kong and Chinese authorities, he looked like a normal businessman, not someone skulking off the grid. "I'm not planning to hide what or who I am," he said, "so I have no reason to go into hiding and feed conspiracy theories or demonization campaigns."

Then I asked the question that had been on my mind since we first spoke online: Why had he chosen Hong Kong as his destination once he was ready to disclose the documents? Characteristically, Snowden's answer showed that the decision was based on careful analysis.

His first priority, he said, was to ensure his physical safety from US interference as he worked with Laura and me on the documents. If the American authorities discovered his plan to leak the documents, they would try to stop him, arresting him or worse. Hong Kong, though semi-independent, was part of Chinese territory, he reasoned, and American agents would find it harder to operate against him there than in the other places he considered as candidates for seeking ultimate refuge, such as a small Latin American nation like Ecuador or Bolivia. Hong Kong would also be more willing and able to resist US pressure to turn him over than a small European nation, such as Iceland.

Though getting the documents out to the public was Snowden's main consideration in the choice of destination, it was not the only one. He also wanted to be in a place where the people had a commitment to political values that were important to him. As he explained, the people of Hong Kong, though ultimately subject to the repressive rule of the Chinese government, had fought to preserve some basic political freedoms and created a vibrant climate of dissent. Snowden pointed out that Hong Kong had democratically elected leaders and was also the site of large street protests, including an annual march against the Tiananmen Square crackdown.

There were other places he could have gone to, affording even greater protection from potential US action, including mainland China. And there were certainly countries that enjoyed more political freedom. But

Hong Kong, he felt, provided the best mix of physical security and political strength.

To be sure, there were drawbacks to the decision, and Snowden was aware of them all, including the city's relationship to mainland China, which would give critics an easy way to demonize him. But there were no perfect choices. "All of my options are bad ones," he often said, and Hong Kong did indeed provide him a measure of security and freedom of movement that would have been difficult to replicate elsewhere.

Once I had all the facts of the story, I had one more goal: to be sure that Snowden understood what would likely happen to him once his identity was revealed as the source behind the disclosures.

The Obama administration had waged what people across the political spectrum were calling an unprecedented war on whistle-blowers. The president, who had campaigned on a vow to have the "most transparent administration in history," specifically pledging to protect whistle-blowers, whom he hailed as "noble" and "courageous," had done exactly the opposite.

Obama's administration has prosecuted more government leakers under the Espionage Act of 1917—a total of seven—than all previous administrations in US history *combined*: in fact, more than double that total. The Espionage Act was adopted during World War I to enable Woodrow Wilson to criminalize dissent against the war, and its sanctions are severe: they include life in prison and even the death penalty.

Without question, the full weight of the law would come crashing down on Snowden. The Obama Justice Department would charge him with crimes that could send him to prison for life and he could expect to be widely denounced as a traitor.

"What do you think will happen to you once you reveal yourself as the source?" I asked.

Snowden answered in a rapid clip that made clear he had contemplated this question many times before: "They'll say I violated the Espionage Act. That I committed grave crimes. That I aided America's enemies. That I endangered national security. I'm sure they'll grab every incident they can from my past, and probably will exaggerate or even fabricate some, to demonize me as much as possible."

He did not want to go to prison, he said. "I'm going to try not to. But if that's the outcome from all of this, and I know there's a huge chance that it will be, I decided a while ago that I can live with whatever they do to me. The only thing I can't live with is knowing I did nothing."

That first day and every day since, Snowden's resolution and calm contemplation of what might happen to him have been profoundly surprising and affecting. I have never seen him display an iota of regret or fear or anxiety. He explained unblinkingly that he had made his choice, understood the possible consequences, and was prepared to accept them.

Snowden seemed to derive a sense of strength from having made this decision. He exuded an extraordinary equanimity when talking about what the US government might do to him. The sight of this twenty-nine-year-old young man responding this way to the threat of decades, or life, in a super-max prison—a prospect that, by design, would scare almost anyone into paralysis—was deeply inspiring. And his courage was contagious: Laura and I vowed to each other repeatedly and to Snowden that every action we would take and every decision we would make from that point forward would honor his choice. I felt a duty to report the story in the spirit that had animated Snowden's original act: fearlessness rooted in the conviction of doing what one believes is right, and a refusal to be intimidated or deterred by baseless threats from malevolent officials eager to conceal their own actions.

After five hours of questioning, I was convinced beyond any doubt that all of Snowden's claims were authentic and his motives were considered and genuine. Before we left him, he returned to the point he had already raised many times: he insisted on identifying himself as the source for the documents, and doing so publicly in the first article we published. "Anyone who does something this significant has the obligation to explain to the public why he did it and what he hopes to achieve," he said. He also did not want to heighten the climate of fear the US government had fostered by hiding.

Besides, Snowden was sure that the NSA and FBI would quickly pinpoint the source of the leaks once our stories started appearing. He had not taken all possible steps to cover his tracks because he did not want his colleagues to be subjected to investigations or false accusations. He insisted that, using the skills he had acquired and given the incredibly lax NSA systems, he could have covered his tracks had he chosen to do so, even downloading as many top secret documents as he had done. But he had chosen instead to leave at least some electronic footprints to be discovered, which meant that remaining hidden was no longer an option.

Although I did not want to help the government learn the identity of my source by revealing him, Snowden convinced me that discovery of his identity was inevitable. More important, he was determined to define himself in the eyes of the public rather than allow the government to define him.

Snowden's only fear about outing himself was that he would distract from the substance of his revelations. "I know the media personalizes everything, and the government will want to make me the story, to attack the messenger," he said. His plan was to identify himself early on, and then disappear from view to allow the focus to remain fixed on the NSA and its spying activities. "Once I identify and explain myself," he said, "I won't do any media. I don't want to be the story."

I argued that rather than revealing Snowden's identity in the first article, we should wait for one week so that we could report the initial set of stories without that distraction. Our idea was simple: to churn out one huge story after the next, every day, a journalistic version of shock and awe, beginning as soon as possible and culminating with unveiling our source. At the end of our meeting that first day, we were all in agreement; we had a plan.

For the remainder of my time in Hong Kong, I met and spoke with Snowden every day at length. I never slept more than two hours in any night, and even that was possible only with the use of sleeping aids. The rest of my time was spent writing articles based on Snowden's documents and, once they started publishing, doing interviews to discuss them.

Snowden left it up to Laura and me to decide which stories should be reported, in what sequence, and how they would be presented. But on the first day, Snowden—as he did on many occasions both before and since—stressed how urgent it was that we vet all the material carefully. "I selected these documents based on what's in the public interest," he told us, "but I'm relying on you to use your journalistic judgment to only publish those documents that the public should see and that can be revealed without harm to any innocent people." If for no other reason, Snowden knew that our ability to generate a real public debate depended on not allowing the US government any valid claims that we had endangered lives through publishing the documents.

He also stressed that it was vital to publish the documents journalistically—meaning working with the media and writing articles that provided the context for the materials, rather than just publishing them in bulk. That approach, he believed, would provide more legal protection, and, more important, would allow the public to process the revelations in a more orderly and rational way. "If I wanted the documents just put on the Internet en masse, I could have done that myself," he said. "I want you to make sure these stories are done, one by one, so that people can understand what they should know." We all agreed that this framework would govern how we reported.

On several occasions, Snowden explained that he had wanted Laura and me to be involved in the stories from the start because he knew we would report them aggressively and not be susceptible to government threats. He frequently referred to the *New York Times* and other major media outlets that had held up big stories at the government's request. But while he wanted aggressive reporting, he also wanted meticulous journalists to take as long as necessary to ensure that the facts of the story were unassailable and that all of the articles had been thoroughly vetted. "Some of the documents I'm giving you are not for publication, but for your own understanding of how this system works so you can report the right way," he said.

After my first full day in Hong Kong, I left Snowden's hotel room, returned to my own, and stayed up all night to write four articles, hoping the *Guardian* would start publishing them immediately. There was some urgency: we needed Snowden to review with us as many documents as we could before he became, one way or another, unavailable to speak further.

There was another source of urgency, too. In the cab on the way to JFK Airport, Laura had told me that she had spoken with several large media outlets and reporters about Snowden's documents.

Included among them was Barton Gellman, the two-time Pulitzer Prize winner who had been on the staff at the *Washington Post* and now worked with the paper on a freelance basis. Laura had difficulty convincing people to travel with her to Hong Kong, but Gellman, who had long had an interest in surveillance issues, was very interested in the story.

On Laura's recommendation, Snowden had agreed to have "some documents" given to Gellman, with the intention that he and the *Post*, along with Laura, would report on certain specific revelations.

I respected Gellman but not the *Washington Post*, which, to me, is the belly of the Beltway media beast, embodying all the worst attributes of US political media: excessive closeness to the government, reverence for the institutions of the national security state, routine exclusion of dissenting voices. The paper's own media critic, Howard Kurtz, had documented in 2004 how the paper had systematically amplified pro-war voices in the run-up to the invasion of Iraq while downplaying or excluding opposition. The *Post*'s news coverage, concluded Kurtz, had been "strikingly one-sided" in favor of the invasion. The *Post* editorial page in my opinion remained one of the most vociferous and mindless cheerleaders for US militarism, secrecy, and surveillance.

The *Post* had been handed a major scoop that it had not worked to obtain and which the source—Snowden—had not selected (but had consented to on Laura's recommendation). Indeed, my first encrypted chat with Snowden arose out of his anger over the *Post*'s fear-driven approach.

One of my few criticisms of WikiLeaks over the years had been that they, too, had at times similarly handed major scoops to the very establishment media organizations that do the most to protect the government, thereby enhancing their stature and importance. Exclusive scoops on top secret documents uniquely elevate a publication's status and empower the journalist who breaks the news. It makes much more sense to give such scoops to independent journalists and media organizations, thereby amplifying their voices, raising their profile, and maximizing their impact.

Worse, I knew that the *Post* would dutifully abide by the unwritten protective rules that govern how the establishment media report on official secrets. According to these rules, which allow the government to control disclosures and minimize, even neuter, their impact, editors first go to officials and advise them what they intend to publish. National security officials then tell the editors all the ways in which national security will supposedly be damaged by the disclosures. A protracted negotiation takes place over what will and will not be published. At best, substantial delay results. Often, patently newsworthy information is suppressed. This is most likely what led the *Post*, when reporting the existence of CIA black sites in 2005, to conceal the identities of those countries in which prisons were based, thus allowing the lawless CIA torture sites to continue.

This same process caused the *New York Times* to conceal the existence of the NSA's warrantless eavesdropping program for *more than a year* after its reporters, James Risen and Eric Lichtblau, were ready to report it in mid-2004. President Bush had summoned the paper's publisher, Arthur Sulzberger, and its editor in chief, Bill Keller, to the Oval Office to insist, ludicrously, that they would be helping terrorists if they revealed that the NSA was spying on Americans without the warrants required by law. The *New York Times* obeyed these dictates and blocked publication of the article *for fifteen months*—until the end of 2005, after Bush had been reelected (thereby allowing him to stand for reelection while concealing from the public that he was eavesdropping on Americans without warrants). Even then, the *Times* eventually ran the NSA story only because a frustrated Risen was about to publish the revelations in his book and the paper did not want to be scooped by its own reporter.

Then there's the tone that establishment media outlets use to discuss government wrongdoing. The culture of US journalism mandates that reporters avoid any clear or declarative statements and incorporate government assertions into their reporting, treating them with respect no matter how frivolous they are. They use what the *Post*'s own media columnist, Erik Wemple, derides as *middle-of-the-road-ese*: never saying anything definitive but instead vesting with equal credence the government's defenses and the actual facts, all of which has the effect of diluting revelations to a muddled, incoherent, often inconsequential mess. Above all else, they invariably give great weight to official claims, even when those claims are patently false or deceitful.

It was that fear-driven, obsequious journalism that led the *Times*, the *Post*, and many other outlets to refuse to use the word "torture" in their reporting on Bush interrogation techniques, even though they freely used that word to describe the exact same tactics when used by other governments around the world. It was also what produced the debacle of media outlets laundering baseless government claims about Saddam and Iraq to sell the American public on a war built of false pretenses that the US media amplified rather than investigated.

Yet another unwritten rule designed to protect the government is that media outlets publish only a few such secret documents, and then stop. They would report on an archive like Snowden's so as to limit its impact— publish a handful of stories, revel in the accolades of a "big scoop," collect prizes, and then walk away, ensuring that nothing had really changed. Snowden, Laura, and I agreed that real reporting on the NSA documents meant that we had to publish aggressively, one story after the next, and not stop until all of the issues in the public interest had been covered, no matter the anger they caused or the threats they provoked.

Snowden had been clear from our first conversation about his ratio- nale for distrusting the establishment media with his story, repeatedly referring to the *New York Times*'s concealment of NSA eavesdropping. He had come to believe that the paper's concealment of that information may very well have changed the outcome of the 2004 election. "Hiding that story changed history," he said.

He was determined to expose the extremity of NSA spying revealed by the documents, so as to enable an enduring public debate with real consequences, rather than achieve a one-off scoop that would accom- plish nothing beyond accolades for the reporters. That would take fear- less disclosures, expressed scorn for flimsy government excuses and fearmongering, steadfast defense of the rightness of Snowden's actions, and unambiguous condemnation of the NSA—exactly what the *Post* would bar its reporters from doing when talking about the govern- ment. I knew that anything the *Post* did would dilute the impact of the disclosures. That they had received a stack of Snowden's documents seemed completely counter to everything I thought we were trying to achieve.

As usual, Laura had cogent reasons for her desire to draw in the *Post*. To begin with, she thought it would be beneficial to involve official Washington in the revelations to make it harder to attack or even criminalize them. If Washington's favorite newspaper were to report on the leaks, it would be more difficult for the government to demonize those involved.

Moreover, as Laura fairly pointed out, neither she nor Snowden had been unable to communicate with me for quite some time due to my lack of encryption, and she had thus been the one to bear the initial burden of having thousands of top secret NSA documents furnished to her by our source. She had felt a need to find someone she could trust with this secret material and to work with an institution that would offer her some protection. She also did not want to travel to Hong Kong alone. Since she couldn't speak with me at first, and since the source felt that someone else should help report the PRISM story, she concluded that it made sense to turn to Gellman.

I understood but never agreed with Laura's rationale for talking to the *Post*. The idea that we needed official Washington involved in the story was, to me, exactly the kind of excessively risk-averse, unwritten-rule-abiding approach I wanted to avoid. We were journalists every bit as much as anyone at the *Post*, and giving them documents so that we would be protected was, in my view, bolstering the very premises we should be seeking to subvert. Although Gellman ended up doing some superb and important reporting with the materials, Snowden, during our initial conversations, began to regret the *Post*'s involvement, even though he had been the one who had ultimately decided to accept Laura's recommendation to include them.

Snowden was upset by what he perceived to be the *Post*'s foot-dragging, by the recklessness of involving so many people to talk in unsecured ways about what he had done, and especially by the fear demonstrated by endlessly convening with alarmist lawyers. Snowden was especially angry that Gellman, at the behest of *Post* lawyers and editors, had ultimately declined to travel to Hong Kong to meet him and go over the documents.

At least as both Snowden and Laura conveyed it, the *Post*'s lawyers had told Gellman he shouldn't travel to Hong Kong; they also advised Laura not to go there and rescinded their offer to pay her travel expenses. This was based on an absurd, fear-driven theory; that any discussions about top secret information conducted in China, itself a pervasive surveillance state, might be overheard by the Chinese government. That, in turn, could be viewed by the US government as the *Post* recklessly passing secrets to the Chinese, which could result in criminal liability for the *Post* and for Gellman under espionage laws.

Snowden, in his stoic and understated way, was livid. He had unraveled his life and put everything in jeopardy in order to get this story out. He had almost no protection, yet here was this huge media operation with all sorts of legal and institutional support that would not take the trivial risk of sending a reporter to Hong Kong to meet with him. "I'm ready to hand them this huge story at great personal risk," he said, "and they won't even get on a plane." It was exactly the type of timid, risk-averse government obeisance by our "adversarial press corps" that I had spent years condemning.

The act of giving some of the documents to the *Post* was done, though, and there was nothing he or I could do to reverse it. But that second night in Hong Kong, after I met with Snowden, I resolved that it would not be the *Washington Post*, with its muddled, pro-government voice, its fear, and its middle-of-the-road-ese, that would shape how the NSA and Snowden would forever be understood. Whoever broke this story first would play the predominant role in how it was discussed and framed, and I was determined that this would be the *Guardian* and me. For this story to have the effect it should, the unwritten rules of establishment journalism—designed to soften the impact of revelations and protect the government—had to be broken, not obeyed. The *Post* would do the latter: I would not.

So, once in my hotel room, I finished work on the four separate stories. The first was about the secret order from the FISA court compelling Verizon, one of America's largest telephone companies, to turn over to the NSA all the telephone records of all Americans. The second covered the history of the Bush warrantless eavesdropping program, based on a top secret 2009 internal report from the NSA's inspector general; another detailed the BOUNDLESS INFORMANT program that I had read about on the plane; and the last story laid out the PRISM program, which I had first learned about at home in Brazil. It was this story, above all, that compelled my urgency: this was the document the *Post* was working to report.

To move quickly, we needed the *Guardian* on board to publish right away. As evening approached in Hong Kong—early morning in New York—I waited impatiently until the *Guardian* editors were just waking up in New York and kept checking every five minutes to see if Janine Gibson had signed on to Google chat, our normal way of communicating. As soon as I saw that she had, I immediately sent her a message: "We have to talk."

By that point, we knew that speaking by telephone or by Google chat was out of the question. Both were far too insecure. We somehow failed to connect via OTR, the encrypted chat program we had been using, so Janine suggested that we try Cryptocat, a recently released program designed to impede state surveillance that became our primary means of communication throughout my time in Hong Kong.

I told her about my meeting that day with Snowden, that I was convinced of his authenticity and of the documents he provided. I told her I had already written a number of articles. Janine was particularly excited by the Verizon story.

"Great," I said. "That article is ready. If there are minor edits, fine, let's do them." I stressed to Janine the urgency of publishing quickly. "Let's get it out now."

But there was a problem. The *Guardian* editors had been meeting with the paper's lawyers and were hearing alarming warnings. Janine conveyed what she had been told by the *Guardian* lawyers: publishing classified information can be depicted (albeit dubiously) as a crime by the US government, a violation of the Espionage Act, even for newspapers. The danger was particularly acute for documents relating to signals intelligence. The government had refrained from prosecuting media outlets in the past, but only as long as the media observed the unwritten rules giving officials an advance look and the opportunity to argue that publication would damage national security. This consultative process with the government, the *Guardian* lawyers explained, is what enables newspapers to demonstrate they have no intent to harm national security by publishing top secret documents and thus lack the requisite criminal intent to be prosecuted.

There had never been a leak of documents from the NSA, let alone one of this magnitude and sensitivity. The lawyers thought there was potential criminal exposure—not only for Snowden but, given the Obama administration's history, for the paper as well. Just weeks before my arrival in Hong Kong, it was revealed that the Obama Justice Department had obtained a court order to read through the emails and telephone records of reporters and editors from the Associated Press to find their source for a story.

Almost immediately after that, a new report revealed an even more extreme attack on the news-gathering process: the Department of Justice had filed a court affidavit accusing Fox News Washington bureau chief James Rosen of being a "co-conspirator" in his source's alleged crimes, on the grounds that the journalist had "aided and abetted" the source's disclosure of classified information by working with him closely to receive the materials.

Journalists had noted for several years that the Obama administration was waging unprecedented attacks on journalism. But the Rosen episode was a major escalation. To criminalize cooperation with one's source as "aiding and abetting" is to criminalize investigative journalism itself: no reporter ever obtains secret information without working with his source to get it. This climate had made all media lawyers, including the *Guardian*'s, extra cautious and even fearful.

"They're saying that the FBI could come in and shut down our office and take our files," Gibson told me.

I thought that was ridiculous: the very idea that the US government would shut down a major newspaper like the *Guardian US* and raid its office was the kind of overanxious advice that had made me, during my legal career, learn to hate lawyers' forbiddingly excessive warnings. But I knew Gibson wouldn't—and couldn't—simply dismiss those concerns out of hand.

"What does this mean for what we're doing?" I asked. "When can we publish?"

"I'm really not sure, Glenn," Gibson told me. "We need to get every-thing sorted first. We're meeting with the lawyers again tomorrow and we'll know more then."

I was truly concerned. I had no idea how the *Guardian* editors were going to react. My independence at the *Guardian* and the fact that I had written few articles with editorial consulation, and certainly none as sen-sitive as this, meant that I was dealing with unknown factors. Indeed, the entire story was sui generis: it was impossible to know how anyone would react because nothing quite like this had happened before. Would the editors be cowed and bullied by US threats? Would they opt to spend weeks in negotiations with the government? Would they prefer to let the *Post* break the story so as to feel safer?

I was eager to publish the Verizon story immediately: we had the FISA document and it was clearly genuine. There was no reason to deny Amer-icans the right to see what the government was doing to their privacy, not even for one more minute. Equally urgent was the obligation I felt to Snowden. He had made his choice in a spirit of fearlessness, passion, and strength. I was determined that the reporting I did would be driven by the same spirit, to do justice to the sacrifice our source had made. Only audacious journalism could give the story the power it needed to over-come the climate of fear the government had imposed on journalists and their sources. Anxious legal concerns and the *Guardian*'s hesitancy were the antithesis of such audacity.

That night, I called David and confessed my growing worry about the *Guardian*. Laura and I discussed my concerns as well. We agreed to give the *Guardian* until the next day to publish the first article or we would explore other options.

Some hours later, Ewen MacAskill came to my room to get an update on Snowden, whom he hadn't yet met. I shared with him my concern about delays. "You don't need to worry," he said about the *Guardian*. "They're very aggressive." Alan Rusbridger, the *Guardian*'s longtime edi-tor in chief in London was, Ewen assured me, "very engaged" with the story and "committed to publishing."

I still viewed Ewen as a company man but was feeling a little bet-ter about him, given his own desire to publish quickly. After he left, I now told Snowden about Ewen traveling with us, referring to him as the *Guardian*'s "babysitter" and said that I wanted them to meet the next day. I explained that getting Ewen on board was an important step in making the *Guardian* editors feel sufficiently comfortable to publish. "No problem," Snowden said. "But you know you have a minder. That's why they sent him."

Their meeting was important. The next morning, Ewen came with us to Snowden's hotel and spent roughly two hours questioning him, covering much of the same ground I had the day before. "How can I know you are what you say you are?" Ewen asked at the end. "Do you have any proof?" Snowden pulled out from his suitcase a pile of documents: his now-expired diplomatic passport, a former CIA identification card, a driver's license, and other government ID.

We left the hotel room together. "I'm completely convinced he's real," Ewen said. "I have zero doubts." In his view, there was no longer any reason to wait. "I'm going to call Alan as soon as we get back to the hotel and tell him we should start publishing now."

From that point forward, Ewen was fully integrated into our team. Laura and Snowden had both felt instantly comfortable with him, and I had to confess to feeling the same way. We realized that our suspicions had been entirely unfounded: lurking under the surface of Ewen's mild-mannered, avuncular exterior was a fearless reporter eager to pursue this story in exactly the way that we all thought necessary. Ewen, at least as he viewed himself, wasn't there to impose institutional constraints but to report and, at times, to help overcome those constraints. In fact, during our stay in Hong Kong, Ewen was often the most radical voice, arguing in favor of disclosures that not even Laura or I—or, for that matter, Snowden—were sure should be made yet. I quickly realized that his advocacy for aggressive reporting inside the *Guardian* would be vital in keeping London fully behind what we were doing, and it was.

As soon as it was morning in London, Ewen and I called Alan together. I wanted to convey as clearly as possible that I expected—demanded, even—that the *Guardian* begin publishing that day, and to get a clear sense of the paper's position. By that point—only my second full day in

Hong Kong—I had mentally committed to taking the story elsewhere if I sensed any substantial institutional hesitation.

I was blunt. "I'm ready to publish this Verizon article and I don't understand at all why we're not doing it now," I told Alan. "What's the delay?"

He assured me that there was no delay. "I agree. We're ready to publish. Janine has to have one final meeting with the lawyers this afternoon. I'm sure we'll publish after that."

I brought up the *Post*'s involvement with the PRISM story, which was only fueling my sense of urgency. Alan then surprised me: he not only wanted to be first to publish NSA stories in general, but also wanted to be the first to publish the PRISM story specifically, clearly eager to scoop the *Post*. "There's no reason we should defer to them," he said.

"That's great with me."

London was four hours ahead of New York, so it was going to be some time before Janine got into the office and even longer still before she met with the lawyers. So I spent the Hong Kong evening with Ewen finalizing our own PRISM story, reassured that Rusbridger was being as aggressive as necessary.

We finished the PRISM article that day and used encryption to email it to Janine and Stuart Millar in New York. Now we had two major, blockbuster scoops ready to be published: Verizon and PRISM. My patience, my willingness to wait, was wearing very thin.

Janine started her meeting with the lawyers at 3:00 p.m. New York time—3:00 a.m. in Hong Kong—and sat with them for two hours. I stayed up, waiting to learn the outcome. When I spoke with Janine, I wanted to hear one thing only: that we were immediately running the Verizon article.

That's not what happened, not even close. There were still "considerable" legal questions to be addressed, she told me. Once those were resolved, the *Guardian* had to advise government officials of our plans to give them an opportunity to persuade us not to publish—the process I loathed and had long condemned. I accepted that the *Guardian* would have to let the government make its case for non-publication, provided that the process did not become some protracted means of delaying the story for weeks or diluting its impact.

"It sounds like we're days or even weeks away from publishing—not hours," I told Janine, trying to pack all my irritation and impatience into an online chat. "Let me reiterate that I will take any steps necessary to ensure that this story runs now." The threat was implicit but unambiguous: if I couldn't get the articles out immediately at the *Guardian*, I would go somewhere else.

"You've already made yourself very clear on that," she curtly replied.

It was now the end of the day in New York, and I knew that nothing would happen until at least the following day. I was frustrated and, by this point, very anxious. The *Post* was working on its PRISM article, and Laura, who was going to have a byline on that story, had heard from Gellman that they were planning to publish on Sunday, which was five days away.

Talking it over with David and Laura, I realized I was no longer willing to wait for the *Guardian*. We all agreed I should start exploring alternatives as a Plan B in the event that there was more delay. Calls to *Salon*, my publishing home for years, as well as the *Nation*, quickly bore fruit. Both told me within a matter of hours that they would be happy to run the NSA stories right away, and they offered all the support I would need, with lawyers ready to vet the articles immediately.

Knowing that there were two established venues ready and eager to print the NSA articles was emboldening. But in conversations with David, we decided there was an even more powerful alternative: to simply create our own website, entitled NSAdisclosures.com, and begin releasing the articles there, without the need for any existing media outlet. Once we went public with the fact that we had in our possession this huge trove of secret documents about NSA spying, we would easily recruit volunteer editors, lawyers, researchers, and financial backers: an entire team, motivated by nothing but a passion for transparency and real adversarial journalism, devoted to reporting what we knew was one of the most significant leaks in US history.

From the start, I believed that the documents presented an opportunity to shine a light not only on secret NSA spying but on the corrupting

dynamics of establishment journalism. Breaking one of the most important stories in years through a new and independent model of reporting,
separate from any large media organization, was extremely appealing to
me. It would boldly underscore that the First Amendment's guarantee
of a free press and the ability to do important journalism were not de-
pendent on affiliation with a large media outlet. The free press guarantee
does not only protect corporate reporters but anyone engaged in journalism, whether employed or not. And the fearlessness conveyed by taking
such a step—*We're going publish thousands of top secret NSA documents
without the protection of a large media corporation*—would embolden
others and help shatter the current climate of fear.

That night, I again barely slept. I spent the early morning hours in
Hong Kong calling people whose opinions I trust: friends, lawyers, journalists, people with whom I had worked closely. They all gave me the
same advice, which didn't really surprise me: it's too risky to do this
alone, without an existing media structure. I wanted to hear the arguments against acting independently, and they provided many good ones.

By late morning, after I had heard all the warnings, I called David
again while I simultaneously spoke online with Laura. David was particularly adamant that going to *Salon* or the *Nation* would be too cautious
and fear-driven—"a step backward," he called it—and that, if the *Guardian* delayed further, only releasing the stories at a newly created website
could capture the intrepid spirit driving the reporting we wanted to do.
He was also convinced that it would inspire people everywhere. Though
initially skeptical, Laura was persuaded that taking such a bold step—
creating a global network of people devoted to NSA transparency—
would unleash a massive and powerful surge of passion.

So as afternoon approached in Hong Kong, we resolved jointly that
if the *Guardian* was unwilling to publish by the end of that day—which
had not yet begun on the East Coast—I would leave and immediately
post the Verizon article on our new website. Though I understood the
risks involved, I was incredibly excited by our decision. I also knew that
having this alternative plan in place would make me much stronger in
my discussions that day with the *Guardian*: I felt I didn't need to stay

attached to them to do this reporting, and freeing oneself of attachments is always empowering.

When I spoke with Snowden that same afternoon, I told him about our plan. "Risky. But bold," he typed. "I like it."

I managed to get a couple of hours of sleep, woke in the middle of the Hong Kong afternoon, and then confronted the fact that I had hours to wait for the start of Wednesday morning in New York. I knew that, in some fashion, I was going to communicate an ultimatum to the *Guardian*. I wanted to get on with it.

As soon as I saw Janine come online, I asked her what the plan was. "Are we going to publish today?"

"I hope so," she replied. Her uncertainty made me agitated. The *Guardian* still intended to contact the NSA that morning to advise them of our intentions. She said we would know our publishing schedule only once we heard back from them.

"I don't get why we're going to wait," I said, now having lost patience with the *Guardian*'s delays. "For a story this clean and straightforward, who cares what they think we should and shouldn't publish?"

Aside from my contempt for the process—the government should not be a collaborative editorial partner with newspapers in deciding what gets published—I knew there was no plausible national security argument against our specific Verizon report, which involved a simple court order showing the systematic collection of Americans' telephone records. The idea that "terrorists" would benefit from exposing the order was laughable: any terrorists capable of tying their own shoes would already know that the government was trying to monitor their telephone communications. The people who would learn something from our article weren't the "terrorists" but the American people.

Janine repeated what she had heard from the *Guardian*'s lawyers and insisted that I was operating under a wrong assumption if I thought the paper was going to be bullied out of publishing. Instead, she said, it was a legal requirement that they hear what US officials have to say. But, she assured me, she would not be intimidated or swayed by vague and frivolous appeals to national security.

I didn't assume that the *Guardian* would be bullied; I just didn't know.

And I was worried that, at the very least, talking to the government would significantly delay things. The *Guardian* did have a history of aggressive and defiant reporting, which is one of the reasons I went there in the first place. And I knew that they had the right to demonstrate what they would do in this situation rather than have me assume the worst. Janine's proclamation of independence was somewhat reassuring.

"OK," I said, willing to wait and see. "But again, from my perspective, this has to be published *today*," I typed. "I'm not willing to wait any longer."

At around noon New York time, Janine told me that they had called the NSA and the White House to tell them they were planning on publishing top secret material. But nobody had called them back. The White House that morning had named Susan Rice as its new national security adviser. The *Guardian*'s national security reporter, Spencer Ackerman, had good contacts in Washington. He told Janine that officials were "preoccupied" with Susan Rice.

"Right now, they don't think they need to call us back," Janine wrote. "They're going to learn quickly that they need to return my calls."

At 3:00 a.m.—3:00 p.m. New York time—I still had not heard anything. Nor had Janine.

"Do they have any sort of deadline, or is it just whenever they feel like getting back to us?" I asked sarcastically.

She replied that the *Guardian* had asked to hear from the NSA "before the end of the day."

"What if they don't respond by then?" I asked.

"We'll make our decision then," she said.

Janine then added another complicating factor: Alan Rusbridger, her boss, had just boarded a plane from London to New York to oversee publication of the NSA stories. But that meant he would be unavailable for the next seven hours or so.

"Are you able to publish this article without Alan?" If the answer was "no," then there was no chance the article would be published that day. Alan's plane wasn't even scheduled to arrive at JKF until late at night.

"We'll see," she said.

I felt like I was running into exactly the sort of institutional barriers to doing aggressive reporting that I had joined the *Guardian* to avoid: Legal worries. Consultation with government officials. Institutional hierarchies. Risk aversion. Delay.

Moments later, at roughly 3:15 p.m. New York time, Stuart Millar, Janine's deputy, sent me an instant message: "The government called back. Janine is talking to them now."

I waited for what felt like an eternity. Around an hour later, Janine called me and recounted what had happened. There had been close to a dozen senior officials on the phone from numerous agencies, including NSA, DOJ, and the White House. At first they were patronizing but friendly, telling her she didn't understand the meaning or "context" of the Verizon court order. They wanted to schedule a meeting with her "sometime next week" to meet and explain things.

When Janine told them she wanted to publish that day, and would do so unless she heard very specific and concrete reasons not to do so, they became more belligerent, even bullying. They told her she was not a "serious journalist" and the *Guardian* was not a "serious newspaper" because of its refusal to give the government more time to argue in favor of suppressing the story.

"No normal journalistic outlet would publish this quickly without first meeting with us," they said, clearly playing for time.

They're probably right, I remember thinking. That's the point. The rules in place allow the government to control and neuter the newsgathering process and eliminate the adversarial relationship between press and government. To me, it was vital for them to know from the start that those corrupting rules were not going to apply in this case. These stories would be released by a different set of rules, one that would define an independent rather than subservient press corps.

I was encouraged by Janine's tone: strong and defiant. She stressed that, despite her repeatedly asking, they had failed to provide a single specific way in which national security would be harmed by publication. But she still wouldn't commit to publishing that day. At the end of the call, she said: "I'm going to see if I can reach Alan, then we'll decide what to do."

I waited for half an hour and then asked her bluntly: "Are we going to publish today or not? That's all I want to know."

She evaded the question. Alan was unreachable. It was clear that she was in an extremely difficult situation: on one side, US officials were bitterly accusing her of recklessness; on the other, she had me making increasingly uncompromising demands. And to top that off, the paper's top editor was on an airplane, meaning that one of the most difficult and consequential decisions in the paper's 190-year history had fallen squarely on her shoulders.

As I stayed online with Janine, I was on the phone the whole time with David. "It's close to five p.m.," David argued. "That's the deadline you gave them. It's time for a decision. They need to publish now or you need to tell them you quit."

He was right, but I was hesitant. Quitting the *Guardian* right before I published one of the biggest national security leaks in US history would cause a huge media scandal. It would be damaging in the extreme to the *Guardian*, as I would have to offer some kind of public explanation, which would in turn compel them to defend themselves, probably by attacking me. We'd have a circus on our hands, a huge sideshow that would damage all of us. Worse, it would distract from where the focus should be: on the NSA disclosures.

I also had to acknowledge my personal fear: publishing hundreds if not thousands of top secret NSA files was going to be risky enough, even as part of a large organization like the *Guardian*. Doing it alone, without institutional protection, would be far riskier. All the smart warnings from the friends and lawyers I had called played loudly in my head.

As I hesitated, David said, "You have no choice. If they're scared to publish, this isn't the place for you. You can't operate by fear or you won't achieve anything. That's the lesson Snowden just showed you."

Together, we composed what I was going to tell Janine in our chat box: "It's now 5:00 p.m., which was the deadline I gave you. If we don't publish immediately—in the next thirty minutes—then I hereby terminate my contract with the *Guardian*." I almost hit "send," and then reconsidered. The note was way too much of an explicit threat, a virtual ransom note.

If I left the *Guardian* under those circumstances, everything would be made public, including that line. So I softened the tone: "I understand that you have your concerns and have to do what you feel is right. I'm going to go ahead and now do what I think needs to be done, too. I'm sorry it didn't work out." I then hit "send."

Within fifteen seconds, the phone rang in my hotel room. It was Janine. "I think you're being terribly unfair," she said, clearly distraught. If I left, then the *Guardian*—which had none of the documents—would lose the entire story.

"I think you're the one being unfair," I replied. "I've repeatedly asked you when you intend to publish, and you refuse to give me an answer, just offering coy evasions."

"We *are* going to publish today," Janine said. "We're thirty minutes away at most. We're just making a few final edits, working on headlines, and formatting. It will be up no later than five thirty."

"OK. If that's the plan, then there's no problem," I said. "I'm obviously willing to wait thirty minutes."

At 5:40 p.m., Janine sent me an instant message with a link, the one I had been waiting to see for days. "It's live," she said.

"NSA Collecting Phone Records of Millions of Verizon Customers Daily," the headline read, followed by a subhead: "Exclusive: Top Secret Court Order Requiring Verizon to Hand Over All Call Data Shows Scale of Domestic Surveillance Under Obama."

That was followed by a link to the full FISA court order. The first three paragraphs of our article told the entire story:

> The National Security Agency is currently collecting the telephone records of millions of US customers of Verizon, one of America's largest telecom providers, under a top secret court order issued in April.
>
> The order, a copy of which has been obtained by the Guardian, requires Verizon on an "ongoing, daily basis" to give the NSA information on all telephone calls in its systems, both within the US and between the US and other countries.
>
> The document shows for the first time that under the Obama administration the communication records of millions of US citizens are being

collected indiscriminately and in bulk—regardless of whether they are suspected of any wrongdoing.

The impact of the article was instant and enormous, beyond anything I had anticipated. It was the lead story on every national news broadcast that night and dominated political and media discussions. I was inundated with interview requests from virtually every national TV outlet: CNN, MSNBC, NBC, the *Today* show, *Good Morning America*, and others. I spent many hours in Hong Kong talking to numerous sympathetic television interviewers—an unusual experience in my career as a political writer often at odds with the establishment press —who all treated the story as a major event and a real scandal.

In response, the White House spokesman predictably defended the bulk collection program as "a critical tool in protecting the nation from terrorist threats." The Democratic chairwoman of the Senate Intelligence Committee, Dianne Feinstein, one of the most steadfast congressional supporters of the national security state generally and US surveillance specifically, invoked standard post-9/11 fearmongering by telling reporters that the program was necessary because "people want the homeland kept safe."

But almost nobody took those claims seriously. The pro-Obama *New York Times* editorial page issued a harsh denunciation of the administration. In an editorial entitled "President Obama's Dragnet," the paper announced: "Mr. Obama is proving the truism that the executive branch will use any power it is given and very likely abuse it." Mocking the administration's rote invocation of "terrorism" to justify the program, the editorial proclaimed: "the administration has now lost all credibility." (Generating some controversy, the *New York Times*, without comment, softened that denunciation several hours after it was first published by adding the phrase "on this issue.")

Democratic senator Mark Udall issued a statement saying that "this sort of wide-scale surveillance should concern all of us and is the kind of government overreach I've said Americans would find shocking." The ACLU said that "from a civil liberties perspective, the program could hardly be any more alarming. . . . It is beyond Orwellian, and it provides

further evidence of the extent to which basic democratic rights are being surrendered in secret to the demands of unaccountable intelligence
agencies." Former vice president Al Gore took to Twitter, linked to our
story, and wrote: "Is it just me, or is blanket surveillance obscenely outra-
geous?"

Soon after the story ran, the Associated Press confirmed from an un-
named senator what we had strongly suspected: that the bulk phone record collection program had been going on for years, and was directed at
all major US telecom carriers, not just Verizon.

In the seven years I had been writing and speaking about the NSA, I
had never seen any revelation produce anything near this level of interest
and passion. There was no time to analyze why it had resonated so powerfully and prompted such a tidal wave of interest and indignation; for
the moment, I intended to ride the wave rather than try to understand it.

When I was finally finished with TV interviews at around noon Hong
Kong time, I went directly to Snowden's hotel room. When I walked in,
he had CNN on. Guests were discussing the NSA, expressing shock at the
scope of the spying program. Hosts were indignant that this was all being done in secret. Almost every guest they brought on denounced bulk
domestic spying.

"It's everywhere," Snowden said, clearly excited. "I watched all your
interviews. Everyone seemed to get it."

At that moment, I felt a real sense of accomplishment. Snowden's
great fear—that he would throw his life away for revelations nobody
would care about—had proved unfounded on the very first day: we had
seen not a trace of indifference or apathy. Laura and I had helped him
unleash precisely the debate we all believed was urgently necessary—and
now I was able to see him watch it all unfold.

Given Snowden's plan to out himself after the first week of stories, we
both knew that his freedom was likely to come to an end very shortly.
For me, the depressing certainty that he would soon be under attack—
hunted if not caged as a criminal—hovered over everything we did. It
didn't seem to bother him at all, but it made me determined to vindicate
his choice, to maximize the value of the revelations he had risked every-

thing to bring to the world. We were off to a good start, and it was just the beginning.

"Everyone thinks this is a onetime story, a stand-alone scoop," Snowden observed. "Nobody knows this is just the very tip of the iceberg, that there's so much more to come." He turned to me. "What's next and when?"

"PRISM," I said. "Tomorrow."

I went back to my hotel room and, despite now approaching a sixth night of sleeplessness, simply could not switch off. The adrenaline was way too potent. At 4:30 p.m., as my only hope of catching some rest, I took a sleeping aid and set the alarm for 7:30 p.m., when I knew *Guardian* editors in New York would be coming online.

That day, Janine got online early. We exchanged congratulations and marveled at the reaction to the article. Instantly, it was obvious that the tone of our exchange had changed radically. We had just navigated a significant journalistic challenge together. Janine was proud of the article and I was proud of her resistance to government bullying and her decision to publish the piece. The *Guardian* had fearlessly, admirably, come through.

Although it had seemed at the time that there was substantial delay, it was clear in retrospect that the *Guardian* had moved forward with remarkable speed and boldness: more so, I'm certain, than any news venue of comparable size and stature would have done. And Janine was now clear that the paper had no intention of resting on its laurels. "Alan is insistent that we publish PRISM today," she said. I, of course, could not have been happier.

What made the PRISM revelations so important was that the program allowed the NSA to obtain virtually anything it wanted from the Internet companies that hundreds of millions of people around the world now use as their primary means to communicate. This move was made possible by the laws that the US government had implemented in the wake of 9/11, which vested the NSA with sweeping powers to surveil Americans and with virtually unlimited authority to carry out indiscriminate mass surveillance of entire foreign populations.

The 2008 FISA Amendments Act is the current governing law for NSA surveillance. It was enacted by a bipartisan Congress in the wake of the Bush-era NSA warrantless eavesdropping scandal, and a key result was that it effectively legalized the crux of Bush's illegal program. As the scandal revealed, Bush had secretly authorized the NSA to eavesdrop on Americans and others within the United States, justifying the order by the need to search for terrorist activity. The order overrode the requirement to obtain the court-approved warrants ordinarily necessary for domestic spying, and resulted in the secret surveillance of at least thousands of people within the United States.

Despite the outcry that this program was illegal, the 2008 FISA law sought to institutionalize some of the scheme, not end it. The law is based on a distinction between "US persons" (American citizens and those legally on US soil) and all other people. To directly target a US person's telephone calls or emails, the NSA must still obtain an individual warrant from the FISA court.

But for all other people, wherever they are, no individual warrant is needed, *even if they are communicating with US persons*. Under section 702 of the 2008 law, the NSA is merely required once a year to submit to the FISA court its general guidelines for determining that year's targets—the criteria is merely that the surveillance will "aid legitimate foreign intelligence gathering"—and then receives blanket authorization to proceed. Once the FISA court stamps "approved" on those permits, the NSA is then empowered to target any foreign nationals it wants for surveillance, and can compel telecoms and Internet companies to provide access to all the communications of any non-American, including those with US persons—Facebook chats, Yahoo! emails, Google searches. There is no need to persuade a court that the person is guilty of anything, or even that there is reason to regard the target with suspicion, and there is no need to filter out the US persons who end up surveilled in the process.

The first order of business was for *Guardian* editors to advise the government of our intentions to publish the PRISM story. Again, we would give them a deadline of the end of that day, New York time. That ensured they would have a full day to convey any objections, rendering invalid their inevitable complaints that they hadn't had long enough to respond. But it was equally vital to get comments from the Internet companies that had, according to the NSA documents, provided the agency with direct access to their servers as part of PRISM: Facebook, Google, Apple, YouTube, Skype, and the rest.

With hours to wait again, I returned to Snowden's hotel room, where Laura was working with him on various issues. At this point, having crossed a significant threshold—with the publication of the first explosive revelation—Snowden was becoming visibly more vigilant about his security. After I walked in, he put extra pillows against the door. At several points, when he wanted to show me something on his computer, he put a blanket over his head to prevent ceiling cameras from picking up his passwords. When the telephone rang, we all froze: Who could be calling? Snowden picked up, very tentatively, after several rings: the hotel housekeepers, seeing the DO NOT DISTURB sign on his door, were checking to see if he wanted his room cleaned. "No thanks," he said curtly.

The climate was always tense when we met in Snowden's room; it only intensified once we began publishing. We had no idea whether the NSA had identified the source of the leak. If they had, did they know where Snowden was? Did Hong Kong or Chinese agents know? There could be a knock on Snowden's door at any moment that would put an immediate and unpleasant end to our work together.

In the background, the television was always on, and it seemed someone was always talking about the NSA. After the Verizon story broke, the news programs talked of little beyond "indiscriminate bulk collection" and "local telephone records" and "surveillance abuses." As we discussed our next stories, Laura and I watched Snowden watching the frenzy he had triggered.

Then at 2:00 a.m. Hong Kong time, when the PRISM article was about to run, I heard from Janine.

"Something extremely weird has happened," she said. "The tech companies vehemently deny what's in the NSA documents. They insist they've never heard of PRISM."

We went through the possible explanations for their denials. Perhaps the NSA documents overstated the agency's capabilities. Perhaps the tech companies were simply lying, or the specific individuals interviewed were unaware of their company's arrangements with the NSA. Or perhaps PRISM was just an internal NSA code name, never shared with the companies. ✕

Whatever the explanation, we had to rewrite our story, not just to include the denials but to change the focus to the strange disparity between the NSA documents and the tech companies' position.

"Let's not take a position on who's right. Let's just air the disagreement and let them work it out in public," I proposed. Our intention was that the story would force an open discussion of what the Internet industry had agreed to do with their users' communications; if their version clashed with the NSA documents, they would need to resolve it with the world watching, which is how it should be.

Janine agreed and two hours later sent me the new draft of the PRISM story. The headline read:

NSA Prism Program Taps In to User Data of Apple, Google and Others

- Top-secret Prism program claims direct access to servers of firms including Google, Apple and Facebook
- Companies deny any knowledge of program in operation since 2007

After quoting the NSA documents describing PRISM, the article noted: "Although the presentation claims the program is run with the assistance of the companies, all those who responded to a *Guardian* request for comment on Thursday denied knowledge of any such program." The article looked great to me, and Janine pledged that it would run within half an hour.

As I waited impatiently for the minutes to go by, I heard the chime indicating the arrival of a chat message. I was hoping for confirmation from Janine, letting me know that the PRISM article was up. The message was from Janine, but not what I expected.

"The *Post* just published their PRISM story," she said.

What? Why, I wanted to know, had the *Post* suddenly changed its publishing schedule to rush their article into publication three days ahead of their plan?

Laura shortly learned from Barton Gellman that the *Post* had got wind of our intentions after US officials had been contacted by the *Guardian* about the PRISM program that morning. One of those officials, knowing that the *Post* was working on a similar story, had passed on the news of our article on PRISM. The *Post* had then rapidly sped up their schedule to avoid being scooped.

Now I loathed the deliberation even more: a US official had exploited this prepublication procedure, supposedly designed to protect national security, to ensure that his favored newspaper would run the story first.

Once I had absorbed the information, I noticed the explosion on Twitter about the *Post*'s PRISM article. But when I went to read it, I saw something missing: the inconsistency between the NSA version and the Internet companies' statements.

Headlined "U.S., British Intelligence Mining Data from Nine U.S. Internet Companies in Broad Secret Program," and with Gellman and Laura's byline, the piece stated that "the National Security Agency and the FBI are tapping directly into the central servers of nine leading U.S. Internet companies, extracting audio and video chats, photographs, e-mails, documents, and connection logs that enable analysts to track foreign targets." Most significantly, it alleged that the nine companies "participate knowingly in PRISM operations."

Our own PRISM article was published ten minutes later, with its rather different focus and more cautious tone, prominently touting the Internet companies' vehement denials.

Once again, the reaction was explosive. Moreover, it was international. Unlike telephone carriers such as Verizon, which are generally based in one country, Internet giants are global. Billions of people all over the world—in countries on every continent—use Facebook, Gmail, Skype, and Yahoo! as a primary means of communication. To learn that these companies had entered into secret arrangements with the NSA to provide access to their customers' communications was globally shocking.

And now people began speculating that the earlier Verizon story was not a onetime event: the two articles signaled a serious NSA leak.

The PRISM story's publication marked the last day for many months when I was able to read, let alone respond to, all the emails I received. Scanning my in-box, I saw the names of almost every major media outlet in the world wanting an interview: the worldwide debate Snowden had wanted to trigger was well under way—after only two days of stories. I thought about the massive trove of documents still to come, what this would mean for my life, the impact it would have on the world, and how the US government would respond once it realized what it faced.

In a repeat of the previous day, I spent the early hours of Hong Kong's morning doing prime-time TV shows in the United States. The pattern that I followed my entire time in Hong Kong was thus set: working on stories throughout the night with the *Guardian*, doing interviews by day with the media, and then joining Laura and Snowden in his hotel room.

I frequently took cabs around Hong Kong at 3:00 or 4:00 a.m., going to television studios, always with Snowden's "operational security" instructions in mind: never to part with my computer or the thumb drives full of documents to prevent tampering or theft. I traveled the desolate streets of Hong Kong with my heavy backpack permanently attached to my shoulders, no matter where or what the hour. I fought paranoia every step of the way and often found myself looking over my shoulder, grabbing my bag just a bit more tightly each time someone approached.

When I was done with the bevy of TV interviews, I would head back to Snowden's room, where Laura, Snowden, and I—sometimes joined by MacAskill—continued our work, interrupting our progress only to glance at the TV. We were amazed at the positive reaction, how substantive the media's engagement with the revelations appeared to be, and how angry most commentators were: not at those who brought the transparency but at the extraordinary level of state surveillance we had exposed.

I now felt able to implement one of our intended strategies, responding defiantly and scornfully toward the government's tactic of invoking 9/11 as the justification for this spying. I began denouncing Washington's tired and predictable accusations—that we had endangered national security, that we were aiding terrorism, that we had committed a crime by revealing national secrets.

I felt emboldened to argue that these were the transparent, manipulative strategies of government officials who had been caught doing things that embarrassed them and damaged their reputations. Such attacks would not deter our reporting: we would publish many more stories from the documents, regardless of fearmongering and threats, carrying out our duty as journalists. I wanted to be clear: the usual intimidation and demonization were futile. Despite this defiant posture, most of the media, in those first days, were supportive of our work.

This surprised me because, especially since 9/11 (though before that as well), the US media in general had been jingoistic and intensely loyal to the government and thus hostile, sometimes viciously so, to anyone who exposed its secrets.

When WikiLeaks began publishing classified documents related to the Iraq and Afghanistan wars and especially diplomatic cables, calls for the prosecution of WikiLeaks were led by American journalists themselves, which was in itself astounding behavior. The very institution ostensibly devoted to bringing transparency to the actions of the powerful not only denounced but attempted to criminalize one of the most significant acts of transparency in many years. What WikiLeaks did—receiving classified information from a source within the government and then revealing it to the world—is essentially what media organizations do all the time.

I had expected the American media to direct its hostility toward me, especially as we continued to publish documents and the unprecedented scope of the leak began to be clear. And as a harsh critic of the journalist establishment and many of its leading members, I was, I reasoned, a natural magnet for such hostility. I had few allies in the traditional media. Most were people whose work I had attacked publicly, frequently, and unsparingly. I expected them to turn on me at the first opportunity, but that first week of media appearances was a virtual lovefest, and not just when I was on.

On Thursday, day five in Hong Kong, I went to Snowden's hotel room and he immediately said he had news that was "a bit alarming." An Internet-connected security device at the home he shared with his longtime girlfriend in Hawaii had detected that two people from the NSA—a human resources person and an NSA "police officer"—had come to their house searching for him.

Snowden was almost certain this meant that the NSA had identified him as the likely source of the leaks, but I was skeptical. "If they thought you did this, they'd send hordes of FBI agents with a search warrant and probably SWAT teams, not a single NSA officer and a human resources person." I figured this was just an automatic and routine inquiry, triggered when an NSA employee goes absent for a few weeks without explanation. But Snowden suggested that perhaps they were being purposely low-key to avoid drawing media attention or setting off an effort to suppress evidence.

Whatever the news meant, it underscored the need to quickly prepare our article and video unveiling Snowden as the source of the disclosures. We were determined that the world would first hear about Snowden, his actions and his motives, from Snowden himself, not through a demonization campaign spread by the US government while he was in hiding or in custody and unable to speak for himself.

Our plan was to publish two more articles, one on Friday, the next day, and one after that, on Saturday. Then on Sunday, we would release a long piece on Snowden, accompanied by a videotaped interview, and a printed Q and A with him that Ewen would conduct.

Laura had spent the prior forty-eight hours editing the footage from my first interview with Snowden, but she said it was too detailed, lengthy, and fragmented to use. She wanted to film a new interview right away, one that was more concise and focused, and wrote a list of twenty or so specific questions for me to ask him. I added several of my own as Laura set up her camera and directed us where to sit.

"Um, my name is Ed Snowden," the now-famous film begins. "I'm twenty-nine years old. I work for Booz Allen Hamilton as an infrastructure analyst for NSA in Hawaii."

Snowden went on to provide crisp, stoic, rational responses to each question: Why had he decided to disclose these documents? Why was this important enough for him to sacrifice his freedom? What were the most significant revelations? Was there anything criminal or illegal shown in these documents? What did he expect would happen to him?

As he gave examples of illegal and invasive surveillance, he became animated and passionate. But only when I asked him whether he expected repercussions did he show distress, fearing that the government would target his family and girlfriend for retaliation. He would avoid contact with them to reduce the risk, he said, but he knew he could not fully protect them. "That's the one thing that keeps me up at night, what will happen to them," he said as his eyes welled up, the first and only time I saw that happen.

As Laura worked on editing the video, Ewen and I finalized our next two stories. The third article, published that same day, disclosed a top secret presidential directive signed by President Obama in November 2012 ordering the Pentagon and related agencies to prepare for a series of aggressive offensive cyber operations around the world. "Senior national security and intelligence officials," the first paragraph explained, have been asked "to draw up a list of potential overseas targets for US cyber-attacks, a top secret presidential directive obtained by the Guardian reveals."

The fourth article, which ran as planned on Saturday, was about BOUNDLESS INFORMANT, the NSA's data-tracking program, and it described the reports showing that the NSA was collecting, analyzing, and storing billions of telephone calls and emails sent across the American telecommunications infrastructure. It also raised the question of whether NSA officials had lied to Congress when they had refused to answer senators about the number of domestic communications intercepted, claiming that they did not keep such records and could not assemble such data.

After the "BOUNDLESS INFORMANT" article was published, Laura and I planned to meet at Snowden's hotel. But before leaving my room, out of nowhere, as I sat on my hotel bed, I remembered Cincinnatus, my anonymous email correspondent from six months earlier, who had bombarded me with requests to install PGP so that he could provide me with important information. Amid the excitement of everything that was happening, I thought that perhaps he, too, had an important story to give me. Unable to remember his email name, I finally located one of his old messages by searching for keywords.

"Hey: good news," I wrote to him. "I know it took me a while, but I'm finally using PGP email. So I'm ready to talk any time if you're still interested." I hit "send."

Soon after I arrived at his room, Snowden said, with more than a small trace of mockery, "By the way, that Cincinnatus you just emailed, that's me."

It took me a few moments to process this and regain my composure. That person, many months earlier, who desperately tried to get me to use email encryption . . . was Snowden. My first contact with him hadn't been in May, just a month earlier, but many months ago. Before contacting Laura about the leaks, before contacting anyone, he had tried to reach me.

Now, with each passing day, the hours and hours the three of us spent together created a tighter bond. The awkwardness and tension of our initial meeting had quickly transformed into a relationship of collaboration, trust, and common purpose. We knew that we had together embarked on one of the most significant events of our lives.

But with the "BOUNDLESS INFORMANT" article now behind us, the relatively lighter mood we had managed to keep up over the prior few days turned to palpable anxiety: we were less than twenty-four hours away from revealing Snowden's identity, which we knew would change everything, for him most of all. The three of us had lived through a short but exceptionally intense and gratifying experience. One of us, Snowden, was soon to be removed from the group, likely to go to prison for a long time—a fact that had depressingly lurked in the air from the outset, dampening the atmosphere, at least for me. Only Snowden had seemed unbothered by this. Now, a giddy gallows humor crept into our dealings.

"I call the bottom bunk at Gitmo," Snowden joked as he contemplated our prospects. As we talked about future articles, he would say things like, "That's going into the indictment. The only question is whether it's going into yours or mine." Mostly he remained inconceivably calm. Even now, with the clock winding down on his freedom, Snowden still went to bed at ten thirty, as he had every night during my time in Hong Kong.

While I could barely catch more than two hours of restless sleep at a time, he kept consistent hours. "Well, I'm going to hit the hay," he would announce casually each night before retiring for seven and a half hours of sound sleep, appearing completely refreshed the next day.

When we asked him about his ability to sleep so well under the circumstances, Snowden said that he felt profoundly at peace with what he had done and so the nights were easy. "I figure I have very few days left with a comfortable pillow," he joked, "so I might as well enjoy them."

On Sunday afternoon Hong Kong time, Ewen and I put the final touches on our article introducing Snowden to the world while Laura finished editing the video. I talked to Janine, who signed in to chat as morning began in New York, about the particular importance of handling this news with care and my sense of personal obligation to Snowden to do justice to his choices. I had come to trust my *Guardian* colleagues more and more, both editorially and for their bravery. But in this case I wanted to vet every edit, large and small, to the piece that would reveal Snowden to the world.

Later that afternoon in Hong Kong, Laura came to my hotel room to show her video to Ewen and me. The three of us watched it in silence. Laura's work was brilliant—the video was spare and the editing superb—but mostly the power lay in hearing Snowden speak for himself. He cogently conveyed the conviction, passion, and force of commitment that had driven him to act. His boldness in coming forward to claim what he had done and take responsibility for his actions, his refusal to hide and be hunted, would, I knew, inspire millions.

What I wanted more than anything was for the world to see Snowden's fearlessness. The US government had worked very hard over the past decade to demonstrate unlimited power. It had started wars, tortured and imprisoned people without charges, drone-bombed targets in extrajudicial killings. And the messengers were not immune: whistle-blowers had been abused and prosecuted, journalists had been threatened with jail. Through a carefully cultivated display of intimidation to anyone who contemplated a meaningful challenge, the government had striven to show people around the world that its power was constrained by neither law nor ethics, neither morality nor the Constitution: *look what we can do and will do to those who impede our agenda.*

Snowden had defied the intimidation as directly as possible. Courage is contagious. I knew that he could rouse so many people to do the same.

At 2:00 p.m. Eastern time on Sunday, June 9, the *Guardian* published the story that revealed Snowden to the world: "Edward Snowden: The Whistleblower Behind the NSA Surveillance Revelations." The top of the article featured Laura's twelve-minute video; the first line read, "The individual responsible for one of the most significant leaks in US political history is Edward Snowden, a 29-year-old former technical assistant for the CIA and current employee of the defence contractor Booz Allen Hamilton." The article told Snowden's story, conveyed his motives, and proclaimed that "Snowden will go down in history as one of America's most consequential whistleblowers, alongside Daniel Ellsberg and Bradley Manning." We quoted from Snowden's early note to Laura and me: "I understand that I will be made to suffer for my actions . . . but I will be satisfied if the federation of secret law, unequal pardon and irresistible executive powers that rule the world that I love are revealed even for an instant."

The reaction to the article and the video was more intense than anything I had experienced as a writer. Ellsberg himself, writing the following day in the *Guardian*, proclaimed that "there has not been in American history a more important leak than Edward Snowden's release of NSA material—and that definitely includes the Pentagon Papers 40 years ago."

Several hundred thousand people posted the link to their Facebook accounts in the first several days alone. Almost three million people watched the interview on YouTube. Many more saw it at the *Guardian* online. The overwhelming response was shock and inspiration at Snowden's courage.

Laura, Snowden, and I followed the reaction to his exposure together, while I also debated with two *Guardian* media strategists over which Monday morning TV interviews I should agree to do. We settled on *Morning Joe* on MSNBC, followed by NBC's *Today* show—the two earliest shows, which would shape the coverage of Snowden throughout the day.

But before I could get to those interviews, we were diverted by a call at 5:00 a.m.—just hours after the Snowden article was published—from a longtime reader of mine who lives in Hong Kong, with whom I had been communicating periodically throughout the week. On this early-morning call, he pointed out that the entire world would soon be looking for Snowden in Hong Kong, and he insisted that Snowden urgently needed to retain well-connected lawyers in the city. He had two of the best human-rights lawyers standing by, willing to represent him. Could the three of them come over to my hotel right away?

We agreed to meet a short time later, at around 8:00 a.m. I slept for a couple of hours until he called, an hour early, at 7:00 a.m.

"We're already here," he said, "downstairs in your hotel. I have the two lawyers with me. Your lobby is filled with cameras and reporters. The media is searching for Snowden's hotel and will find it imminently, and the lawyers say that it's vital they get to him before the media finds him."

Barely awake, I threw on the nearest clothes I could find and I stumbled to the door. As soon as I opened it, the flashes from multiple cameras went off in my face. The media horde had obviously paid off someone on the hotel staff to get my room number. Two women identified themselves as Hong Kong–based *Wall Street Journal* reporters; others, including one with a large camera, were from Associated Press.

They hurled questions and formed a moving half-circle around me as I walked to the elevator. They pushed their way into the elevator with me, asking one question after the next, most of which I answered with short, curt, unhelpful replies.

Down in the lobby, a new swarm of cameras and reporters joined the group. I tried to look for my reader and the lawyers but could not move two feet without having my path blocked.

I was particularly concerned that the swarm would try to follow me and make it impossible for the lawyers to get to Snowden. I finally decided to hold an impromptu press conference in the lobby, answering

questions so that the reporters would go away. After fifteen minutes or
so, most of them dispersed.

I was then relieved to stumble into Gill Phillips, the *Guardian*'s chief
lawyer, who had stopped in Hong Kong on her way from Australia to
London to provide Ewen and me with legal counsel. She said she wanted
to explore all possible ways for the *Guardian* to protect Snowden. "Alan
is adamant that we give him all the support we legally can," she said. We
tried to talk more but had no privacy with the last few reporters lurking.

I finally found my reader, along with the two Hong Kong lawyers he
had brought with him. We plotted how we could speak without being
followed, and all decamped for Gill's room. Still trailed by a handful of
reporters, we shut the door in their faces.

We got right down to business. The lawyers wished urgently to speak
to Snowden to get his formal permission to represent him, at which point
they could begin acting on his behalf.

Gill frantically used her phone to investigate these lawyers, whom we
had only just met, before turning Snowden over to them. She was able to
determine that they were indeed well-known and established in the human rights and asylum community and seemed quite well connected politically in Hong Kong. As Gill performed her impromptu due diligence,
I signed on to the chat program. Both Snowden and Laura were online.

Laura, who was now staying at Snowden's hotel, was certain that it
was only a matter of time before the reporters found their location, too.
Snowden was clearly eager to leave. I told him about the lawyers, who
were ready to go to his hotel room. Snowden said they should pick him
up and bring him to a safe place. It was, he said, "time to enter the part of
the plan where I ask the world for protection and justice."

"But I need to get out of the hotel without being recognized by reporters," he said. "Otherwise they'll just follow me wherever I go."

I conveyed these concerns to the lawyers. "Does he have any ideas
how to prevent that?" one of them asked.

I passed the question on to Snowden.

"I'm in the process of taking steps to change my appearance," he said,
clearly having thought about this previously. "I can make myself unrec-
ognizable."

At that point, I thought the lawyers should speak to him directly. Before being able to do so, they needed Snowden to recite a formalistic phrase about hereby retaining them. I sent Snowden the phrase and he then typed it back to me. The lawyers then took over the computer and began speaking with Snowden.

After ten minutes, the two lawyers announced they were heading over to his hotel immediately to meet Snowden as he attempted to leave the hotel undetected.

"What do you intend to do with him after that?" I asked.

They would likely take him to the UN mission in Hong Kong and formally seek the UN's protection from the US government, on the grounds that Snowden was a refugee seeking asylum. Or, they said, they would try to arrange a "safe house."

But how to get the lawyers out of the hotel without being followed? We came up with a plan: I would walk out of the hotel room with Gill and go down to the lobby to lure the reporters, still waiting outside our door, to follow me. The lawyers would then wait for a few minutes and exit the hotel, hopefully without being noticed.

The ruse worked. After thirty minutes of chatting with Gill in a mall attached to the hotel, I went back up to my room and anxiously called one of the lawyers on his cell phone.

"He got out right before journalists started swarming the floor," he said. "We met him in his hotel room and then we crossed a bridge into an adjacent mall"—in front of the room with the alligator where Snowden had first met us, I later learned—"and then into our waiting car. He's with us now."

Where were they taking him?

"It's best not to talk about that on the phone," the lawyer replied. "He'll be safe for now."

I was immensely relieved that Snowden was in good hands, but we knew there was a strong chance we might never see or speak to him again, at least not as a free man. Most likely, I thought, we would next see him on television, dressed in an orange prison jumpsuit and wearing shackles, inside a US courtroom, being arraigned on espionage charges.

As I digested the news, there was a knock on my door. It was the general manager of the hotel, who had come to tell me that the phone was ringing nonstop for my room (I had given an instruction to the front desk to block all calls). There were also throngs of reporters, photographers, and camera people down in the lobby waiting for me to appear.

"If you like," he said, "we can take you out a back elevator and through an exit nobody will see. And the *Guardian*'s lawyer has made a reservation for you at another hotel under a different name, if that's what you want to do."

That was clearly hotel-manager-ese for: *we want you to leave because of the ruckus you are creating.* I knew it was a good idea anyway: I wanted to continue to work with some privacy and was still hoping to maintain contact with Snowden. So I packed my bags, followed the manager out the back exit, met Ewen in a waiting car, and then checked into a different hotel under the name of the *Guardian*'s lawyer.

The first thing I did was sign on to the Internet, hoping to hear from Snowden. Several minutes later, he appeared online.

"I'm fine," he told me. "In a safe house for now. But I have no idea how safe it is, or how long I'll be here. I'll have to move from place to place, and my Internet access is unreliable, so I don't know when or how often I'll be online."

He was obviously reluctant to give any details about his location and I did not want them. I knew that my ability to be involved in his hiding was very limited. He was now the world's most wanted man by the world's most powerful government. The United States had already demanded that Hong Kong authorities arrest him and turn him over to American custody.

So we spoke briefly and vaguely, expressing mutual hope that we would be in touch. I told him to stay safe.

When I finally got to the studio for the interviews for *Morning Joe* and the *Today* show, I noticed immediately that the tenor of the questioning had changed significantly. Rather than dealing with me as a reporter, the hosts preferred to attack a new target: Snowden himself, now a shadowy figure in Hong Kong. Many US journalists resumed their accustomed role as servants to the government. The story was no longer that reporters had exposed serious NSA abuses but that an American working for the government had "betrayed" his obligations, committed crimes, and then "fled to China."

My interviews with both hosts, Mika Brzezinski and Savannah Guthrie, were acrimonious and acerbic. Sleep-deprived for more than a full week now, I had no patience for the criticisms of Snowden embedded in their questions: journalists, I felt, should be celebrating, not demonizing someone who had brought more transparency to the national security state than anyone in years.

After a few more days of interviews, I decided it was time to leave Hong Kong. Clearly, it would now be impossible to meet or otherwise help Snowden from Hong Kong, and at that point I was completely exhausted, physically, emotionally, and psychologically. I was eager to return to Rio.

I thought about flying home through New York and stopping for one day to do interviews—just to make the point that I could and would. But I was advised by a lawyer against doing so, arguing that it made little sense to take legal risks of that sort until we knew how the government planned to react. "You've just enabled the biggest national security leak in US history and gone all over TV with the most defiant message possible," he said. "It will only make sense to plan a trip to the US once we get a sense of the Justice Department's response."

I didn't agree: I thought it was unlikely in the extreme that the Obama administration would arrest a journalist in the middle of such high-profile reporting. But I was too drained to argue or take the risk. So I had the *Guardian* book my flight back to Rio through Dubai, nowhere near the United States. For the moment, I reasoned, I had done enough.

3

COLLECT IT ALL

The archive of documents Edward Snowden had assembled was stunning in both size and scope. Even as someone who had spent years writing about the dangers of secret US surveillance, I found the sheer vastness of the spying system genuinely shocking, all the more so because it had clearly been implemented with virtually no accountability, no transparency, and no limits.

The thousands of discrete surveillance programs described by the archive were never intended by those who implemented them to become public knowledge. Many of the programs were aimed at the American population, but dozens of countries around the planet—including democracies typically considered US allies, such as France, Brazil, India, and Germany—were also targets of indiscriminate mass surveillance.

Snowden's archive was elegantly organized, but its size and complexity made it extremely difficult to process. The tens of thousands of NSA documents in it had been produced by virtually every unit and subdivision within the sprawling agency, and it also contained some files from closely aligned foreign intelligence agencies. The documents were startlingly recent: mostly from 2011 and 2012, and many from 2013. Some even dated from March and April of that year, just months before we met Snowden in Hong Kong.

The vast majority of the files in the archive were designated "top secret." Most of those were marked "FVEY," meaning that they were approved for distribution only to the NSA's four closest surveillance allies, the "Five Eyes" English-speaking alliance composed of Britain, Canada, Australia, and New Zealand. Others were meant for US eyes only, marked "NOFORN" for "no foreign distribution." Certain documents, such as the FISA court order allowing collection of telephone records and Obama's presidential directive to prepare offensive cyber-operations, were among the US government's most closely held secrets.

Deciphering the archive and the NSA's language involved a steep learning curve. The agency communicates with itself and its partners in an idiosyncratic language of its own, a lingo that is bureaucratic and stilted yet at times boastful and even snarky. Most of the documents were also quite technical, filled with forbidding acronyms and code names, and sometimes required that other documents be read first before they could be understood.

But Snowden had anticipated the problem, providing glossaries of acronyms and program names, as well as internal agency dictionaries for terms of art. Still, some documents were impenetrable on the first, second, or even third reading. Their significance emerged only after I had put together different parts of other papers and consulted with some of the world's foremost experts on surveillance, cryptography, hacking, the history of the NSA, and the legal framework governing American spying.

Compounding the difficulty was the fact that the mountains of documents were often organized not by subject but by branch of the agency where they had originated, and dramatic revelations were mixed in with large amounts of banal or highly technical material. Although the *Guardian* devised a program to search through the files by keyword, which was of great help, that program was far from perfect. The process of digesting the archive was painstakingly slow, and many months after we first received the documents, some terms and programs still required further reporting before they could be safely and coherently disclosed.

Despite such problems, though, Snowden's files indisputably laid bare a complex web of surveillance aimed at Americans (who are explicitly beyond the NSA's mission) and non-Americans alike. The archive revealed the technical means used to intercept communications: the NSA's tapping of Internet servers, satellites, underwater fiber-optic cables, local and foreign telephone systems, and personal computers. It identified individuals targeted for extremely invasive forms of spying, a list that ranged from alleged terrorists and criminal suspects to the democratically elected leaders of the nation's allies and even ordinary American citizens. And it shed light on the NSA's overall strategies and goals.

Snowden had placed crucial, overarching documents at the front of the archive, flagging them as especially important. These files disclosed the agency's extraordinary reach, as well as its deceit and even criminality. The BOUNDLESS INFORMANT program was one of the first such revelations, showing that the NSA counts all the telephone calls and emails collected every day from around the world with mathematical exactitude. Snowden had placed these files so prominently not only because they quantified the volume of calls and emails collected and stored by the NSA—literally billions each day—but also because they proved that NSA chief Keith Alexander and other officials had lied to Congress. Repeatedly, NSA officials had claimed that they were incapable of providing specific numbers—exactly the data that BOUNDLESS INFORMANT was constructed to assemble.

For the one-month period beginning March 8, 2013, for example, a BOUNDLESS INFORMANT slide showed that a single unit of the NSA, Global Access Operations, had collected data on more than 3 billion telephone calls and emails that had passed through the US telecommunications system. ("DNR," or "Dialed Number Recognition," refers to telephone calls; "DNI," or "Digital Network Intelligence," refers to Internet-based communications such as emails.) That exceeded the collection from the systems each of Russia, Mexico, and virtually all the countries in Europe, and was roughly equal to the collection of data from China.

Overall, in just thirty days the unit had collected data on more than 97 billion emails and 124 billion phone calls from around the world. Another BOUNDLESS INFORMANT document detailed the international data collected in a single thirty-day period from Germany (500 million), Brazil (2.3 billion), and India (13.5 billion). And yet other files showed collection of metadata in cooperation with the governments of France (70 million), Spain (60 million), Italy (47 million), the Netherlands (1.8 million), Norway (33 million), and Denmark (23 million).

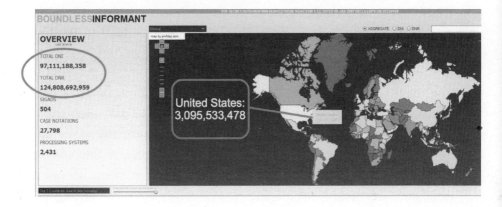

Despite the NSA's statutorily defined focus on "foreign intelligence," the documents confirmed that the American public was an equally important target for the secret surveillance. Nothing made that clearer than the April 25, 2013, top secret order from the FISA court compelling Verizon to turn over to the NSA all information about its American customers' telephone calls, the "telephony metadata." Marked "NOFORN," the language of the order was as clear as it was absolute:

> IT IS HEREBY ORDERED that, the Custodian of Records shall produce to the
>
> National Security Agency (NSA) upon service of this Order, and continue production
>
> on an ongoing daily basis thereafter for the duration of this Order, unless otherwise
>
> ordered by the Court, an electronic copy of the following tangible things: all call detail
>
> records or "telephony metadata" created by Verizon for communications (i) between
>
> the United States and abroad; or (ii) wholly within the United States, including local
>
> telephone calls.

. . . continued

> Telephony metadata includes comprehensive communications routing information, including but not limited to session identifying information (*e.g.*, originating and terminating telephone number, International Mobile Subscriber Identity (IMSI) number, International Mobile station Equipment Identity (IMEI) number, etc.), trunk identifier, telephone calling card numbers, and time and duration of call.

This bulk telephone collection program was one of the most significant discoveries in an archive suffused with all types of covert surveillance programs—from the large-scale PRISM (involving collection of data directly from the servers of the world's biggest Internet companies) and PROJECT BULLRUN, a joint effort between the NSA and its British counterpart, the Government Communications Headquarters (GCHQ), to defeat the most common forms of encryption used to safeguard online transactions, to smaller-scale enterprises with names that reflect the contemptuous and boastful spirit of supremacy behind them: EGOTISTICAL GIRAFFE, which targets the Tor browser that is meant to enable anonymity in online browsing; MUSCULAR, a means to invade the private networks of Google and Yahoo!; and OLYMPIA, Canada's program to surveil the Brazilian Ministry of Mines and Energy.

Some of the surveillance was ostensibly devoted to terrorism suspects. But great quantities of the programs manifestly had nothing to do with national security. The documents left no doubt that the NSA was equally involved in economic espionage, diplomatic spying, and suspicionless surveillance aimed at entire populations.

Taken in its entirety, the Snowden archive led to an ultimately simple conclusion: the US government had built a system that has as its goal the complete elimination of electronic privacy worldwide. Far from hyperbole, that is the literal, explicitly stated aim of the surveillance state: to collect, store, monitor, and analyze all electronic communication by all people around the globe. The agency is devoted to one overarching mission: to prevent the slightest piece of electronic communication from evading its systemic grasp.

This self-imposed mandate requires endlessly expanding the NSA's reach. Every day, the NSA works to identify electronic communications that are not being collected and stored and then develops new technologies and methods to rectify the deficiency. The agency regards itself as needing no specific justification to collect any particular electronic communication, nor any grounds for regarding its targets with suspicion. What the NSA calls "SIGINT"—all signals intelligence—is its target. And the mere fact that it has the capability to collect those communications has become one rationale for doing so.

A military branch of the Pentagon, the NSA is the largest intelligence agency in the world, with the majority of its surveillance work conducted through the Five Eyes alliance. Until the spring of 2014, when controversy over the Snowden stories became increasingly intense, the agency was headed by four-star general Keith B. Alexander, who had overseen it for the previous nine years, aggressively increasing the NSA's size and influence during his tenure. In the process, Alexander became what reporter James Bamford described as "the most powerful intelligence chief in the nation's history."

The NSA "was already a data behemoth when Alexander took over," *Foreign Policy* reporter Shane Harris noted, "but under his watch, the breadth, scale, and ambition of its mission have expanded beyond anything ever contemplated by his predecessors." Never before had "one agency of the U.S. government had the capacity, as well as the legal authority, to collect and store so much electronic information." A former administration official who worked with the NSA chief told Harris that "Alexander's strategy" was clear: "I need to get all of the data." And, Harris added, "He wants to hang on to it for as long as he can."

Alexander's personal motto, "Collect it all," perfectly conveys the central purpose of the NSA. He first put this philosophy into practice in 2005 while collecting signals intelligence relating to the occupation of Iraq. As the *Washington Post* reported in 2013, Alexander grew dissatisfied with the limited focus of American military intelligence, which targeted only suspected insurgents and other threats to US forces, an approach that the newly appointed NSA chief viewed as too constraining. "He wanted everything: Every Iraqi text message, phone call, and e-mail that could be vacuumed up by the agency's powerful computers." So the government deployed technological methods indiscriminately to collect all communications data from the entire Iraqi population.

Alexander then conceived of applying this system of ubiquitous surveillance—originally created for a foreign population in an active war zone—to American citizens. "And, as he did in Iraq, Alexander has pushed hard for everything he can get," the *Post* reported: "tools, resources, and the legal authority to collect and store vast quantities of raw information on American and foreign communications." Thus, "in his eight years at the helm of the country's electronic surveillance agency, Alexander, 61, has quietly presided over a revolution in the government's ability to scoop up information in the name of national security."

Alexander's reputation as a surveillance extremist is well documented. In describing his "all-out, barely legal drive to build the ultimate spy machine," *Foreign Policy* called him "the cowboy of the NSA." Even Bush-era CIA and NSA chief General Michael Hayden—who himself oversaw the implementation of Bush's illegal warrantless eavesdropping program and is notorious for his aggressive militarism—often had "heartburn" over Alexander's no-holds-barred approach, according to *Foreign Policy*. A former intelligence official characterized Alexander's view: "Let's not worry about the law. Let's just figure out how to get the job done." The *Post* similarly noted that "even his defenders say Alexander's aggressiveness has sometimes taken him to the outer edge of his legal authority."

Although some of the more extreme statements from Alexander—such as his blunt question "Why can't we collect all the signals, all the time?," which he reportedly asked during a 2008 visit to Britain's GCHQ—have been dismissed by agency spokespeople as mere lighthearted quips taken out of context, the agency's own documents demonstrate that Alexander was not joking. A top secret presentation to the 2011 annual conference of the Five Eyes alliance, for instance, shows that the NSA has explicitly embraced Alexander's motto of omniscience as its core purpose:

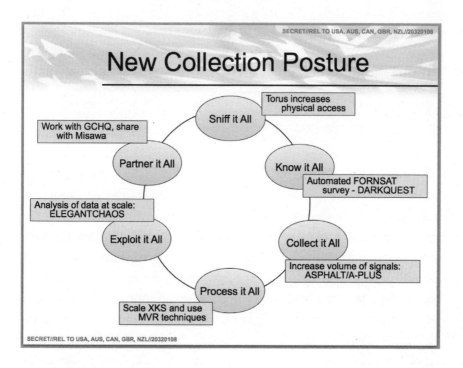

A 2010 document presented to the Five Eyes conference by the GCHQ—referring to its ongoing program to intercept satellite communications, code-named TARMAC—makes it clear that the British spy agency also uses this phrase to describe its mission:

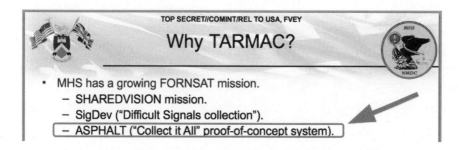

Even routine internal NSA memoranda invoke the slogan to justify expanding the agency's capabilities. One 2009 memo from the technical director of the NSA's Mission Operations, for example, touts recent improvements to the agency's collection site in Misawa, Japan:

Future Plans (U)

(TS//SI//REL) In the future, MSOC hopes to expand the number of WORDGOPHER platforms to enable demodulation of thousands of additional low-rate carriers.

These targets are ideally suited for software demodulation. Additionally, MSOC has developed a capability to automatically scan and demodulate signals as they activate on the satellites. There are a multitude of possibilities, bringing our enterprise one step closer to "collecting it all."

Far from being a frivolous quip, "collect it all" defines the NSA's aspiration, and it is a goal the NSA is increasingly closer to reaching. The quantity of telephone calls, emails, online chats, online activities, and telephonic metadata collected by the agency is staggering. Indeed, the NSA frequently, as one 2012 document put it, "collects far more content than is routinely useful to analysts." As of mid-2012, the agency was processing more than twenty billion communications events (both Internet and telephone) from around the world *each day*:

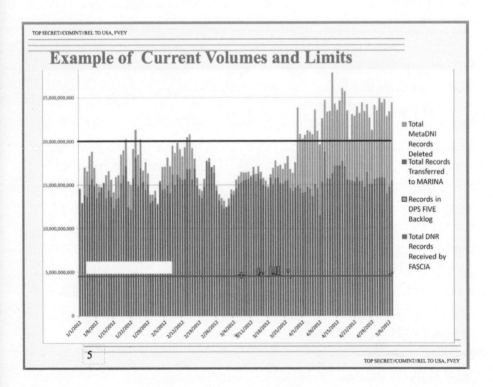

For each individual country, the NSA also produces a daily breakdown quantifying the number of calls and emails collected. The chart below, for Poland, shows more than three million telephone calls on some days, for a thirty-day total of seventy-one million:

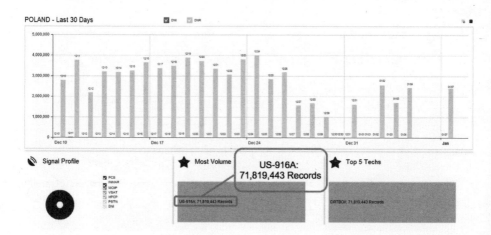

The domestic total collected by the NSA is equally stunning. Even prior to Snowden's revelations, the *Washington Post* reported in 2010 that "every day, collection systems at the National Security Agency intercept and store 1.7 billion emails, phone calls, and other types of communications" from Americans. William Binney, a mathematician who worked for the NSA for three decades and resigned in the wake of 9/11 in protest over the agency's increasing domestic focus, has likewise made numerous statements about the quantities of US data collected. In a 2012 interview with *Democracy Now!*, Binney said that "they've assembled on the order of 20 trillion transactions about U.S. citizens with other U.S. citizens."

After Snowden's revelations, the *Wall Street Journal* reported that the overall interception system of the NSA "has the capacity to reach roughly 75% of all U.S. Internet traffic in the hunt for foreign intelligence, including a wide array of communications by foreigners and Americans." Speaking anonymously, current and former NSA officials told the *Journal* that in some cases the NSA "retains the written content of emails sent between citizens within the U.S. and also filters domestic phone calls made with Internet technology."

Britain's GCHQ similarly collects such a great quantity of communications data that it can barely store what it has. As one 2011 document prepared by the British put it:

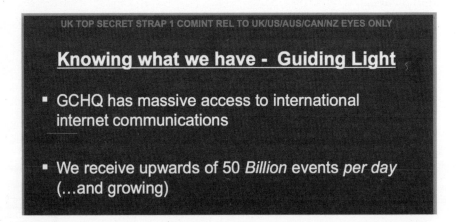

So fixated is the NSA on collecting it all that the Snowden archive is sprinkled with celebratory internal memos heralding particular collection milestones. This December 2012 entry from an internal messaging board, for instance, proudly proclaims that the SHELLTRUMPET program has processed its one trillionth record:

```
(S//SI//REL TO USA, FVEY) SHELLTRUMPET Processes it's One Trillionth
Metadata Record
```

By [NAME REDACTED] on 2012-12-31 0738

```
(S//SI//REL TO USA, FVEY) On December 21, 2012 SHELLTRUMPET processed its
One Trillionth metadata record.  SHELLTRUMPET began as a near-real-time
metadata analyzer on Dec 8, 2007 for a CLASSIC collection system. In its
five year history, numerous other systems from across the Agency have come
to use SHELLTRUMPET's processing capabilities for performance monitoring,
direct E-Mail tip alerting, TRAFFICTHIEF tipping, and Real-Time Regional
Gateway (RTRG) filtering and ingest.  Though it took five years to get to
the one trillion mark, almost half of this volume was processed in this
calendar year, and half of that volume was from SSO's DANCINGOASIS.
SHELLTRUMPET is currently processing Two Billion call events/day from
select SSO (Ram-M, OAKSTAR, MYSTIC and NCSC enabled systems), MUSKETEER,
and Second Party systems. We will be expanding its reach into other SSO
systems over the course of 2013. The Trillion records processed have
resulted in over 35 Million tips to TRAFFICTHIEF.
```

To collect such vast quantities of communications, the NSA relies on a multitude of methods. These include tapping directly into fiber-optic lines (including underwater cables) used to transmit international communications; redirecting messages into NSA repositories when they traverse the US system, as most worldwide communications do; and cooperating with the intelligence services in other countries. With increasing frequency, the agency also relies on Internet companies and telecoms, which indispensably pass on information they have collected about their own customers.

While the NSA is officially a public agency, it has countless overlapping partnerships with private sector corporations, and many of its core functions have been outsourced. The NSA itself employs roughly thirty thousand people, but the agency also has contracts for some sixty thousand employees of private corporations, who often provide essential services. Snowden himself was actually employed not by the NSA but by the Dell Corporation and the large defense contractor Booz Allen Hamilton. Still, he, like many other private contractors, worked in the NSA offices, on its core functions, with access to its secrets.

According to Tim Shorrock, who has long chronicled the NSA-corporate relationship, "70 percent of our national intelligence budget is being spent on the private sector." When Michael Hayden said that "the largest concentration of cyber power on the planet is the intersection of the Baltimore Parkway and Maryland Route 32," Shorrock noted, "he was referring not to the NSA itself but to the business park about a mile down the road from the giant black edifice that houses NSA's headquarters in Fort Meade, Md. There, all of NSA's major contractors, from Booz to SAIC to Northrop Grumman, carry out their surveillance and intelligence work for the agency."

These corporate partnerships extend beyond intelligence and defense contractors to include the world's largest and most important Internet corporations and telecoms, precisely those companies that handle the bulk of the world's communications and can facilitate access to private exchanges. After describing the agency's missions of "Defense (Protect

U.S. Telecommunications and Computer Systems Against Exploitation)" and "Offense (Intercept and Exploit Foreign Signals)," one top secret NSA document enumerates some of the services supplied by such corporations:

These corporate partnerships, which provide the systems and the access on which the NSA depends, are managed by the NSA's highly secret Special Sources Operations unit, the division that oversees corporate partnerships. Snowden described the SSO as the "crown jewel" of the organization.

BLARNEY, FAIRVIEW, OAKSTAR, and STORMBREW are some of the programs overseen by the SSO within its Corporate Partner Access (CPA) portfolio.

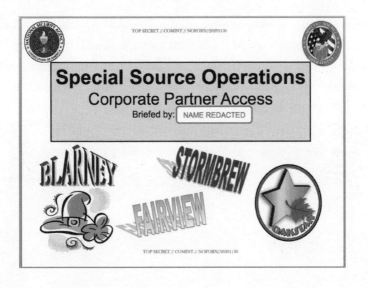

As part of these programs, the NSA exploits the access that certain telecom companies have to international systems, having entered into contracts with foreign telecoms to build, maintain, and upgrade their networks. The US companies then redirect the target country's communications data to NSA repositories.

The core purpose of BLARNEY is depicted in one NSA briefing:

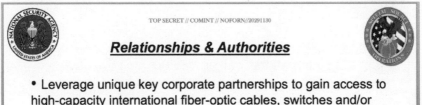

BLARNEY relied on one relationship in particular—a long-standing partnership with AT&T Inc., according to the *Wall Street Journal*'s reporting on the program. According to the NSA's own files, in 2010 the list of countries targeted by BLARNEY included Brazil, France, Germany, Greece, Israel, Italy, Japan, Mexico, South Korea, and Venezuela, as well as the European Union and the United Nations.

FAIRVIEW, another SSO program, also collects what the NSA touts as "massive amounts of data" from around the world. And it, too, relies mostly on a single "corporate partner" and, in particular, that partner's access to the telecommunications systems of foreign nations. The NSA's internal summary of FAIRVIEW is simple and clear:

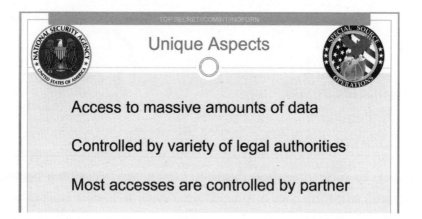

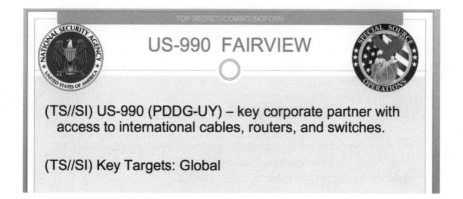

According to NSA documents, FAIRVIEW "is typically in the top five at NSA as a collection source for serialized production"—meaning on-going surveillance—"and one of the largest providers of metadata." Its overwhelming reliance on one telecom is demonstrated by its claim that "approximately 75% of reporting is single source, reflecting the unique access the program enjoys to a wide variety of target communications." Though the telecom is not identified, one description of the FAIRVIEW partner makes clear its eagerness to cooperate:

FAIRVIEW –   Corp partner since 1985 with access to int. cables, routers, switches. The partner operates in the U.S., but has access to information that transits the nation and through its corporate relationships provide unique accesses to other telecoms and ISPs. Aggressively involved in shaping traffic to run signals of interest past our monitors.

Thanks to such cooperation, the FAIRVIEW program collects vast quantities of information about telephone calls. One chart, which covers the thirty-day period beginning December 10, 2012, shows that just this program alone was responsible for the collection of some two hundred million records each day that month, for a thirty-day total of more than six billion records. The light bars are collections of "DNR" (telephone calls), while the dark bars are "DNI" (Internet activity):

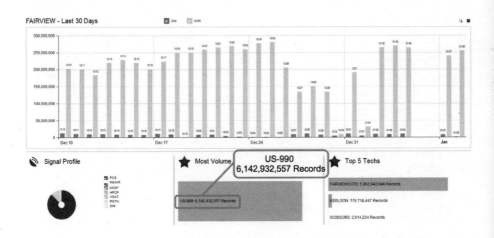

To collect these billions of phone records, the SSO collaborates with the NSA's corporate partners as well as with foreign government agencies—for instance, the Polish intelligence service:

(TS//SI//NF) ORANGECRUSH, part of the OAKSTAR program under SSO's
corporate portfolio, began forwarding metadata from a third party partner
site (Poland) to NSA repositories as of 3 March and content as of 25 March.
This program is a collaborative effort between SSO, NCSC, ETC, FAD, an NSA
Corporate Partner and a division of the Polish Government. ORANGECRUSH is
only known to the Poles as BUFFALOGREEN. This multi-group partnership
began in May 2009 and will incorporate the OAKSTAR project of ORANGEBLOSSOM
and its DNR capability. The new access will provide SIGINT from commercial
links managed by the NSA Corporate Partner and is anticipated to include
Afghan National Army, Middle East, limited African continent, and European
communications. A notification has been posted to SPRINGRAY and this
collection is available to Second Parties via TICKETWINDOW.

The OAKSTAR program similarly exploits the access that one of the
NSA's corporate partners (code-named STEELKNIGHT) has to foreign
telecommunications systems, using that access to redirect data into the
NSA's own repositories. Another partner, code-named SILVERZEPHYR,
appears in a November 11, 2009, document describing work done with
the company to obtain "internal communications" from both Brazil and
Colombia:

SILVERZEPHYR FAA DNI Access Initiated at NSAW (TS//SI//NF)

By [NAME REDACTED] on 2009-11-06 0918

(TS//SI//NF) On Thursday, 11/5/09, the SSO-OAKSTAR
SILVERZEPHYR (SZ) access began forwarding FAA DNI records
to NSAW via the FAA WealthyCluster2/Tellurian system
installed at the partner's site. SSO coordinated with the
Data Flow Office and forwarded numerous sample files to a
test partition for validation, which was completely
successful. SSO will continue to monitor the flow and
collection to ensure a ny anomalies are identified and
corrected as required. SILVERZEPHYR will continue to
provide customers with authorized, transit DNR collection.
SSO is working with the partner to gain access to an
additional 80Gbs of DNI data on their peering network,
bundled in 10 Gbs increments. The OAKSTAR team, along with
support from NSAT and GNDA, just completed a 12 day SIGINT
survey at site, which identified over 200 new links. During
the survey, GNDA worked with the partner to test the output
of their ACS system. OAKSTAR is also working with NSAT to
examine snapshots taken by the partner in Brazil and
Colombia, both of which may contain internal communications
for those countries.

Meanwhile, the STORMBREW program, conducted in "close partnership with the FBI," gives the NSA access to Internet and telephone traffic that enters the United States at various "choke points" on US soil. It exploits the fact that the vast majority of the world's Internet traffic at some point flows through the US communications infrastructure—a residual by-product of the central role that the United States had played in developing the network. Some of these designated choke points are identified by cover names:

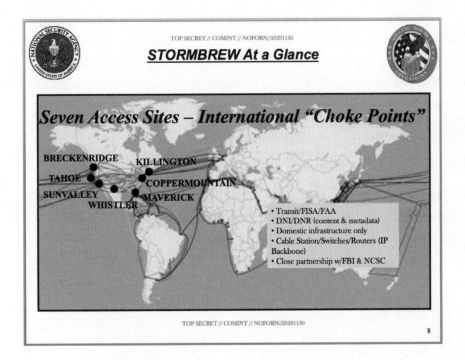

According to the NSA, STORMBREW "is currently comprised of very sensitive relationships with two U.S. telecom providers (cover terms ARTIFICE and WOLFPOINT)." Beyond its access to US-based choke points, "the STORMBREW program also manages two submarine cable landing access sites; one on the USA west coast (cover term, BRECKENRIDGE), and the other on the USA east coast (cover term QUAILCREEK)."

As the profusion of cover names attests, the identity of its corpo-

rate partners is one of the most closely guarded secrets in the NSA. The
documents containing the key to those code names are vigilantly safe-
guarded by the agency and Snowden was unable to obtain many of them.
Nonetheless, his revelations did unmask some of the companies cooperating with the NSA. Most famously, his archive included the PRISM
documents, which detailed secret agreements between the NSA and the
world's largest Internet companies—Facebook, Yahoo!, Apple, Google—
as well as extensive efforts by Microsoft to provide the agency with access
to its communications platforms such as Outlook.

Unlike BLARNEY, FAIRVIEW, OAKSTAR, and STORMBREW,
which entail tapping into fiber-optic cables and other forms of infrastructure ("upstream" surveillance, in NSA parlance), PRISM allows the
NSA to collect data directly from the servers of nine of the biggest Internet companies:

The companies listed on the PRISM slide denied allowing the NSA unlimited access to their servers. Facebook and Google, for instance, claimed that they only give the NSA information for which the agency has a warrant, and tried to depict PRISM as little more than a trivial technical detail: a slightly upgraded delivery system whereby the NSA receives data in a "lockbox" that the companies are legally compelled to provide.

But their argument is belied by numerous points. For one, we know that Yahoo! vigorously fought in court against the NSA's efforts to force it to join PRISM—an unlikely effort if the program were simply a trivial change to a delivery system. (Yahoo!'s claims were rejected by the FISA court, and the company was ordered to participate in PRISM.) Second, the *Washington Post*'s Bart Gellman, after receiving heavy criticism for "overstating" the impact of PRISM, reinvestigated the program and confirmed that he stood by the *Post*'s central claim: "From their workstations anywhere in the world, government employees cleared for PRISM access may 'task' the system"—that is, run a search—"and receive results from an Internet company without further interaction with the company's staff."

Third, the Internet companies' denials were phrased in evasive and legalistic fashion, often obfuscating more than clarifying. For instance, Facebook claimed not to provide "direct access," while Google denied having created a "back door" for the NSA. But as Chris Soghoian, the ACLU's tech expert, told *Foreign Policy*, these were highly technical terms of art denoting very specific means to get at information. The companies ultimately did not deny that they had worked with the NSA to set up a system through which the agency could directly access their customers' data.

Finally, the NSA itself has repeatedly hailed PRISM for its unique collection capabilities and noted that the program has been vital for increasing surveillance. One NSA slide details PRISM's special surveillance powers:

TOP SECRET//SI//ORCON//NOFORN

(TS//SI//NF) FAA702 Operations
Why Use Both: PRISM vs. Upstream

	PRISM	Upstream
DNI Selectors	✓ 9 U.S. based service providers	✓ Worldwide sources
DNR Selectors	⊘ Coming soon	✓ Worldwide sources
Access to Stored Communications (Search)	✓	⊘
Real-Time Collection (Surveillance)	✓	✓
"Abouts" Collection	⊘	✓
Voice Collection	✓ Voice over IP	✓
Direct Relationship with Comms Providers	⊘ Only through FBI	✓

TOP SECRET//SI//ORCON//NOFORN

Another details the wide range of communications that PRISM enables the NSA to access:

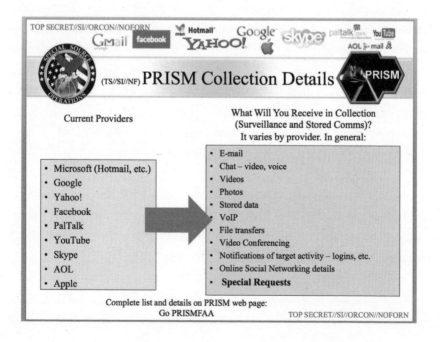

TOP SECRET//SI//ORCON//NOFORN

(TS//SI//NF) PRISM Collection Details

Current Providers

- Microsoft (Hotmail, etc.)
- Google
- Yahoo!
- Facebook
- PalTalk
- YouTube
- Skype
- AOL
- Apple

What Will You Receive in Collection (Surveillance and Stored Comms)?
It varies by provider. In general:

- E-mail
- Chat – video, voice
- Videos
- Photos
- Stored data
- VoIP
- File transfers
- Video Conferencing
- Notifications of target activity – logins, etc.
- Online Social Networking details
- **Special Requests**

Complete list and details on PRISM web page:
Go PRISMFAA

TOP SECRET//SI//ORCON//NOFORN

And another NSA slide details how the PRISM program has steadily and substantially increased the agency's collection:

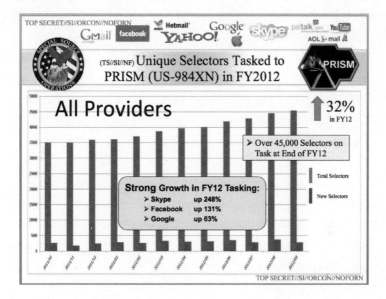

On its internal messaging boards, the Special Source Operation division frequently hails the massive collection value PRISM has provided. One message, from November 19, 2012, is entitled "PRISM Expands Impact: FY12 Metrics":

```
(TS//SI//NF) PRISM (US-984XN) expanded its impact on NSA's reporting
mission in FY12 through increased tasking, collection and operational
improvements. Here are some highlights of the FY12 PRISM program:

    PRISM is the most cited collection source in NSA 1st Party end-product
reporting. More NSA product reports were based on PRISM than on any other
single SIGAD for all of NSA's 1st Party reporting during FY12: cited in
15.1% of all reports (up from 14% in FY11). PRISM was cited in 13.4% of all
1st, 2nd, and 3rd Party NSA reporting (up from 11.9% in FY11), and is also
the top cited SIGAD overall
    Number of PRISM-based end-product reports issued in FY12: 24,096, up
27% from FY11
    Single-source reporting percentage in FY12 and FY11: 74%
    Number of product reports derived from PRISM collection and cited as
sources in articles in the President's Daily Brief in FY12: 1,477 (18% of
all SIGINT reports cited as sources in PDB articles - highest single SIGAD
for NSA); In FY11: 1,152 (15% of all SIGINT reports cited as sources in PDB
articles - highest single SIGAD for NSA)
    Number of Essential Elements of Information contributed to in FY12:
4,186 (32% of all EEIs for all Information Needs); 220 EEIs addressed
solely by PRISM
    Tasking: The number of tasked selectors rose 32% in FY12 to 45,406 as
of Sept 2012
    Great success in Skype collection and processing; unique, high value
targets acquired
    Expanded PRISM taskable e-mail domains from only 40, to 22,000
```

Such congratulatory proclamations do not support the notion of PRISM as only a trivial technicality, and they give the lie to Silicon Valley's denials of cooperation. Indeed, the *New York Times*, reporting on the PRISM program after Snowden's revelations, described a slew of secret negotiations between the NSA and Silicon Valley about providing the agency with unfettered access to the companies' systems. "When government officials came to Silicon Valley to demand easier ways for the world's largest Internet companies to turn over user data as part of a secret surveillance program, the companies bristled," reported the *Times*. "In the end, though, many cooperated at least a bit." In particular:

> Twitter declined to make it easier for the government. But other companies were more compliant, according to people briefed on the negotiations. They opened discussions with national security officials about developing technical methods to more efficiently and securely share the personal data of foreign users in response to lawful government requests. And in some cases, they changed their computer systems to do so.

These negotiations, the *New York Times* said, "illustrate how intricately the government and tech companies work together, and the depth of their behind-the-scenes transactions." The article also contested the companies' claims that they provide the NSA only with access that is legally compelled, noting: "While handing over data in response to a legitimate FISA request is a legal requirement, making it easier for the government to get the information is not, which is why Twitter could decline to do so."

The Internet companies' claim that they hand over to the NSA just the information that they are legally required to provide is also not particularly meaningful. That's because the NSA only needs to obtain an individual warrant when it wants to specifically target a US person. No such special permission is required for the agency to obtain the communications data of any non-American on foreign soil, *even when that person is communicating with Americans*. Similarly, there is no check or limit on the NSA's bulk collection of metadata, thanks to the government's interpretation of the Patriot Act—an interpretation so broad that even the law's original authors were shocked to learn how it was being used.

The close collaboration between the NSA and private corporations is perhaps best seen in the documents relating to Microsoft, which reveal the company's vigorous efforts to give the NSA access to several of its most used online services, including SkyDrive, Skype, and Outlook.com.

SkyDrive, which allows people to store their files online and access them from various devices, has more than 250 million users worldwide. "We believe it's important that you have control over who can and cannot access your personal data in the cloud," Microsoft's SkyDrive website proclaims. Yet as an NSA document details, Microsoft spent "many months" working to provide the government with easier access to that data:

```
(TS//SI//NF) SSO HIGHLIGHT — Microsoft Skydrive Collection Now Part of
PRISM Standard Stored Communications Collection

By    NAME REDACTED    on 2013-03-08 1500
```

```
(TS//SI//NF) Beginning on 7 March 2013, PRISM now collects Microsoft
Skydrive data as part of PRISM's standard Stored Communications collection
package for a tasked FISA Amendments Act Section 702 (FAA702) selector.
This means that analysts will no longer have to make a special request to
SSO for this — a process step that many analysts may not have known about.
This new capability will result in a much more complete and timely
collection response from SSO for our Enterprise customers. This success is
the result of the FBI working for many months with Microsoft to get this
tasking and collection solution established. "SkyDrive is a cloud service
that allows users to store and access their files on a variety of devices.
The utility also includes free web app support for Microsoft Office
programs, so the user is able to create, edit, and view Word, PowerPoint,
Excel files without having MS Office actually installed on their device."
(source: S314 wiki)
```

In late 2011, Microsoft purchased Skype, the Internet-based telephone and chat service with over 663 million registered users. At the time of its purchase, Microsoft assured users that "Skype is committed to respecting your privacy and the confidentiality of your personal data, traffic, and communications content." But in fact, this data, too, was readily available to the government. By early 2013, there were multiple messages on the NSA system celebrating the agency's steadily improving access to the communications of Skype users:

```
(TS//SI//NF) New Skype Stored Comms Capability For PRISM

By [ NAME REDACTED ] on 2013-04-03 0631


(TS//SI//NF) PRISM has a new collection capability: Skype stored
communications.  Skype stored communications will contain unique data which
is not collected via normal real-time surveillance collection. SSO expects
to receive buddy lists, credit card info, call data records, user account
info, and other material. On 29 March 2013, SSO forwarded approximately 2000
Skype selectors for stored communications to be adjudicated in SV41 and the
Electronic Communications Surveillance Unit (ECSU) at FBI. SV41 had been
working on adjudication for the highest priority selectors ahead of time and
had about 100 ready for ECSU to evaluate. It could take several weeks for
SV41 to work through all 2000 selectors to get them approved, and ECSU will
likely take longer to grant the approvals. As of 2 April, ESCU had approved
over 30 selectors to be sent to Skype for collection. PRISM Skype collection
has carved out a vital niche in NSA reporting in less than two years with
terrorism, Syrian opposition and regime, and exec/special series reports
being the top topics. Over 2800 reports have been issued since April 2011
based on PRISM Skype collection, with 76% of them being single source.



(TS//SI//NF) SSO Expands PRISM Skype Targeting Capability

By [ NAME REDACTED ] on 2013-04-03 0629


(TS//SI//NF) On 15 March 2013, SSO's PRISM program began tasking all
Microsoft PRISM selectors to Skype because Skype allows users to log in
using account identifiers in addition to Skype usernames. Until now, PRISM
would not collect any Skype data when a user logged in using anything other
than the Skype username which resulted in missing collection; this action
will mitigate that.  In fact, a user can create a Skype account using any
e-mail address with any domain in the world. UTT does not currently allow
analysts to task these non-Microsoft e-mail addresses to PRISM, however,
SSO intends to fix that this summer. In the meantime, NSA, FBI and Dept of
Justice coordinated over the last six months to gain approval for PRINTAURA
to send all current and future Microsoft PRISM selectors to Skype. This
resulted in about 9800 selectors being sent to Skype and successful
collection has been received which otherwise would have been missed.
```

Not only was all this collaboration conducted with no transparency, but it contradicted public statements made by Skype. ACLU technology expert Chris Soghoian said the revelations would surprise many Skype customers. "In the past, Skype made affirmative promises to users about their inability to perform wiretaps," he said. "It's hard to square Microsoft's secret collaboration with the NSA with its high-profile efforts to compete on privacy with Google."

In 2012, Microsoft began upgrading its email portal, Outlook.com, to merge all of its communications services—including the widely used

Hotmail—into one central program. The company touted the new Outlook by promising high levels of encryption to protect privacy, and the NSA quickly grew concerned that the encryption Microsoft offered to Outlook customers would block the agency from spying on their communications. One SSO memo from August 22, 2012, frets that "using this portal means that email emerging from it will be encrypted with the default setting" and that "chat sessions conducted within the portal are also encrypted when both communicants are using a Microsoft encrypted chat client."

But that worry was short-lived. Within a few months, the two entities got together and devised methods for the NSA to circumvent the very encryption protections Microsoft was publicly advertising as vital for protecting privacy:

```
(TS//SI//NF) Microsoft releases new service, affects FAA 702 collection

By [ NAME REDACTED ]   on 2012-12-26 0811


(TS//SI//NF) On 31 July, Microsoft (MS) began encrypting web-based chat
with the introduction of the new outlook.com service.   This new Secure
Socket Layer (SSL) encryption effectively cut off collection of the new
service for FAA 702 and likely 12333 (to some degree) for the Intelligence
Community (IC).  MS, working with the FBI, developed a surveillance
capability to deal with the new SSL. These solutions were successfully
tested and went live 12 Dec 2012. The SSL solution was applied to all
current FISA and 702/PRISM requirements - no changes to UTT tasking
procedures were required.  The SSL solution does not collect server-based
voice/video or file transfers.  The MS legacy collection system will remain
in place to collect voice/video and file transfers.  As a result there will
be some duplicate collection of text-based chat from the new and legacy
systems which will be addressed at a later date.  An increase in collection
volume as a result of this solution has already been noted by CES.
```

Another document describes further collaboration between Microsoft and the FBI, as that agency also sought to ensure that new Outlook features did not interfere with its surveillance habits: "The FBI Data Intercept Technology Unit (DITU) team is working with Microsoft to understand an additional feature in Outlook.com which allows users to create email aliases, which may affect our tasking process. . . . There are compartmented and other activities underway to mitigate these problems."

Finding this mention of FBI surveillance in Snowden's archive of internal NSA documents was not an isolated occurrence. The entire intelligence community is able to access the information that the NSA collects: it routinely shares its vast trove of data with other agencies, including the FBI and the CIA. One principal purpose of the NSA's great spree of data collection was precisely to boost the spread of information across the board. Indeed, almost every document pertaining to the various collection programs mentions the inclusion of other intelligence units. This 2012 entry from the NSA's SSO unit, on sharing PRISM data, gleefully declares that "PRISM is a team sport!":

(TS//SI//NF) Expanding PRISM Sharing With FBI and CIA

By [NAME REDACTED] on 2012-08-31 0947

(TS//SI//NF) Special Source Operations (SSO) has recently expanded sharing with the Federal Bureau of Investigations (FBI) and the Central Intelligence Agency (CIA) on PRISM operations via two projects. Through these efforts, SSO has created an environment of sharing and teaming across the Intelligence Community on PRISM operations. First, SSO's PRINTAURA team solved a problem for the Signals Intelligence Directorate (SID) by writing software which would automatically gather a list of tasked PRISM selectors every two weeks to provide to the FBI and CIA. This enables our partners to see which selectors the National Security Agency (NSA) has tasked to PRISM. The FBI and CIA then can request a copy of PRISM collection from any selector, as allowed under the 2008 Foreign Intelligence Surveillance Act (FISA) Amendments Act law. Prior to PRINTAURA's work, SID had been providing the FBI and CIA with incomplete and inaccurate lists, preventing our partners from making full use of the PRISM program. PRINTAURA volunteered to gather the detailed data related to each selector from multiple locations and assemble it in a usable form. In the second project, the PRISM Mission Program Manager (MPM) recently began sending operational PRISM news and guidance to the FBI and CIA so that their analysts could task the PRISM system properly, be aware of outages and changes, and optimize their use of PRISM. The MPM coordinated an agreement from the SID Foreign Intelligence Surveillance Act Amendments Act (FAA) Team to share this information weekly, which has been well-received and appreciated. These two activities underscore the point that PRISM is a team sport!

"Upstream" collection (from fiber-optic cables) and direct collection from the servers of Internet companies (PRISM) account for most of the records gathered by the NSA. In addition to such sweeping surveillance, though, the NSA also carries out what it calls Computer Network Exploitation (CNE), placing malware in individual computers to surveil their users. When the agency succeeds in inserting such malware, it is able, in NSA terminology, to "own" the computer: to view every keystroke entered and every screen viewed. The Tailored Access Operations (TAO) division responsible for this work is, in effect, the agency's own private hacker unit.

The hacking practice is quite widespread in its own right: one NSA document indicates that the agency has succeeded in infecting at least fifty thousand individual computers with a type of malware called "Quantum Insertion." One map shows the places where such operations have been performed and the number of successful insertions:

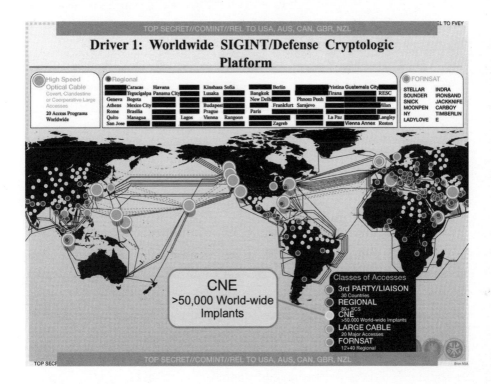

Using Snowden documents, the *New York Times* reported that the NSA has in fact implanted this particular software "in nearly 100,000 computers around the world." Although the malware is usually installed by "gaining access to computer networks, the NSA has increasingly made use of a secret technology that enables it to enter and alter data in computers even if they are not connected to the Internet."

Beyond its work with compliant telecoms and Internet companies, the NSA has also colluded with foreign governments to construct its far-reaching surveillance system. Broadly speaking, the NSA has three different categories of foreign relationships. The first is with the Five Eyes group: the US spies with these countries, but rarely on them, unless requested to by those countries' own officials. The second tier involves countries that the NSA works with for specific surveillance projects while also spying on them extensively. The third group is comprised of countries on which the United States routinely spies but with whom it virtually never cooperates.

Within the Five Eyes group, the closest NSA ally is the British GCHQ. As the *Guardian* reported, based on documents provided by Snowden, "The U.S. government has paid at least £100m to the UK spy agency GCHQ over the last three years to secure access to and influence over Britain's intelligence gathering programs." Those payments were an incentive to GCHQ to support the NSA's surveillance agenda. "GCHQ must pull its weight and be seen to pull its weight," a secret GCHQ strategy briefing said.

The Five Eyes members share most of their surveillance activities and meet each year at a Signals Development conference, where they boast of their expansion and the prior year's successes. Former NSA deputy director John Inglis has said of the Five Eyes alliance that they "practice intelligence in many regards in a combined way—essentially make sure that we leverage one another's capabilities for mutual benefit."

Many of the most invasive surveillance programs are carried out by the Five Eyes partners, a substantial number of these involving the GCHQ. Of special note are the British agency's joint efforts with the NSA to break the common encryption techniques that are used to safeguard personal Internet transactions, such as online banking and retrieval of medical records. The two agencies' success in setting up backdoor access to those encryption systems not only allowed them to peer at people's private dealings, but also weakened the systems for everyone, making them more vulnerable to malicious hackers and to other foreign intelligence agencies.

The GCHQ has also conducted mass interception of communications data from the world's underwater fiber-optic cables. Under the program name Tempora, the GCHQ developed the "ability to tap into and store huge volumes of data drawn from fibre-optic cables for up to 30 days so that it can be sifted and analysed," the *Guardian* reported, and the "GCHQ and the NSA are consequently able to access and process vast quantities of communications between entirely innocent people." The intercepted data encompass all forms of online activity, including "recordings of phone calls, the content of email messages, entries on Facebook, and the history of any internet user's access to websites."

The GCHQ's surveillance activities are every bit as comprehensive— and unaccountable—as the NSA's. As the *Guardian* noted:

> The sheer scale of the agency's ambition is reflected in the titles of its two principal components: Mastering the Internet and Global Telecoms Exploitation, aimed at scooping up as much online and telephone traffic as possible. This is all being carried out without any form of public acknowledgement or debate.

Canada is also a very active partner with the NSA and an energetic surveillance force in its own right. At the 2012 SigDev conference, the Communications Services Establishment Canada (CSEC) boasted about targeting the Brazilian Ministry of Mines and Energy, the agency in Brazil that regulates the industry of greatest interest to Canadian companies:

**AND THEY SAID TO THE
TITANS: « WATCH OUT
OLYMPIANS IN THE
HOUSE! »**

CSEC – Advanced Network Tradecraft
SD Conference June 2012

Overall Classification: TOP SECRET//SI

OLYMPIA & THE CASE STUDY

OLYMPIA

CSEC's Network Knowledge Engine

Various data sources
Chained enrichments
Automated analysis

Brazilian Ministry of Mines and Energy (MME)

New target to develop
Limited access/target knowledge

Advanced Network Tradecraft - CSEC   TOP SECRET // SI

There is evidence of widespread CSEC/NSA cooperation, including Canada's efforts to set up spying posts for communications surveillance around the world at the behest and for the benefit of the NSA, and spying on trading partners targeted by the US agency.

TOP SECRET//SI//REL USA, FVEY

National Security Agency/   3 April 2013
Central Security Service

Information Paper

Subject: (U//FOUO) NSA Intelligence Relationship with Canada's Communications Security Establishment Canada (CSEC)

TOP SECRET//SI//REL TO USA, CAN

(U) What NSA provides to the partner:

(S//SI//REL TO USA, CAN) SIGINT: NSA and CSEC cooperate in targeting approximately 20 high-priority countries ▮▮▮▮▮▮▮▮▮▮▮▮▮▮▮▮▮▮▮▮▮▮▮▮▮▮▮▮▮ NSA shares technological developments, cryptologic capabilities, software and resources for state-of-the-art collection, processing and analytic efforts, and IA capabilities. The intelligence exchange with CSEC covers worldwide national and transnational targets. No Consolidated Cryptologic Program (CCP) money is allocated to CSEC, but NSA at times pays R&D and technology costs on shared projects with CSEC.

(U) What the partner provides to NSA:

(TS//SI///REL TO USA, CAN) CSEC offers resources for advanced collection, processing and analysis, and has opened covert sites at the request of NSA. CSEC shares with NSA their unique geographic access to areas unavailable to the U.S. ▮▮▮▮▮▮▮▮▮▮▮▮▮▮ and provides cryptographic products, cryptanalysis, technology, and software. CSEC has increased its investment in R&D projects of mutual interest.

The Five Eyes relationship is so close that member governments place the NSA's desires above the privacy of their own citizens. The *Guardian* reported on one 2007 memo, for instance, describing an agreement "that allowed the agency to 'unmask' and hold on to personal data about Britons that had previously been off limits." Additionally, the rules were changed in 2007 "to allow the NSA to analyse and retain any British citizens' mobile phone and fax numbers, emails and IP addresses swept up by its dragnet."

Going a step further, in 2011 the Australian government explicitly pleaded with the NSA to "extend" their partnership and subject Australian citizens to greater surveillance. In a February 21 letter, the acting deputy director of Australia's Intelligence Defence Signals Directorate wrote to the NSA's Signals Intelligence Directorate, claiming that Australia "now face[s] a sinister and determined threat from 'home grown' extremists active both abroad and within Australia." He requested increased surveillance on the communications of Australian citizens deemed suspicious by their government:

> While we have invested significant analytic and collection effort of our own to find and exploit these communications, the difficulties we face in obtaining regular and reliable access to such communications impacts on our ability to detect and prevent terrorist acts and diminishes our capacity to protect the life and safety of Australian citizens and those of our close friends and allies.
>
> We have enjoyed a long and very productive partnership with NSA in obtaining minimised access to United States warranted collection against our highest value terrorist targets in Indonesia. This access has been critical to DSD's efforts to disrupt and contain the operational capabilities of terrorists in our region as highlighted by the recent arrest of fugitive Bali bomber Umar Patek.
>
> We would very much welcome the opportunity to extend that partnership with NSA to cover the increasing number of Australians involved in international extremist activities – in particular Australians involved with AQAP.

Beyond the Five Eyes partners, the NSA's next level of cooperation is with its Tier B allies: countries that have some limited cooperation with the agency and are also targeted themselves for aggressive, unrequested surveillance. The NSA has clearly delineated these two levels of alliances:

CONFIDENTIAL//NOFORN//20291123

TIER A Comprehensive Cooperation	Australia Canada New Zealand United Kingdom
TIER B Focused Cooperation	Austria Belgium Czech Republic Denmark Germany Greece Hungary
	Iceland Italy Japan Luxemberg Netherlands Norway Poland Portugal South Korea Spain Sweden Switzerland Turkey

Using different designations (referring to Tier B as Third Parties), a more recent NSA document—from the Fiscal Year 2013 "Foreign Partner Review"—shows an expanding list of NSA partners, including international organizations such as NATO:

TOP SECRET// COMINT //REL USA, AUS, CAN, GBR, NZL

Approved SIGINT Partners

Second Parties: Australia, Canada, New Zealand, United Kingdom

Coalitions/Multi-lats: AFSC, NATO, SSEUR, SSPAC

Third Parties: Algeria, Austria, Belgium, Croatia, Czech Republic, Denmark, Ethiopia, Finland, France, Germany, Greece, Hungary, India, Israel, Italy, Japan, Jordan, Korea, Macedonia, Netherlands, Norway, Pakistan, Poland, Romania, Saudi Arabia, Singapore, Spain, Sweden, Taiwan, Thailand, Tunisia, Turkey, UAE

As with the GCHQ, the NSA often maintains these partnerships by paying its partner to develop certain technologies and engage in surveillance, and can thus direct how the spying is carried out. The Fiscal Year 2012 "Foreign Partner Review" reveals numerous countries that have received such payments, including Canada, Israel, Japan, Jordan, Pakistan, Taiwan, and Thailand:

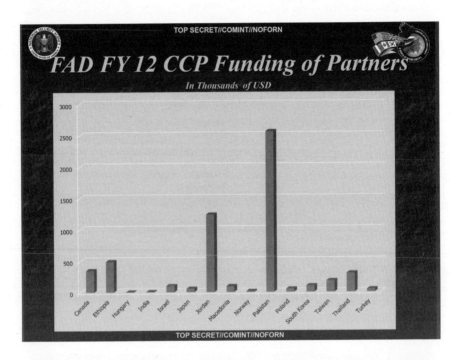

In particular, the NSA has a surveillance relationship with Israel that often entails cooperation as close as the Five Eyes partnership, if not sometimes even closer. A Memorandum of Understanding between the NSA and the Israeli intelligence service details how the United States takes the unusual step of routinely sharing with Israel raw intelligence containing the communications of American citizens. Among the data furnished to Israel are "unevaluated and unminimized transcripts, gists, facsimiles, telex, voice, and Digital Network Intelligence metadata and content."

What makes this sharing particularly egregious is that the material is sent to Israel without having undergone the legally required process of "minimization." The minimization procedures are supposed to ensure that when the NSA's bulk surveillance sweeps up some communications data that even the agency's very broad guidelines do not permit it to collect, such information is destroyed as soon as possible and not disseminated further. As the law is written, the minimization requirements already have plenty of loopholes, including exemptions for "significant foreign intelligence information" or any "evidence of a crime." But when it comes to disseminating data to Israeli intelligence, the NSA has apparently dispensed with such legalities altogether.

The memo flatly states: "NSA routinely sends ISNU [the Israeli SIGINT National Unit] minimized and unminimized raw collection."

Highlighting how a country can both cooperate on surveillance and be a target at the same time, an NSA document recounting the history of Israel's cooperation noted "trust issues which revolve around previous ISR operations," and identified Israel as one of the most aggressive surveillance services acting against the United States:

(TS//SI//REL) There are also a few surprises... France targets the US DoD through technical intelligence collection, and Israel also targets us. On the one hand, the Israelis are extraordinarily good SIGINT partners for us, but on the other, they target us to learn our positions on Middle East problems. A NIE [National Intelligence Estimate] ranked them as the third most aggressive intelligence service against the US.

The same report observed that, despite the close relationship between American and Israeli intelligence agencies, the extensive information provided to Israel by the United States produced little in return. Israeli intelligence was only interested in collecting data that helped them. As the NSA complained, the partnership was geared "almost totally" to Israel's needs.

Balancing the SIGINT exchange equally between US and Israeli needs has been a constant challenge in the last decade, it arguably tilted heavily in favor of Israeli security concerns. 9/11 came, and went, with NSA's only true Third Party CT relationship being driven almost totally by the needs of the partner.

Another rung lower, below the Five Eyes partners and second-tier countries such as Israel, the third tier is composed of countries who are often targets but never partners of US spying programs. Those predictably include governments viewed as adversaries, such as China, Russia, Iran, Venezuela, and Syria. But the third tier also includes countries ranging from the generally friendly to neutral, such as Brazil, Mexico, Argentina, Indonesia, Kenya, and South Africa.

When the NSA revelations first came out, the US government tried to defend its actions by saying that, unlike foreign nationals, American citizens are protected from warrantless NSA surveillance. On June 18, 2013, President Obama told Charlie Rose: "What I can say unequivocally is that if you are a U.S. person, the NSA cannot listen to your telephone calls . . . by law and by rule, and unless they . . . go to a court, and obtain a warrant, and seek probable cause, the same way it's always been." The GOP chairman of the House Intelligence Committee, Mike Rogers, similarly told CNN that the NSA "is not listening to Americans' phone calls. If it did, it is illegal. It is breaking the law."

This was a rather odd line of defense: in effect, it told the rest of the world that the NSA does assault the privacy of non-Americans. Privacy protections, apparently, are only for American citizens. This message prompted such international outrage that even Facebook CEO Mark Zuckerberg, not exactly known for his vehement defense of privacy, complained that the US government "blew it" in its response to the NSA scandal by jeopardizing the interests of international Internet companies: "The government said don't worry, we're not spying on any Americans. Wonderful, that's really helpful for companies trying to work with people around the world. Thanks for going out there and being clear. I think that was really bad."

Aside from being a strange strategy, the claim is also patently false. In fact, contrary to the repeated denials of President Obama and his top officials, the NSA continuously intercepts the communications of American citizens, without any individual "probable cause" warrants to justify such surveillance. That's because the 2008 FISA law, as noted earlier, allows the NSA—without an individual warrant—to monitor the content of any American's communications as long as those communications are exchanged with a targeted foreign national. The NSA labels this "incidental" collection, as though it's some sort of minor accident that the agency has been spying on Americans. But the implication is deceitful. As Jameel Jaffer, the deputy legal director of the ACLU, explained:

> The government often says that this surveillance of Americans' communications is "incidental," which makes it sound like the NSA's surveillance of Americans' phone calls and emails is inadvertent and, even from the government's perspective, regrettable.
>
> But when the Bush administration officials asked Congress for this new surveillance power, they said quite explicitly that Americans' communications were the communications of most interest to them. See, for example, FISA for the 21st century, Hearing Before the S. Comm. On the Judiciary, 109th Cong. (2006) (statement of Michael Hayden), that certain communications "with one end in the United States" are the ones "that are most important to us."
>
> The principal purpose of the 2008 law was to make it possible for the government to collect *Americans'* international communications—and to collect those communications without reference to whether any party to those communications was doing anything illegal. And a lot of the government's advocacy is meant to obscure this fact, but it's a crucial one: The government doesn't need to "target" Americans in order to collect huge volumes of their communications.

Yale Law School professor Jack Balkin concurred that the FISA law of 2008 effectively gave the president the authority to run a program "similar in effect to the warrantless surveillance program" that had been secretly implemented by George Bush. "These programs may inevitably include many phone calls involving Americans, who may have absolutely no connection to terrorism or to Al Qaeda."

Further discrediting Obama's assurances is the subservient posture of the FISA court, which grants almost every surveillance request that the NSA submits. Defenders of the NSA frequently tout the FISA court process as evidence that the agency is under effective oversight. However, the court was set up not as a genuine check on the government's power but as a cosmetic measure, providing just the appearance of reform to placate public anger over surveillance abuses revealed in the 1970s.

The uselessness of this institution as a true check on surveillance abuses is obvious because the FISA court lacks virtually every attribute of what our society generally understands as the minimal elements of a justice system. It meets in complete secrecy; only one party—the government—is permitted to attend the hearings and make its case; and the court's rulings are automatically designated "Top Secret." Tellingly, for years the FISA court was housed in the Department of Justice, making clear its role as a part of the executive branch rather than as an independent judiciary exercising real oversight.

The results have been exactly what one would expect: the court almost never rejects specific NSA applications to target Americans with surveillance. From its inception, FISA has been the ultimate rubber stamp. In its first twenty-four years, from 1978 to 2002, the court rejected a total of *zero* government applications while approving many thousands. In the subsequent decade, through 2012, the court has rejected just eleven government applications. In total, it has approved more than twenty thousand requests.

One of the provisions of the 2008 FISA law requires the executive branch annually to disclose to Congress the number of eavesdropping applications the court receives and then approves, modifies, or rejects. The disclosure for 2012 showed that the court approved every single one of the 1,788 applications for electronic surveillance that it considered, while "modifying"—that is, narrowing the purview of the order—in just 40 cases, or less than 3 percent.

Applications Made to the Foreign Intelligence Surveillance Court During Calendar Year 2012 (section 107 of the Act, 50 U.S.C. § 1807)

During calendar year 2012, the Government made 1,856 applications to the Foreign Intelligence Surveillance Court (the "FISC") for authority to conduct electronic surveillance and/or physical searches for foreign intelligence purposes. The 1,856 applications include applications made solely for electronic surveillance, applications made solely for physical search, and combined applications requesting authority for electronic surveillance and physical search. Of these, 1,789 applications included requests for authority to conduct electronic surveillance.

Of these 1,789 applications, one was withdrawn by the Government. The FISC did not deny any applications in whole or in part.

Much the same was true of 2011, when the NSA reported 1,676 applications; the FISA court, while modifying 30 of them, "did not deny any applications in whole, or in part."

The court's subservience to the NSA is demonstrated by other statistics as well. Here, for instance, is the FISA court's reaction over the last six years to various requests made by the NSA under the Patriot Act to obtain the business records—telephone, financial or medical—of US persons:

Gov't surveillance requests to FISA court

Year	Number of business records requests made by U.S. Gov't	Number of requests rejected by FISA court
2005	155	0
2006	43	0
2007	17	0
2008	13	0
2009	21	0
2010	96	0
2011	205	0

[Source: Documents released by ODNI, 18/Nov/2013]

Thus, even in those limited cases when approval from the FISA court is needed to target someone's communications, the process is more of an empty pantomime than a meaningful check on the NSA.

Another layer of oversight for the NSA is ostensibly provided by the congressional intelligence committees, also created in the aftermath of the surveillance scandals of the 1970s, but they are even more supine than the FISA court. While they are supposed to conduct "vigilant legislative oversight" over the intelligence community, those committees are in fact currently headed by the most devoted NSA loyalists in Washington: Democrat Dianne Feinstein in the Senate and Republican Mike Rogers in the House. Rather than offer any sort of adversarial check on the NSA's operations, the Feinstein and Rogers committees exist primarily to defend and justify anything the agency does.

As the New Yorker's Ryan Lizza put it in a December 2013 article, instead of providing oversight, the Senate committee more often "treats senior intelligence officials like matinée idols." Observers of the committee's hearings on NSA activities were shocked by how the senators approached the questioning of NSA officials who appeared before them. The "questions" typically contained nothing more than long monologues by the senators about their recollections of the 9/11 attack and how vital it was to prevent attacks in the future. The committee members waved away the opportunity to interrogate those officials and perform their oversight responsibilities, instead propagandizing in defense of the NSA. The scene perfectly captured the true function of the intelligence committees over the last decade.

Indeed, the chairs of the congressional committees have sometimes defended the NSA even more vigorously than the agency's officials themselves have done. At one point, in August 2013, two members of Congress—Democrat Alan Grayson of Florida and Republican Morgan Griffith of Virginia—separately approached me to complain that the House Permanent Select Committee on Intelligence was blocking them and other members from accessing the most basic information about the NSA. They each gave me letters they had written to the staff of Chairman Rogers requesting information about NSA programs being discussed in the media. Those requests were rebuffed again and again.

In the wake of our Snowden stories, a group of senators from both parties who had long been concerned with surveillance abuses began efforts to draft legislation that would impose real limits on the NSA's powers.

But these reformers, led by Democratic senator Ron Wyden of Oregon, ran into an immediate roadblock: counterefforts by the NSA's defenders in the Senate to write legislation that would provide only the appearance of reform, while in fact retaining or even increasing the NSA's powers. As *Slate*'s Dave Weigel reported in November:

> Critics of the NSA's bulk data collection and surveillance programs have never been worried about congressional *inaction*. They've expected Congress to come up with something that looked like reform but actually codified and excused the practices being exposed and pilloried. That's what's always happened—every amendment or reauthorization to the 2001 USA Patriot Act has built more back doors than walls.
>
> "We will be up against a 'business-as-usual brigade'—made up of influential members of the government's intelligence leadership, their allies in thinktanks [*sic*] and academia, retired government officials, and sympathetic legislators," warned Oregon Sen. Ron Wyden last month. "Their endgame is ensuring that any surveillance reforms are only skin-deep. . . . Privacy protections that don't actually protect privacy are not worth the paper they're printed on."

The "fake reform" faction was led by Dianne Feinstein, the very senator who is charged with exercising primary oversight over the NSA. Feinstein has long been a devoted loyalist of the US national security industry, from her vehement support for the war on Iraq to her steadfast backing of Bush-era NSA programs. (Her husband, meanwhile, has major stakes in various military contracts.) Clearly, Feinstein was a natural choice to head a committee that claims to carry out oversight over the intelligence community but has for years performed the opposite function.

Thus, for all the government's denials, the NSA has no substantial constraints on whom it can spy on and how. Even when such constraints nominally exist—when American citizens are the surveillance target—the process has become largely hollow. The NSA is the definitive rogue agency: empowered to do whatever it wants with very little control, transparency, or accountability.

Very broadly speaking, the NSA collects two types of information: content and metadata. "Content" here refers to actually listening to people's phone calls or reading their emails and online chats, as well as reviewing Internet activity such as browsing histories and search activities. "Metadata" collection, meanwhile, involves amassing data *about* those communications. The NSA refers to that as "information about content (but not the content itself)."

Metadata about an email message, for instance, records who emailed whom, when the email was sent, and the location of the person sending it. When it comes to telephone calls, the information includes the phone numbers of the caller and the receiver, how long they spoke for, and often their locations and the types of devices they used to communicate. In one document about telephone calls, the NSA outlined the metadata it accesses and stores:

SECRET//COMINT//NOFORN//20320108

Communications Metadata Fields in ICREACH

(S//NF) NSA populates these fields in PROTON:
- Called & calling numbers, date, time & duration of call

(S//SI//REL) ICREACH users will see telephony metadata* in the following fields:

DATE & TIME	IMEI – International Mobile Equipment Identifier
DURATION – Length of Call	
CALLED NUMBER	MSISDN – Mobile Subscriber Integrated Services Digital Network
CALLING NUMBER	
CALLED FAX (CSI) – Called Subscriber ID	MDN – Mobile Dialed Number
	CLI – Call Line Identifier (Caller ID)
TRANSMITTING FAX (TSI) – Transmitting Subscriber ID	DSME – Destination Short Message Entity
IMSI – International Mobile Subscriber Identifier	OSME – Originating Short Message Entity
TMSI – Temporary Mobile Subscriber Identifier	VLR – Visitor Location Register

SECRET//COMINT//NOFORN//20320108

The US government has insisted that much of the surveillance revealed in the Snowden archive involves the collection of "metadata, not content," trying to imply that this kind of spying is not intrusive—or at least not to the same degree as intercepting content. Dianne Feinstein has explicitly argued in *USA Today* that the metadata collection of all Americans' telephone records "is not surveillance" at all because it "does not collect the content of any communication." ✗

These disingenuous arguments obscure the fact that metadata surveillance can be at least as intrusive as content interception, and often even more so. When the government knows everyone you call and everyone who calls you, plus the exact length of all those phone conversations; when it can list every single one of your email correspondents and every location from where your emails were sent, it can create a remarkably comprehensive picture of your life, your associations, and your activities, including some of your most intimate and private information.

In an affidavit filed by the ACLU challenging the legality of the NSA's metadata collection program, Princeton computer science and public affairs professor Edward Felten explained why metadata surveillance can be especially revealing:

> Consider the following hypothetical example: A young woman calls her gynecologist; then immediately calls her mother; then a man who, during the past few months, she had repeatedly spoken to on the telephone after 11pm; followed by a call to a family planning center that also offers abortions. A likely storyline emerges that would not be as evident by examining the record of a single telephone call.

Even for a single phone call, the metadata can be more informative than the call's content. Listening in on a woman calling an abortion clinic might reveal nothing more than someone confirming an appointment with a generic-sounding establishment ("East Side Clinic" or "Dr. Jones's office"). But the metadata would show far more than that: it would reveal the identity of those who were called. The same is true of calls to a dating service, a gay and lesbian center, a drug addiction clinic, an HIV specialist, or a suicide hotline. Metadata would likewise unmask a conversation between a human rights activist and an informant in a repressive regime, or a confidential source calling a journalist to reveal high-level wrong-doing. And if you frequently call someone late at night who is not your spouse, the metadata will reveal that, too. What's more, it will record not only all the people with whom you communicate and how often, but also all the people with whom your friends and associates communicate, cre-ating a comprehensive picture of your network of contacts.

Indeed, as Professor Felten notes, eavesdropping on calls can be quite difficult due to language differences, meandering conversations, the use of slang or deliberate codes, and other attributes that either by design or accident obfuscate the meaning. "The content of calls are far more difficult to analyze in an automated fashion due to their unstructured nature," he argued. By contrast, metadata is mathematical: clean, precise, and thus easily analyzed. And as Felten put it, it is often "a proxy for content":

> Telephony metadata can . . . expose an extraordinary amount about our habits and our associations. Calling patterns can reveal when we are awake and asleep; our religion, if a person regularly makes no calls on the Sabbath, or makes a large number of calls on Christmas day; our work habits and our social aptitude; the number of friends we have; and even our civil and political affiliations.

In sum, writes Felten, "mass collection not only allows the government to learn information about more people, but it also enables the govern-ment to learn new, previously private facts that it could not have learned simply by collecting the information about a few, specific individuals."

Concern about the many uses that the government could find for this kind of sensitive information is especially justified because, contrary to repeated claims from President Obama and the NSA, it is already clear that a substantial number of the agency's activities have nothing to do with antiterrorism efforts or even with national security. Much of the Snowden archive revealed what can only be called economic espionage: eavesdropping and email interception aimed at the Brazilian oil giant Petrobras, economic conferences in Latin America, energy companies in Venezuela and Mexico, and spying by the NSA's allies—including Canada, Norway, and Sweden—on the Brazilian Ministry of Mines and Energy and energy companies in several other countries.

One remarkable document presented by the NSA and the GCHQ detailed numerous surveillance targets that were plainly economic in nature: Petrobras, the SWIFT banking system, the Russian oil company Gazprom, and the Russian airline Aeroflot.

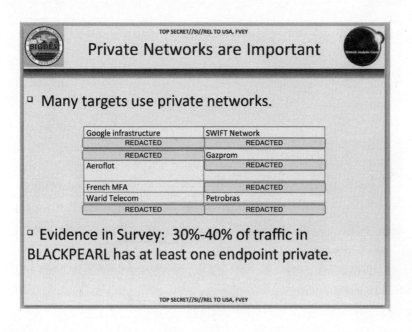

For years, President Obama and his top officials vehemently denounced China for using its surveillance capabilities for economic advantage while insisting that the United States and its allies never do any such thing. The *Washington Post* quoted an NSA spokesperson saying that the Department of Defense, of which the agency is a part, "'does engage' in computer network exploitation," but "does ***not*** engage in economic espionage in any domain, including 'cyber'" [emphatic asterisks in the original].

That the NSA spies for precisely the economic motive it has denied is proven by its own documents. The agency acts for the benefit of what it calls its "customers," a list that includes not only the White House, the

State Department, and the CIA, but also primarily economic agencies, such as the US Trade Representative and the Departments of Agriculture, Treasury, and Commerce:

In its description of the BLARNEY program, the NSA lists the types of information it is supposed to provide to its customers as "counter terrorism," "diplomatic"—and "economic":

US-984 BLARNEY

(TS//SI) US-984 (PDDG: AX) – provides collection against DNR and DNI FISA Court Order authorized communications.

(TS//SI) Key Targets: Diplomatic establishment, counterterrorism, Foreign Government, Economic

Further evidence of the NSA's economic interest appears in a PRISM document showing a "sampling" of the "Reporting Topics" for the week of February 2–8, 2013. A list of the types of information gathered from various countries clearly includes economic and financial categories, among them "energy," "trade," and "oil":

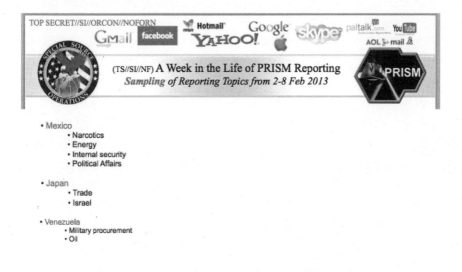

TOP SECRET//SI//ORCON//NOFORN

(TS//SI/NF) A Week in the Life of PRISM Reporting
Sampling of Reporting Topics from 2-8 Feb 2013

- Mexico
    - Narcotics
    - Energy
    - Internal security
    - Political Affairs

- Japan
    - Trade
    - Israel

- Venezuela
    - Military procurement
    - Oil

One 2006 memorandum from the global capabilities manager of the agency's International Security Issues (ISI) mission spells out the NSA's economic and trade espionage—against countries as diverse as Belgium, Japan, Brazil, and Germany—in stark terms:

(U) NSA Washington Mission

(U) Regional

(TS//SI) ISI is responsible for 13 individual nation states in three continents. One significant tie that binds all these countries together is their importance to U.S. economic, trade, and defense concerns. The Western Europe and Strategic Partnerships division primarily focuses on foreign policy and trade activities of Belgium, France, Germany, Italy, and Spain, as well as Brazil, Japan and Mexico.

(TS//SI) The Energy and Resource branch provides unique intelligence on worldwide energy production and development in key countries that affect the world economy. Targets of current emphasis are ▇▇▇▇▇▇▇▇ and the ▇▇▇▇ ▇▇▇▇▇▇▇▇▇▇▇▇▇▇▇. Reporting has included the monitoring of international investment in the energy sectors of target countries, electrical and Supervisory Control and Data Acquisition (SCADA) upgrades, and computer aided designs of projected energy projects.

Reporting on a group of GCHQ documents leaked by Snowden, the *New York Times* noted that its surveillance targets often included financial institutions and "heads of international aid organizations, foreign energy companies and a European Union official involved in antitrust battles with American technology businesses." It added that the US and British agencies "monitored the communications of senior European Union officials, foreign leaders including African heads of state and sometimes their family members, directors of United Nations and other relief programs [such as UNICEF], and officials overseeing oil and finance ministries."

The reasons for economic espionage are clear enough. When the United States uses the NSA to eavesdrop on the planning strategies of other countries during trade and economic talks, it can gain enormous advantage for American industry. In 2009, for example, Assistant Secretary of State Thomas Shannon wrote a letter to Keith Alexander, offering his "gratitude and congratulations for the outstanding signals intelligence support" that the State Department received regarding the Fifth Summit of the Americas, a conference devoted to negotiating economic accords. In the letter, Shannon specifically noted that the NSA's surveillance provided the United States with negotiating advantages over the other parties:

> The more than 100 reports we received from the NSA gave us deep insight into the plans and intentions of other Summit participants, and ensured that our diplomats were well prepared to advise President Obama and Secretary Clinton on how to deal with contentious issues, such as Cuba, and interact with difficult counterparts, such as Venezuelan President Chavez.

The NSA is equally devoted to diplomatic espionage, as the documents referring to "political affairs" demonstrate. One particularly egregious example, from 2011, shows how the agency targeted two Latin American leaders—Dilma Rousseff, the president of Brazil, along with "her key advisers"; and Enrique Peña Nieto, then Mexico's leading presidential candidate (and now its president), along with "nine of his close associates"—for a "surge" of especially invasive surveillance. The document even features some of the intercepted text messages sent and received by Nieto and a "close associate":

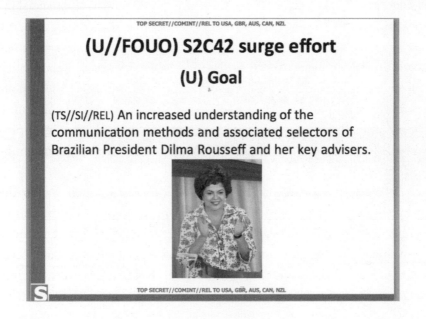

TOP SECRET//COMINT//REL TO USA, GBR, AUS, CAN, NZL

(U//FOUO) S2C42 surge effort

(U) Goal

(TS//SI//REL) An increased understanding of the communication methods and associated selectors of Brazilian President Dilma Rousseff and her key advisers.

TOP SECRET//COMINT//REL TO USA, GBR, AUS, CAN, NZL

(U//FOUO) S2C41 surge effort

(TS//SI//REL) NSA's Mexico Leadership Team (S2C41) conducted a two-week target development surge effort against one of Mexico's leading presidential candidates, Enrique Pena Nieto, and nine of his close associates. Nieto is considered by most political pundits to be the likely winner of the 2012 Mexican presidential elections which are to be held in July 2012.   SATC leveraged graph analysis in the development surge's target development effort.

(U) Results

- (S//SI//REL)85489 Text messages
  Interesting Messages

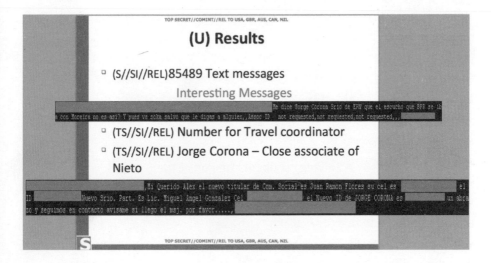

- (TS//SI//REL) Number for Travel coordinator
- (TS//SI//REL) Jorge Corona – Close associate of Nieto

TOP SECRET//COMINT//REL TO USA, GBR, AUS, CAN, NZL

(U) Conclusion

- (S//REL) Contact graph-enhanced filtering is a simple yet effective technique, which may allow you to find previously unobtainable results and empower analytic discovery
- (TS//SI//REL) Teaming with S2C, SATC was able to successfully apply this technique against high-profile, OPSEC-savvy Brazilian and Mexican targets.

TOP SECRET//COMINT//REL TO USA, GBR, AUS, CAN, NZL

One can speculate about why political leaders of Brazil and Mexico were NSA targets. Both countries are rich in oil resources. They are a big and influential presence in the region. And while they are far from adversaries, they are also not America's closest and most trusted allies. Indeed, one NSA planning document—entitled "Identifying Challenges: Geopolitical Trends for 2014–2019"—list both Mexico and Brazil under the heading "Friends, Enemies, or Problems?" Others on that list are Egypt, India, Iran, Saudi Arabia, Somalia, Sudan, Turkey, and Yemen.

But ultimately, in this case as in most others, speculation about any specific target is based on a false premise. The NSA does not need any specific reason or rationale to invade people's private communications. Their institutional mission is to collect everything.

If anything, the revelations about NSA spying on foreign leaders are *less* significant than the agency's warrantless mass surveillance of whole populations. Countries have spied on heads of state for centuries, including allies. This is unremarkable, despite the great outcry that ensued when, for example, the world discovered that the NSA had for many years targeted the personal cell phone of German chancellor Angela Merkel.

More remarkable is the fact that in country after country, revelations

that the NSA was spying on hundreds of millions of their citizens produced little more than muted objections from their political leadership.
True indignation came gushing forward only once those leaders understood that they, and not just their citizens, had been targeted as well.

Still, the sheer scale of diplomatic surveillance the NSA has practiced
is unusual and noteworthy. In addition to foreign leaders, the United
States has also, for example, spied extensively on international organizations such as the United Nations to gain diplomatic advantage. One
April 2013 briefing from SSO is typical, noting how the agency used its
programs to obtain the UN secretary general's talking points prior to his
meeting with President Obama:

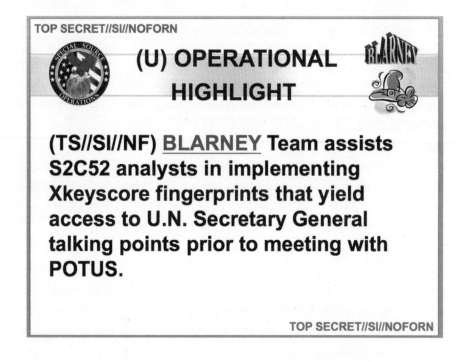

TOP SECRET//SI//NOFORN

(U) OPERATIONAL HIGHLIGHT

**(TS//SI//NF) BLARNEY Team assists
S2C52 analysts in implementing
Xkeyscore fingerprints that yield
access to U.N. Secretary General
talking points prior to meeting with
POTUS.**

TOP SECRET//SI//NOFORN

Numerous other documents detail how Susan Rice, then ambassador to the UN and now President Obama's national security adviser, repeatedly requested that the NSA spy on the internal discussions of key member states to learn their negotiation strategies. A May 2010 SSO report describes this process in connection with a resolution being debated by the UN that involved imposing new sanctions on Iran.

(S//SI) BLARNEY Team Provides Outstanding Support to Enable UN Security Council Collection

By [NAME REDACTED]   on 2010-05-28 1430

(TS//SI//NF) With the UN vote on sanctions against Iran approaching and several countries riding the fence on making a decision, Ambassador Rice reached out to NSA requesting SIGINT on those countries so that she could develop a strategy. With the requirement that this be done rapidly and within our legal authorities, the BLARNEY team jumped in to work with organizations and partners both internal and external to NSA.

(TS//SI//NF) As OGC, SV and the TOPIs aggressively worked through the legal paperwork to expedite four new NSA FISA court orders for Gabon, Uganda, Nigeria and Bosnia, BLARNEY Operations Division personnel were behind the scenes gathering data determining what survey information was available or could be obtained via their long standing FBI contacts. As they worked to obtain information on both the UN Missions in NY and the Embassies in DC, the target development team greased the skids with appropriate data flow personnel and all preparations were made to ensure data could flow to the TOPIs as soon as possible. Several personnel, one from legal team and one from target development team were called in on Saturday 22 May to support the 24 hour drill legal paperwork exercise doing their part to ensure the orders were ready for the NSA Director's signature early Monday morning 24 May.

(S//SI) With OGC and SV pushing hard to expedite these four orders, they went from the NSA Director for signature to DoD for SECDEF signature and then to DOJ for signature by the FISC judge in record time. All four orders were signed by the judge on Wednesday 26 May! Once the orders were received by the BLARNEY legal team, they sprung into action parsing these four orders plus another "normal" renewal in one day. Parsing five court orders in one day — a BLARNEY record! As the BLARNEY legal team was busily parsing court orders the BLARNEY access management team was working with the FBI to pass tasking information and coordinate the engagement with telecommunications partners.

A similar surveillance document from August 2010 reveals that the United States spied on eight members of the UN Security Council regarding a subsequent resolution about sanctions on Iran. The list included France, Brazil, Japan, and Mexico—all considered friendly nations. The espionage gave the US government valuable information about those countries' voting intentions, giving Washington an edge when talking to other members of the Security Council.

TOP SECRET//COMINT//NOFORN

August 2010

 (U//FOUO) Silent Success: SIGINT Synergy Helps Shape US Foreign Policy

(TS//SI//NF) At the outset of these lengthy negotiations, NSA had sustained collection against
France
Japan, Mexico,   Brazil

(TS//SI//REL) In late spring 2010, eleven branches across five Product Lines teamed with NSA enablers to provide the most current and accurate information to USUN and other customers on how UNSC members would vote on the Iran Sanctions Resolution. Noting that Iran continued its non-compliance with previous UNSC resolutions concerning its nuclear program, the UN imposed further sanctions on 9 June 2010. SIGINT was key in keeping USUN informed of how the other members of the UNSC would vote.

(TS//SI//REL) The resolution was adopted by twelve votes for, two against (Brazil and Turkey), and one abstention from Lebanon. According to USUN, SIGINT "helped me to know when the other Permreps [Permanent Representatives] were telling the truth.... revealed their real position on sanctions... gave us an upper hand in negotiations... and provided information on various countries 'red lines.'"

To facilitate diplomatic spying, the NSA has gained various forms of access to the embassies and consulates of many of its closest allies. One 2010 document—shown here with some countries deleted—lists the nations whose diplomatic structures inside the United States were invaded by the agency. A glossary at the end explains the various types of surveillance used.

10 Sep 2010

CLOSE ACCESS SIGADS

CLOSE ACCESS SIGADS

All Close Access domestic collection uses the US-3136 SIGAD with a unique two-letter suffix for each target location and mission. Close Access overseas GENIE collection has been assigned the US-3137 SIGAD with a two-letter suffix.

(Note: Targets marked with an * have either been dropped or are slated to be dropped in the near future. Please check with TAO/RTD/ROS (961-1578s) regarding authorities status.)

SIGAD   US-3136

SUFFIX	TARGET/COUNTRY	LOCATION	COVERTERM	MISSION
BE	Brazil/Emb	Wash,DC	KATEEL	LIFESAVER
SI	Brazil/Emb	Wash,DC	KATEEL	HIGHLANDS
VQ	Brazil/UN	New York	POCOMOKE	HIGHLANDS
HN	Brazil/UN	New York	POCOMOKE	VAGRANT
LJ	Brazil/UN	New York	POCOMOKE	LIFESAVER
YL *	Bulgaria/Emb	Wash, DC	MERCED	HIGHLANDS
QX *	Colombia/Trade Bureau	New York	BANISTER	LIFESAVER
DJ	EU/UN	New York	PERDIDO	HIGHLANDS
SS	EU/UN	New York	PERDIDO	LIFESAVER
KD	EU/Emb	Wash, DC	MAGOTHY	HIGHLANDS
IO	EU/Emb	Wash, DC	MAGOTHY	MINERALIZ
XJ	EU/Emb	Wash,DC	MAGOTHY	DROPMIRE
OF	France/UN	New York	BLACKFOOT	HIGHLANDS
VC	France/UN	New York	BLACKFOOT	VAGRANT
UC	France/Emb	Wash, DC	WABASH	HIGHLANDS
LO	France/Emb	Wash, DC	WABASH	PBX
NK *	Georgia/Emb	Wash, DC	NAVARRO	HIGHLANDS
BY *	Georgia/Emb	Wash, DC	NAVARRO	VAGRANT
RX	Greece/UN	New York	POWELL	HIGHLANDS
HB	Greece/UN	New York	POWELL	LIFESAVER
CD	Greece/Emb	Wash, DC	KLONDIKE	HIGHLANDS
PJ	Greece/Emb	Wash,DC	KLONDIKE	LIFESAVER

JN	Greece/Emb	Wash, DC	KLONDIKE	PBX
MO*	India/UN	New York	NASHUA	HIGHLANDS
QL *	India/UN	New York	NASHUA	MAGNETIC
ON *	India/UN	New York	NASHUA	VAGRANT
IS *	India/UN	New York	NASHUA	LIFESAVER
OX *	India/Emb	Wash,DC	OSAGE	LIFESAVER
CQ *	India/Emb	Wash, DC	OSAGE	HIGHLANDS
TQ *	India/Emb	Wash, DC	OSAGE	VAGRANT
CU *	India/EmbAnx	Wash, DC	OSWAYO	VAGRANT
DS *	India/EmbAnx	Wash, DC	OSWAYO	HIGHLANDS
SU *	Italy/Emb	Wash, DC	BRUNEAU	LIFESAVER
MV*	Italy/Emb	Wash, DC	HEMLOCK	HIGHLANDS
IP *	Japan/UN	New York	MULBERRY	MINERALIZ
HF *	Japan/UN	New York	MULBERRY	HIGHLANDS
BT *	Japan/UN	New York	MULBERRY	MAGNETIC
RU *	Japan/UN	New York	MULBERRY	VAGRANT
LM *	Mexico/UN	New York	ALAMITO	LIFESAVER
UX *	Slovakia/Emb	Wash, DC	FLEMING	HIGHLANDS
SA *	Slovakia/Emb	Wash, DC	FLEMING	VAGRANT
XR *	South Africa/ UN & Consulate	New York	DOBIE	HIGHLANDS
RJ *	South Africa/ UN & Consulate	New York	DOBIE	VAGRANT
YR *	South Korea/UN	New York	SULPHUR	VAGRANT
TZ *	Taiwan/TECO	New York	REQUETTE	VAGRANT
VN *	Venezuela/Emb	Wash, DC	YUKON	LIFESAVER
UR *	Venezuela/UN	New York	WESTPORT	LIFESAVER
NO *	Vietnam/UN	New York	NAVAJO	HIGHLANDS
OU *	Vietnam/UN	New York	NAVAJO	VAGRANT
GV *	Vietnam/Emb	Wash, DC	PANTHER	HIGHLANDS

SIGAD   US-3137

GENERAL TERM DESCRIPTIONS

HIGHLANDS: Collection from Implants

VAGRANT: Collection of Computer Screens

MAGNETIC: Sensor Collection of Magnetic Emanations

MINERALIZE: Collection from LAN Implant

OCEAN: Optical Collection System for Raster-Based Computer Screens

LIFESAVER: Imaging of the Hard Drive

GENIE: Multi-stage operation; jumping the airgap etc.

BLACKHEART: Collection from an FBI Implant

PBX: Public Branch Exchange Switch

CRYPTO ENABLED: Collection derived from AO's efforts to enable crypto

DROPMIRE: passive collection of emanations using an antenna

CUSTOMS: Customs opportunities (not LIFESAVER)

DROPMIRE: Laser printer collection, purely proximal access (**NOT** implanted)

DEWSWEEPER: USB (Universal Serial Bus) hardware host tap that provides COVERT link over USB link into a target network. Operates w/RF relay subsystem to provide wireless Bridge into target network.

RADON: Bi-directional host tap that can inject Ethernet packets onto the same target. Allows bi-directional exploitation of Denied networks using standard on-net tools.

Some of the NSA's methods serve all agendas—economic, diplomatic, security, and obtaining an all-purpose global advantage—and these are among the most invasive, and hypocritical, in the agency's repertoire. For years, the US government loudly warned the world that Chinese routers and other Internet devices pose a "threat" because they are built with backdoor surveillance functionality that gives the Chinese government the ability to spy on anyone using them. Yet what the NSA's documents show is that Americans have been engaged in precisely the activity that the United States accused the Chinese of doing.

The drumbeat of American accusations against Chinese Internet device manufacturers was unrelenting. In 2012, for example, a report from the House Intelligence Committee, headed by Mike Rogers, claimed that Huawei and ZTE, the top two Chinese telecommunications equipment companies, "may be violating United States laws" and have "not followed United States legal obligations or international standards of business behavior." The committee recommended that "the United States should view with suspicion the continued penetration of the U.S. telecommunications market by Chinese telecommunications companies."

The Rogers committee voiced fears that the two companies were enabling Chinese state surveillance, although it acknowledged that it had obtained no actual evidence that the firms had implanted their routers and other systems with surveillance devices. Nonetheless, it cited the failure of those companies to cooperate and urged US firms to avoid purchasing their products:

> Private-sector entities in the United States are strongly encouraged to consider the long-term security risks associated with doing business with either ZTE or Huawei for equipment or services. U.S. network providers and systems developers are strongly encouraged to seek other vendors for their projects. Based on available classified and unclassified information, Huawei and ZTE cannot be trusted to be free of foreign state influence and thus pose a security threat to the United States and to our systems.

The constant accusations became such a burden that Ren Zhengfei, the sixty-nine-year-old founder and CEO of Huawei, announced in November 2013 that the company was abandoning the US market. As *Foreign Policy* reported, Zhengfei told a French newspaper: "'If Huawei gets in the middle of U.S-China relations,' and causes problems, 'it's not worth it.'"

But while American companies were being warned away from supposedly untrustworthy Chinese routers, foreign organizations would have been well advised to beware of American-made ones. A June 2010 report from the head of the NSA's Access and Target Development department is shockingly explicit. The NSA routinely receives—or intercepts—routers, servers, and other computer network devices being exported from the United States before they are delivered to the international customers. The agency then implants backdoor surveillance tools, repackages the devices with a factory seal, and sends them on. The NSA thus gains access to entire networks and all their users. The document gleefully observes that some "SIGINT tradecraft . . . is very hands-on (literally!)":

TOP SECRET//COMINT//NOFORN

June 2010

(U) Stealthy Techniques Can Crack Some of SIGINT's Hardest Targets

By: (U//FOUO) [NAME REDACTED], Chief, Access and Target Development (S3261)

(TS//SI//NF) Not all SIGINT tradecraft involves accessing signals and networks from thousands of miles away... In fact, sometimes it is very hands-on (literally!). Here's how it works: shipments of computer network devices (servers, routers, etc.) being delivered to our targets throughout the world are *intercepted*. Next, they are *redirected to a secret location* where Tailored Access Operations/Access Operations (AO – S326) employees, with the support of the Remote Operations Center (S321), enable the *installation of beacon implants* directly into our targets' electronic devices. These devices are then re-packaged and *placed back into transit* to the original destination. All of this happens with the support of Intelligence Community partners and the technical wizards in TAO.

(TS//SI//NF) Such operations involving **supply-chain interdiction** are some of the most productive operations in TAO, because they pre-position access points into hard target networks around the world.

(TS//SI//NF) Left: Intercepted packages are opened carefully; Right: A "load station" implants a beacon

Eventually, the implanted device connects back to the NSA infrastructure:

(TS//SI//NF) In one recent case, after several months a beacon implanted through supply-chain interdiction called back to the NSA covert infrastructure. This call back provided us access to further exploit the device and survey the network.

Among other devices, the agency intercepts and tampers with routers and servers manufactured by Cisco to direct large amounts of Internet traffic back to the NSA's repositories. (There is no evidence in the documents that Cisco is aware of, or condoned, these interceptions.) In April 2013, the agency grappled with technical difficulties involving the intercepted Cisco network switches, which affected the BLARNEY, FAIRVIEW, OAKSTAR, and STORMBREW programs:

TOP SECRET//COMINT//REL TO USA, FVEY
(Report generated on:4/11/2013 3:31:05PM)

NewCrossProgram		Active ECP Count:	1
CrossProgram-1-13	New	ECP Lead:	NAME REDACTED

Title of Change:	Update Software on all Cisco ONS Nodes

Submitter:	NAME REDACTED	**Approval Priority:**	C-Routine
Site(s):	APPLE1 : CLEVERDEVICE : HOMEMAKER : DOGHUT : QUARTERPOUNDER : QUEENSLAND : SCALLION : SPORTCOAT : SUBSTRATUM : TITAN POINTE : SUBSTRATUM : BIRCHWOOD : MAYTAG : EAGLE : EDEN :	**Project(s):**	No Project(s) Entered
System(s):	Comms/Network : Comms/Network : Comms/Network : Comms/Network :	**SubSystem(s):**	No Subsystem(s) Entered

Description of Change: Udate software on all Cisco Optical Network Switches.

Reason for Change: All of our Cisco ONS SONET multiplexers are experiencing a software bug that causes them to intermittently drop out.

Mission Impact: The mission impact is unknown.   While the existing bug doesn't appear to affect traffic, applying the new software update could. Unfortunately, there is now way to be sure. We can't simulate the bug in our lab and so it's impossible to predict exactly what will happen when we apply the software update. We propose to update one of the nodes in NBP-320 first to determine if the update goes smoothly.

Recently we tried to reset the standby manager card in the HOMEMAKER node. When that failed, we attempted to physically reseat it. Since it was the standby card, we did not expect that would cause any problems. However, upon reseating the card, the entire ONS crashed and we lost all traffic through the box. It took more than an hour to recover from this failure.

The worst case scenario is that we have to blow away the entire configuration and start from scratch. Prior to starting our upgrade, we will save the configuration so that if we have to configure the box from scratch, we can simply upload the saved configuration. We estimate that we will be down for no more than an hour for each node in the system.

Additional Info: 3/26/2013 8:16:13 AM   NAME REDACTED
    We have tested the upgrade in our lab and it works well. However, we can't repeat the bug in our lab, so we don't know if we will encounter problems when we attempt to upgrade a node that is affected by the bug.

Last CCB Entry: 04/10/13 16:08:11 NAME REDACTED
    09 Apr Blarney CCB - Blarney ECP board approved
    ECP lead: NAME REDACTED

Programs Affected: Blarney Fairview Oakstar Stormbrew

No Related Work Tasks

It is quite possible that Chinese firms are implanting surveillance mechanisms in their network devices. But the United States is certainly doing the same.

Warning the world about Chinese surveillance could have been one of the motives behind the US government's claims that Chinese devices cannot be trusted. But an equally important motive seems to have been preventing Chinese devices from supplanting American-made ones, which would have limited the NSA's own reach. In other words, Chinese routers and servers represent not only economic competition but also surveillance competition: when someone buys a Chinese device instead of an American one, the NSA loses a crucial means of spying on a great many communication activities.

If the quantity of collection revealed was already stupefying, the NSA's mission to collect all the signals all the time has driven the agency to expand and conquer more and more ground. The amount of data it captures is so vast, in fact, that the principal challenge the agency complains about is storing the heaps of information accumulated from around the globe. One NSA document, prepared for the Five Eyes SigDev Conference, set forth this central problem:

TOP SECRET//COMINT//REL TO USA, FVEY

The Challenge

Collection is outpacing our ability to ingest, process and store to the "norms" to which we have become accustomed.

The story goes back to 2006, when the agency embarked on what it called "Large Scale Expansion of NSA Metadata Sharing." At that point, the NSA predicted that its metadata collection would grow by six hundred billion records every year, growth that would include one to two billion new telephone call events collected every single day:

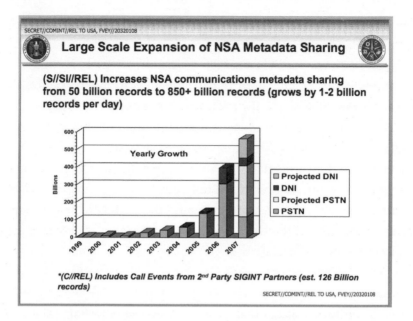

By May 2007, the expansion had evidently borne fruit: the amount of telephone metadata the agency was storing—independent of email and other Internet data, and excluding data the NSA had deleted due to lack of storage space—had increased to 150 billion records:

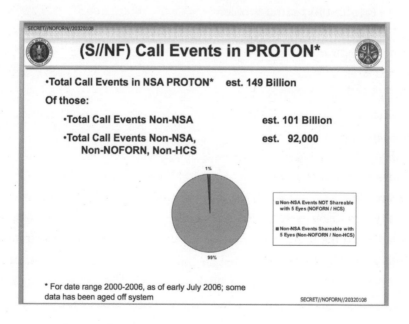

Once Internet-based communications were added to the mix, the total number of communication events stored was close to 1 trillion (this data, it should be noted, was then shared by the NSA with other agencies).

To address its storage problem, the NSA began building a massive new facility in Bluffdale, Utah, that has as one of its primary purposes the retention of all that data. As reporter James Bamford noted in 2012, the Bluffdale construction will expand the agency's capacity by adding "four 25,000-square-foot halls filled with servers, complete with raised floor space for cables and storage. In addition, there will be more than 900,000 square feet for technical support and administration." Considering the size of the building and the fact that, as Bamford says, "a terabyte of data can now be stored on a flash drive the size of a man's pinky," the implications for data collection are profound.

The need for ever-larger facilities is particularly pressing given the agency's current invasions into global online activity, which extend far beyond the collection of metadata to include the actual content of emails, Web browsing, search histories, and chats. The key program used by the NSA to collect, curate, and search such data, introduced in 2007, is X-KEYSCORE, and it affords a radical leap in the scope of the agency's surveillance powers. The NSA calls X-KEYSCORE its "widest-reaching" system for collecting electronic data, and with good reason.

A training document prepared for analysts claims the program captures "nearly everything a typical user does on the internet," including the text of emails, Google searches, and the names of websites visited. X-KEYSCORE even allows "real-time" monitoring of a person's online activities, enabling the NSA to observe emails and browsing activities as they happen.

Beyond collecting comprehensive data about the online activities of hundreds of millions of people, X-KEYSCORE allows any NSA analyst to search the system's databases by email address, telephone number, or identifying attributes such as an IP address. The range of information available and the basic means an analyst uses to search it are illustrated in this slide:

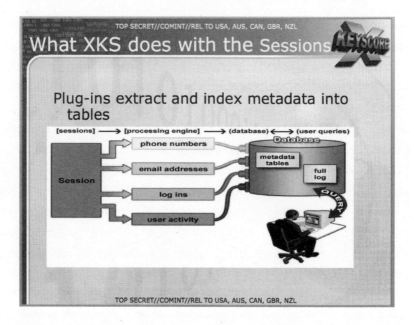

Another X-KEYSCORE slide lists the various fields of information that can be searched via the program's "plug-ins." Those include "every email address seen in a session," "every phone number seen in a session" (including "address book entries"), and "the webmail and chat activity":

TOP SECRET//COMINT//REL TO USA, AUS, CAN, GBR, NZL

Plug-ins

Plug-in	DESCRIPTION
E-mail Addresses	Indexes every E-mail address seen in a session by both username and domain
Extracted Files	Indexes every file seen in a session by both filename and extension
Full Log	Indexes every DNI session collected. Data is indexed by the standard N-tupple (IP, Port, Casenotation etc.)
HTTP Parser	Indexes the client-side HTTP traffic (examples to follow)
Phone Number	Indexes every phone number seen in a session (e.g. address book entries or signature block)
User Activity	Indexes the Webmail and Chat activity to include username, buddylist, machine specific cookies etc.

TOP SECRET//COMINT//REL TO USA, AUS, CAN, GBR, NZL

The program also offers the ability to search and retrieve embedded documents and images that were created, sent, or received:

Other NSA slides openly declare the all-encompassing global ambition of X-KEYSCORE:

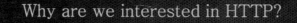

> # Why are we interested in HTTP?
>
> • Almost all web-browsing uses HTTP:
>   - Internet surfing
>   - Webmail (Yahoo/Hotmail/Gmail/etc.)
>   - OSN (Facebook/MySpace/etc.)
>   - Internet Searching (Google/Bing/etc.)
>   - Online Mapping (Google Maps/Mapquest/etc.)

The searches enabled by the program are so specific that any NSA analyst is able not only to find out which websites a person has visited but also to assemble a comprehensive list of all visits to a particular website from specified computers:

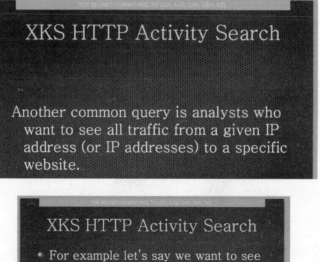

Most remarkable is the ease with which analysts can search for what-ever they want with no oversight. An analyst with access to X-KEY-SCORE need not submit a request to a supervisor or any other authority. Instead, the analyst simply fills out a basic form to "justify" the surveil-lance, and the system returns the information requested.

In the first video interview he gave when in Hong Kong, Edward Snowden made an audacious claim: "I, sitting at my desk, could wire-tap anyone, from you or your accountant, to a federal judge or even the president, if I had a personal email." US officials vehemently denied that this was true. Mike Rogers expressly accused Snowden of "lying," add-ing, "It's impossible for him to do what he was saying he could do." But X-KEYSCORE permits an analyst to do exactly what Snowden said: tar-get any user for comprehensive monitoring, which includes reading the content of their emails. Indeed, the program lets an analyst search for all emails that include targeted users in the "cc" line or mention of them in the body of the text.

The NSA's own instructions for searching through emails demon-strate just how simple and easy it is for analysts to monitor anyone whose address they know:

TOP SECRET//COMINT//REL TO USA, AUS, CAN, GBR, NZL//20320108

Email Addresses Query:

One of the most common queries is (you guessed it) an **Email Address Query** searching for an email address. To create a query for a specific email address, you have to fill in the name of the query, justify it and set a date range then you simply fill in the email address(es) you want to search on and submit.

That would look something like this...

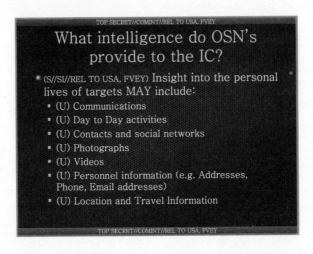

One of X-KEYSCORE's most valuable functions to the NSA is its ability to surveil the activities on online social networks (OSNs), such as Facebook and Twitter, which the agency believes provide a wealth of information and "insight into the personal lives of targets:"

The methods for searching social media activity are every bit as simple as the email search. An analyst enters the desired user name on, say, Facebook, along with the date range of activity, and X-KEYSCORE then returns all of that user's information, including messages, chats, and other private postings.

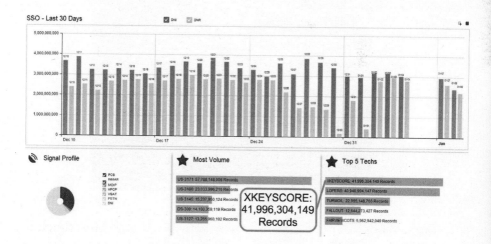

Perhaps the most remarkable fact about X-KEYSCORE is the sheer quantity of data that it captures and stores at multiple collection sites around the world. "At some sites," one report states, "the amount of data we receive per day (20+ terabytes) can only be stored for as little as 24 hours based on available resources." For one thirty-day period beginning in December 2012, the quantity of records collected by X-KEYSCORE just for one unit, the SSO, exceeded forty-one billion:

X-KEYSCORE "stores the full-take content for 3–5 days, effectively 'slowing down the internet,'"—meaning that "analysts can go back and recover sessions." Then "content that is 'interesting' can be pulled out of

X-KEYSCORE and pushed to Agility or PINWALE," storage databases
that provide longer retention.

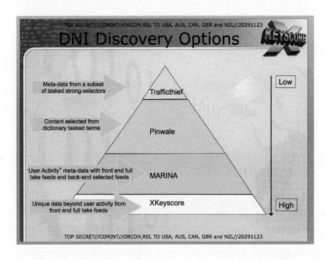

X-KEYSCORE's ability to access Facebook and other social media sites is
boosted by other programs, which include BLARNEY, allowing the NSA
to monitor a "broad range of Facebook data via surveillance and search
activities":

(TS//SI//NF) BLARNEY Exploits the Social Network via
Expanded Facebook Collection

By [NAME REDACTED] on 2011-03-14 0737

(TS//SI//NF) SSO HIGHLIGHT – BLARNEY Exploits the Social
Network via Expanded Facebook Collection

(TS//SI//NF) On 11 March 2011, BLARNEY began delivery of
substantially improved and more complete Facebook content.
This is a major leap forward in NSA's ability to exploit
Facebook using FISA and FAA authorities. This effort was
initiated in partnership with the FBI six months ago to
address an unreliable and incomplete Facebook collection
system. NSA is now able to access a broad range of Facebook
data via surveillance and search activities. OPIs are
excited about receiving many content fields, such as chat,
on a sustained basis that had previously only been
occasionally available. Some content will be completely new
including subscriber videos. Taken together, the new
Facebook collection will provide a robust SIGINT
opportunity against our targets – from geolocation based on
their IP addresses and user agent, to collection of all of
their private messages and profile information. Multiple
elements across NSA partnered to ensure the successful
delivery of this data. An NSA representative at FBI
coordinated the rapid development of the collection system;
SSO's PRINTAURA team wrote new software and made
configuration changes; CES modified their protocol
exploitation systems and the Technology Directorate fast-
tracked upgrades to their data presentation tools so that
OPIs could view the data properly.

In the UK, meanwhile, the GCHQ's Global Telecommunications Exploitation (GTE) division has also devoted substantial resources to the task, detailed in a 2011 presentation to the annual Five Eyes conference.

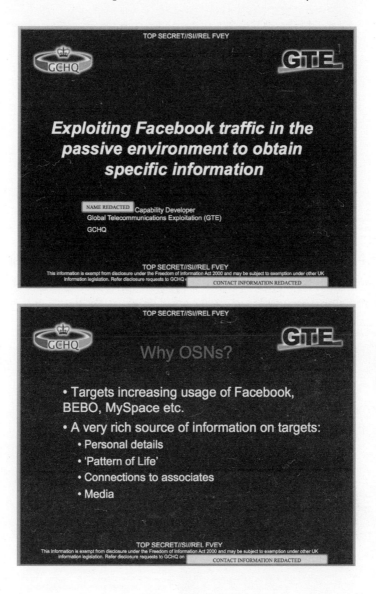

The GCHQ has paid special attention to weaknesses in Facebook's security system and to obtaining the kind of data that Facebook users attempt to shield:

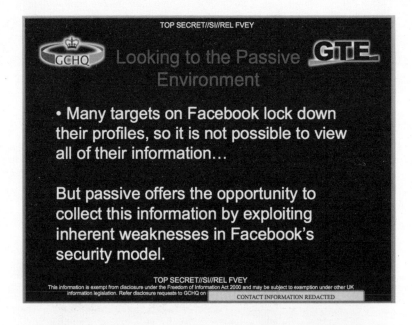

In particular, the GCHQ has found vulnerabilities in the network's system for storing pictures, which can be used to gain access to Facebook IDs and album images:

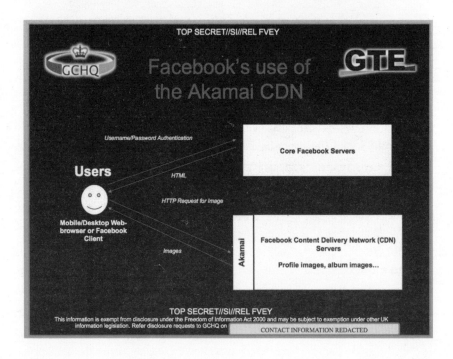

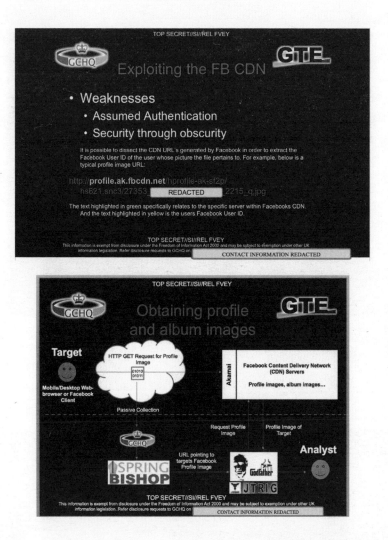

Beyond social media networks, the NSA and the GCHQ continue to look for any gaps in their surveillance net, any communications that remain outside their grasp, and then develop ways to bring them under the agencies' watchful eye. One seemingly obscure program demonstrates this point.

Both the NSA and GCHQ have been consumed by their perceived need to monitor Internet and phone communications of people on commercial airline flights. Because these are rerouted via independent satellite systems, they are extremely difficult to pinpoint. The idea that there is a moment when someone can use the Internet or their phone without detection—even for just a few hours while flying—is intolerable to the surveillance agencies. In response, they have devoted substantial resources to developing systems that will intercept in-flight communications.

At the 2012 Five Eyes conference, the GCHQ presented an interception program named Thieving Magpie, targeting the increasingly available use of cell phones during flights:

The proposed solution envisioned a system to ensure complete "global coverage":

Substantial headway has been made to ensure that certain devices are susceptible to surveillance on passenger jets:

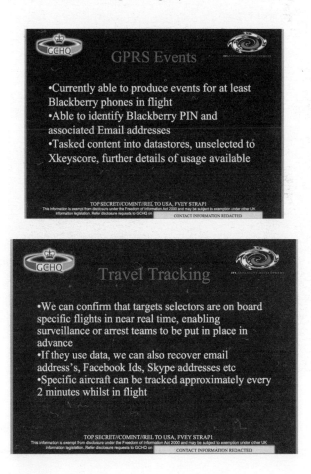

A related NSA document presented at the same conference, for a program entitled Homing Pigeon, also describes efforts to monitor in-air communications. The agency's program was to be coordinated with the GCHQ, and the entire system made available to the Five Eyes group.

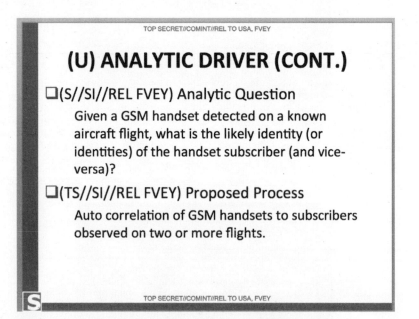

TOP SECRET//COMINT//REL TO USA, FVEY

(U) ANALYTIC DRIVER (CONT.)

❑(S//SI//REL FVEY) Analytic Question

Given a GSM handset detected on a known aircraft flight, what is the likely identity (or identities) of the handset subscriber (and vice-versa)?

❑(TS//SI//REL FVEY) Proposed Process

Auto correlation of GSM handsets to subscribers observed on two or more flights.

TOP SECRET//COMINT//REL TO USA, FVEY

TOP SECRET//COMINT//REL TO USA, FVEY

(U) GOING FORWARD

❑(TS//SI//REL FVEY) SATC will complete development once a reliable THIEVING MAGPIE data feed has been established

❑(TS//SI//REL FVEY) Once the QFD is complete, it will be available to FVEY users as a RESTful web service, JEMA component, and a light weight web page

❑ (TS//SI//REL FVEY) If the S2 QFD Review Panel elects to ask for HOMING PIGEON to be made persistent, its natural home would be incorporation into FASTSCOPE

TOP SECRET//COMINT//REL TO USA, FVEY

There is remarkable candidness, within parts of the NSA, about the true purpose of building so massive a secret surveillance system. A Power-Point presentation prepared for a group of agency officials discussing the prospect of international Internet standards gives the unvarnished view. The author of the presentation is an "NSA/SIGINT National Intelligence Officer (SINIO) for Science and Technology," a self-described "well trained scientist and hacker."

The blunt title of his presentation: "The Role of National Interests, Money, and Egos." These three factors together, he says, are the primary motives driving the United States to maintain global surveillance domination.

He notes that US dominance over the Internet has given the country substantial power and influence, and has also generated vast profit:

Such profit and power have also inevitably accrued, of course, to the surveillance industry itself, providing another motive for its endless expansion. The post-9/11 era has seen a massive explosion of resources dedicated to surveillance. Most of those resources were transferred from the public coffers (i.e., the American taxpayer) into the pockets of private surveillance defense corporations.

Companies like Booz Allen Hamilton and AT&T employ hordes of former top government officials, while hordes of current top defense officials are past (and likely future) employees of those same corporations. Constantly growing the surveillance state is a way to ensure that the government funds keep flowing, that the revolving door stays greased. That is also the best way to ensure that the NSA and its related agencies retain institutional importance and influence inside Washington.

As the scale and ambition of the surveillance industry has grown, so has the profile of its perceived adversary. Listing the various threats supposedly facing the United States, the NSA—in a document entitled "National Security Agency: Overview Briefing"—includes some predictable items: "hackers," "criminal elements," and "terrorists." Revealingly, though, it also goes far broader by including among the threats a list of *technologies*, including the Internet itself:

The Internet has long been heralded as an unprecedented instrument of democratization and liberalization, even emancipation. But in the eyes of the US government, this global network and other types of communications technology threaten to undermine American power. Viewed from this perspective, the NSA's ambition to "collect it all" at last becomes coherent. It is vital that the NSA monitor all parts of the Internet and any other means of communication, so that none can escape US government control.

Ultimately, beyond diplomatic manipulation and economic gain, a system of ubiquitous spying allows the United States to maintain its grip on the world. When the United States is able to know everything that everyone is doing, saying, thinking, and planning—its own citizens, foreign populations, international corporations, other government leaders—its power over those factions is maximized. That's doubly true if the government operates at ever greater levels of secrecy. The secrecy creates a one-way mirror: the US government sees what everyone else in the world does, including its own population, while no one sees its own actions. It is the ultimate imbalance, permitting the most dangerous of all human conditions: the exercise of limitless power with no transparency or accountability.

Edward Snowden's revelations subverted that dangerous dynamic by shining a light on the system and how it functions. For the first time, people everywhere were able to learn the true extent of the surveillance capabilities amassed against them. The news triggered an intense, sustained worldwide debate precisely because the surveillance poses such a grave threat to democratic governance. It also triggered proposals for reform, a global discussion of the importance of Internet freedom and privacy in the electronic age, and a reckoning with the vital question: What does limitless surveillance mean for us as individuals, in our own lives?

4

THE HARM OF SURVEILLANCE

Governments around the world have made vigorous attempts to train citizens to disdain their own privacy. A litany of now-familiar platitudes has convinced people to tolerate severe encroachments into their private realm; so successful are these justifications that many people applaud as the authorities collect vast amounts of data about what they say, read, buy, and do—and with whom.

Those state authorities have been assisted in their assault on privacy by a chorus of Internet moguls—the government's seemingly indispensable partners in surveillance. When Google CEO Eric Schmidt was asked in a 2009 CNBC interview about concerns over his company's retention of user data, he infamously replied: "If you have something that you don't want anyone to know, maybe you shouldn't be doing it in the first place." With equal dismissiveness, Facebook founder and CEO Mark Zuckerberg said in a 2010 interview that "people have really gotten comfortable not only sharing more information and different kinds, but more openly and with more people." Privacy in the digital age is no longer a "social norm," he claimed, a notion that handily serves the interests of a tech company trading on personal information.

But the importance of privacy is evident in the fact that even those who devalue it, who have declared it dead or dispensable, do not believe the things they say. Anti-privacy advocates have often gone to great lengths to maintain control over the visibility of their own behavior and information. The US government itself has used extreme measures to shield its actions from public view, erecting an ever-higher wall of secrecy behind which it operates. As a 2011 report from the ACLU argued, "Today much of our government's business is conducted in secret." So secretive is this shadowy world, "so large, so unwieldy," as the *Washington Post* reported, that no one knows how much money it costs, how many people it employs, how many programs exist within it or exactly how many agencies do the same work."

Similarly, those Internet tycoons who are apparently so willing to devalue our privacy are vehemently protective of their own. Google insisted on a policy of not talking to reporters from CNET, the technology news site, after CNET published Eric Schmidt's personal details—including his salary, campaign donations, and address, all public information obtained via Google—in order to highlight the invasive dangers of his company.

Meanwhile, Mark Zuckerberg purchased the four homes adjacent to his own in Palo Alto, at a cost of $30 million, to ensure his privacy. As CNET put it, "Your personal life is now known as Facebook's data. Its CEO's personal life is now known as mind your own business."

The same contradiction is expressed by the many ordinary citizens who dismiss the value of privacy yet nonetheless have passwords on their email and social media accounts. They put locks on their bathroom doors; they seal the envelopes containing their letters. They engage in conduct when nobody is watching that they would never consider when acting in full view. They say things to friends, psychologists, and lawyers that they do not want anyone else to know. They give voice to thoughts online that they do not want associated with their names.

The many pro-surveillance advocates I have debated since Snowden blew the whistle have been quick to echo Eric Schmidt's view that privacy is for people who have something to hide. But none of them would willingly give me the passwords to their email accounts, or allow video cameras in their homes.

When the Senate Intelligence Committee's chair, Dianne Feinstein, insisted that the NSA's collection of metadata does not constitute surveillance—because it does not include the content of any communication—online protesters demanded that she back up her assertion with action: Would the senator, each month, publish a full list of people she emailed and called, including the length of time they spoke and their physical locations when the call was made? That she would take up the offer was inconceivable precisely because such information is profoundly revealing; making it public would constitute a true breach of one's private realm.

The point is not the hypocrisy of those who disparage the value of privacy while intensely safeguarding their own, although that is striking. It is that the desire for privacy is shared by us all as an essential, not ancillary, part of what it means to be human. We all instinctively understand that the private realm is where we can act, think, speak, write, experiment, and choose how to be, away from the judgmental eyes of others. Privacy is a core condition of being a free person.

Perhaps the most famous formulation of what privacy means and why it is so universally and supremely desired was offered by US Supreme Court Justice Louis Brandeis in the 1928 case *Olmstead v. U.S.*: "The right to be left alone [is] the most comprehensive of rights, and the right most valued by a free people." The value of privacy, he wrote, "is much broader in scope" than mere civic freedoms. It is, he said, fundamental:

> The makers of our Constitution undertook to secure conditions favorable to the pursuit of happiness. They recognized the significance of man's spiritual nature, of his feelings and of his intellect. They knew that only a part of the pain, pleasure and satisfactions of life are to be found in material things. They sought to protect Americans in their beliefs, their thoughts, their emotions and their sensations. They conferred, as against the Government, the right to be let alone.

Even before Brandeis was appointed to the Court, he was an ardent proponent of the importance of privacy. Together with lawyer Samuel Warren, he wrote the seminal 1890 *Harvard Law Review* article "The Right to Privacy," arguing that robbing someone of their privacy was a crime of a deeply different nature than the theft of a material belonging.

"The principle which protects personal writings and all other personal productions, not against theft and physical appropriation, but against publication in any form, is in reality not the principle of private property, but that of an inviolate personality."

Privacy is essential to human freedom and happiness for reasons that are rarely discussed but instinctively understood by most people, as evidenced by the lengths to which they go to protect their own. To begin with, people radically change their behavior when they know they are being watched. They will strive to do that which is expected of them. They want to avoid shame and condemnation. They do so by adhering tightly to accepted social practices, by staying within imposed boundaries, avoiding action that might be seen as deviant or abnormal.

The range of choices people consider when they believe that others are watching is therefore far more limited than what they might do when acting in a private realm. A denial of privacy operates to severely restrict one's freedom of choice.

Several years ago, I attended the bat mitzvah of my best friend's daughter. During the ceremony, the rabbi emphasized that "the central lesson" for the girl to learn was that she was "always being watched and judged." He told her that God always knew what she was doing, every choice, every action, and even every thought, no matter how private. "You are never alone," he said, which meant that she should always adhere to God's will.

The rabbi's point was clear: if you can never evade the watchful eyes of a supreme authority, there is no choice but to follow the dictates that authority imposes. You cannot even consider forging your own path beyond those rules: if you believe you are always being watched and judged, you are not really a free individual.

All oppressive authorities—political, religious, societal, parental—rely on this vital truth, using it as a principal tool to enforce orthodoxies, compel adherence, and quash dissent. It is in their interest to convey that nothing their subjects do will escape the knowledge of the authorities. Far more effectively than a police force, the deprivation of privacy will crush any temptation to deviate from rules and norms.

What is lost when the private realm is abolished are many of the attributes typically associated with quality of life. Most people have experienced how privacy enables liberation from constraint. And we've all, conversely, had the experience of engaging in private behavior when we thought we were alone—dancing, confessing, exploring sexual expression, sharing untested ideas—only to feel shame at having been seen by others.

Only when we believe that nobody else is watching us do we feel free—safe—to truly experiment, to test boundaries, to explore new ways of thinking and being, to explore what it means to be ourselves. What made the Internet so appealing was precisely that it afforded the ability to speak and act anonymously, which is so vital to individual exploration.

For that reason, it is in the realm of privacy where creativity, dissent, and challenges to orthodoxy germinate. A society in which everyone knows they can be watched by the state—where the private realm is effectively eliminated—is one in which those attributes are lost, at both the societal and the individual level.

Mass surveillance by the state is therefore inherently repressive, even in the unlikely case that it is not abused by vindictive officials to do things like gain private information about political opponents. Regardless of how surveillance is used or abused, the limits it imposes on freedom are intrinsic to its existence.

Invoking George Orwell's *1984* is something of a cliché, but the echoes of the world about which he warned in the NSA's surveillance state are unmistakable: both rely on the existence of a technological system with the capacity to monitor every citizen's actions and words. The similarity is denied by the surveillance champions—we're not *always* being watched, they say—but that argument misses the point. In *1984*, citizens were not necessarily monitored at all times; in fact, they had no idea whether they were ever actually being monitored. But the state had the capability to watch them at any time. It was the uncertainty and possibility of ubiquitous surveillance that served to keep everyone in line:

The telescreen received and transmitted simultaneously. Any sound that Winston made, above the level of a very low whisper, would be picked up by it; moreover, so long as he remained within the field of vision which the metal plaque commanded, he could be seen as well as heard. There was of course no way of knowing whether you were being watched at any given moment. How often, or on what system, the Thought Police plugged in on any individual wire was guesswork. It was even conceivable that they watched everybody all the time. But at any rate they could plug in your wire whenever they wanted to. You had to live—did live, from habit that became instinct—in the assumption that every sound you made was overheard, and, except in darkness, every movement scrutinized.

Even the NSA, with its capacity, could not read every email, listen to every telephone call, and track the actions of each individual. What makes a surveillance system effective in controlling human behavior is the knowledge that one's words and actions are susceptible to monitoring.

This principle was at the heart of British philosopher Jeremy Bentham's eighteenth-century conception of the Panopticon, a building design he believed would allow institutions to effectively control human behavior. The building's structure was to be used, in his words, for "any sort of establishment, in which persons of any description are to be kept under inspection." The Panopticon's primary architectural innovation was a large central tower from which every room—or cell, or classroom, or ward—could be monitored at any time by guards. The inhabitants, however, were not able to see into the tower and so could never know whether they were or were not being watched.

Since the institution—any institution—was not capable of observing all of the people all of the time, Bentham's solution was to create "the apparent omnipresence of the inspector" in the minds of the inhabitants. "The persons to be inspected should always feel themselves as if under inspection, at least as standing a great chance of being so." They would thus act as if they were always being watched, even if they weren't. The result would be compliance, obedience, and conformity with expectations.

You are watching your phone.
Your phone is watching you.

Bentham envisioned that his creation would spread far beyond prisons and mental hospitals to all societal institutions. Inculcating in the minds of citizens that they might always be monitored would, he understood, revolutionize human behavior.

In the 1970s, Michel Foucault observed that the principle of Bentham's Panopticon was one of the foundational mechanisms of the modern state. In *Power*, he wrote that Panopticonism is "a type of power that is applied to individuals in the form of continuous individual supervision, in the form of control, punishment, and compensation, and in the form of correction, that is, the moulding and transformation of individuals in terms of certain norms."

In *Discipline and Punish*, Foucault further explained that ubiquitous surveillance not only empowers authorities and compels compliance but also induces individuals to internalize their watchers. Those who believe they are watched will instinctively choose to do that which is wanted of them without even realizing that they are being controlled—the Panopticon induces "in the inmate a state of conscious and permanent visibility that assures the automatic functioning of power." With the control internalized, the overt evidence of repression disappears because it is no longer necessary: "the external power may throw off its physical weight; it tends to be non-corporal; and, the more it approaches this limit, the more constant, profound and permanent are its effects: it is a profound victory that avoids any physical confrontation and which is always decided in advance."

Additionally, this model of control has the great advantage of simultaneously creating the illusion of freedom. The compulsion to obedience exists in the individual's mind. Individuals choose on their own to comply, out of fear that they are being watched. That eliminates the need for all the visible hallmarks of compulsion, and thus enables control over people who falsely believe themselves to be free.

For this reason, every oppressive state views mass surveillance as one of its most critical instruments of control. When the normally restrained German chancellor Angela Merkel learned that the NSA had spent years eavesdropping on her personal cell phone, she spoke to President Obama and angrily likened US surveillance to the Stasi, the notorious security service of East Germany, where she grew up. Merkel did not mean that the United States was the equivalent of the Communist regime; rather that the essence of a menacing surveillance state, be it the NSA or the Stasi or Big Brother or the Panopticon, is the knowledge that one can be watched at any time by unseen authorities.

It is not hard to understand why authorities in the United States and other Western nations have been tempted to construct a ubiquitous system of spying directed at their own citizens. Worsening economic inequality, converted into a full-blown crisis by the financial collapse in 2008, has generated grave internal instability. There has been visible unrest even in relatively stable democracies, such as Spain and Greece. In 2011, there were days of rioting in London. In the United States both the Right—the Tea Party protests of 2008 and 2009—and the Left—the Occupy movement—have launched enduring citizens protests. Polls in these countries revealed strikingly intense levels of discontent with the political class and direction of society.

Authorities faced with unrest generally have two options: to placate the population with symbolic concessions or fortify their control to minimize the harm it can do their interests. Elites in the West seem to view the second option—fortifying their power—as their better, perhaps only viable course of action to protect their position. The response to the Occupy movement was to crush it with force, through tear gas, pepper spray, and prosecution. The para-militarization of domestic police forces was on full display in American cities, as police officers brought out weapons seen on the streets of Baghdad to quell legally assembled and largely peaceful protesters. The strategy was to put people in fear of attending marches and protests, and it generally worked. The more general aim was to cultivate the sense that this sort of resistance is futile against a massive and impenetrable establishment force.

A system of ubiquitous surveillance achieves the same goal but with even greater potency. Merely organizing movements of dissent becomes difficult when the government is watching everything people are doing. But mass surveillance kills dissent in a deeper and more important place as well: in the mind, where the individual trains him- or herself to think only in line with what is expected and demanded. ╳

History leaves no doubt that collective coercion and control is both the intent and effect of state surveillance. The Hollywood screenwriter Walter Bernstein, who was blacklisted and monitored during the Mc-Carthy era, forced to write under pseudonyms to continue working, has described the dynamic of oppressive self-censorship that comes from the sense of being watched:

> Everybody was careful. It was not a time for risk taking. . . . There were writers, non-blacklisted writers who did, I don't know what you'd call them, "cutting-edge things," but not political. They stayed away from politics. . . . I think there was a general feeling of "You don't stick your neck out."
>
> It's not an atmosphere that helps creativity or lets the mind run free. You're always in danger of self-censorship, of saying "no, I won't try this because I know it's not going to get done or it'll alienate the government," or something like that.

Bernstein's observations were eerily echoed in a report released by PEN America in November 2013 entitled *Chilling Effects: NSA Surveillance Drives U.S. Writers to Self Censor*. The organization conducted a survey to look at the effects of the NSA revelations on its members, finding that many writers now "assume that their communications are being monitored" and have changed their behavior in ways that "curtail their freedom of expression and restrict the free flow of information." Specifically, "24% have deliberately avoided certain topics in phone or email conversations."

The pernicious controlling power of ubiquitous surveillance and the self-censorship that results are confirmed in a range of social science experiments and extend far beyond political activism. Ample studies show how this dynamic works at the deepest personal and psychological levels.

One team of researchers, publishing their findings in the journal *Evolutionary Psychology*, presented their subjects with morally questionable actions, such as keeping a sizeable amount of money found in a wallet on the street or knowing that a friend had added false information to his résumé. The subjects were asked to assess the degree of wrongdoing. The study noted that subjects who were shown images hinting at surveillance, such as a large pair of staring eyes, rated the actions as more "reprehensible" than those who were shown a neutral image. The researchers concluded that surveillance encourages those who are being watched to "affirm their endorsement of prevailing social norms" as they attempt to "actively manage their reputations."

A comprehensive experiment conducted in 1975 by Stanford University psychologists Gregory White and Philip Zimbardo, entitled "The Chilling Effects of Surveillance," sought to assess whether being watched had an impact on the expression of controversial political opinions. The impetus for the study was Americans' concerns about surveillance by the government:

> The Watergate scandal, revelations of White House bugging, and Congressional investigations of domestic spying by the Central Intelligence Agency have served to underscore the developing paranoid theme of American life: Big Brother may be watching you! Proposals for national data banks, uses of surveillance helicopters by urban police forces, the presence of observation cameras in banks and supermarkets, and airport security searches of person and property are but some of the signs that our private lives are under such increasing scrutiny.

The participants were placed under varying levels of surveillance and asked to give their views on the legalization of marijuana.

It turned out that "threatened" subjects—those who were told that their statements would be shared with the police "for training purposes"—were more likely to condemn marijuana usage and to use second- and third-person pronouns ("you," "they," "people") in their language. Only 44 percent of subjects under surveillance advocated for legalization, compared to 77 percent of those not so "threatened." Tellingly, 31 percent of the participants being monitored spontaneously sought approval from the researchers (asking, for example, "Is that all right?"), whereas only 7 percent of the other group did so. Participants who were "threatened" also scored significantly higher on feelings of anxiety and inhibition.

White and Zimbardo noted in their conclusion that the "threat or actuality of government surveillance may psychologically inhibit freedom of speech." They added that while their "research design did not allow for the possibility of 'avoiding assembly,'" they expected that "the anxiety generated by the threat of surveillance would cause many people to totally avoid situations" in which they might be monitored. "Since such assumptions are limited only by one's imagination and are encouraged daily by revelations of government and institutional invasion of privacy," they wrote, "the boundaries between paranoid delusions and justified cautions indeed become tenuous."

It is true that surveillance can at times promote what some may consider desirable behavior. One study found that rowdiness in Swedish soccer stadiums—fans throwing bottles and lighters onto the field—declined by 65 percent after the introduction of security cameras. And public health literature on hand washing has repeatedly confirmed that the way to increase the likelihood of someone washing his or her hands is to put someone nearby.

But overwhelmingly, the effect of being watched is to severely constrain individual choice. Even in the most intimate of settings, within the family, for example, surveillance turns insignificant actions into a source of self-judgment and anxiety, just by virtue of being observed. In one UK experiment, researchers provided subjects with tracking devices to keep tabs on family members. Any member's precise location was accessible at any time, and if someone's location had been viewed, he would receive a message. Each time one member tracked another, he was also sent a questionnaire asking why he had done so and whether the information received had matched expectations.

In the debriefing, participants said that while they sometimes found the tracking comforting, they also felt anxious that if they were in an unexpected place, family members would "jump to conclusions" about their behavior. And the option of "going invisible"—blocking the location-sharing mechanism—did not resolve the anxiety: many participants said that the act of avoiding surveillance in and of itself would generate suspicion. The researchers concluded:

> There are trails in our daily life that we cannot explain and that may be completely insignificant. However, their representation via a tracking device . . . gives them significance, seemingly calling for an extraordinary degree of accountability. This generates anxieties, especially within close relationships, in which people may feel under greater pressure to account for things they simply cannot account for.

For a Finnish experiment that carried out one of the most radical simulations of surveillance, cameras were placed in subjects' homes—bathrooms and bedrooms excluded—and all of their electronic communications were tracked. Although the advertisement for the study went viral on social media, the researchers had difficulty getting even ten households to participate.

Among those who signed up, complaints about the project focused on the invasion of ordinary parts of their daily lives. One person felt uncomfortable being naked in her home; another felt conscious of the cameras while fixing her hair after a shower; someone else thought of the surveillance while injecting medicine. Innocuous actions gained layers of significance when surveilled.

Subjects initially described the surveillance as annoying; however, they soon "got used to it." What began as deeply invasive became normalized, transformed into the usual state of affairs and no longer noticed.

As the experiments showed, there are all sorts of things people do that they are eager to keep private, even though these sorts of things do not constitute doing "something wrong." Privacy is indispensable to a wide range of human activities. If someone calls a suicide hotline or visits an abortion provider or frequents an online sex website or makes an appointment with a rehabilitation clinic or is treated for a disease, or if a whistle-blower calls a reporter, there are many reasons for keeping such acts private that have no connection to illegality or wrongdoing.

In sum, everyone has something to hide. Reporter Barton Gellman made the point this way:

Privacy is relational. It depends on your audience. You don't want your employer to know you're job hunting. You don't spill all about your love life to your mom, or your kids. You don't tell trade secrets to your rivals. We don't expose ourselves indiscriminately and we care enough about exposure to lie as a matter of course. Among upstanding citizens, researchers have consistently found that lying is "an everyday social interaction" (twice a day among college students, once a day in the Real World). . . . Comprehensive transparency is a nightmare. . . . Everyone has something to hide.

A prime justification for surveillance—that it's for the benefit of the population—relies on projecting a view of the world that divides citizens into categories of good people and bad people. In that view, the authorities use their surveillance powers only against bad people, those who are "doing something wrong," and only they have anything to fear from the invasion of their privacy. This is an old tactic. In a 1969 *Time* magazine article about Americans' growing concerns over the US government's surveillance powers, Nixon's attorney general, John Mitchell, assured readers that "any citizen of the United States who is not involved in some illegal activity has nothing to fear whatsoever."

The point was made again by a White House spokesman, responding to the 2005 controversy over Bush's illegal eavesdropping program: "This is not about monitoring phone calls designed to arrange Little League practice or what to bring to a potluck dinner. These are designed to monitor calls from very bad people to very bad people." And when President Obama appeared on *The Tonight Show* in August 2013 and was asked by Jay Leno about NSA revelations, he said: "We don't have a domestic spying program. What we do have is some mechanisms that can track a phone number or an email address that is connected to a terrorist attack."

For many, the argument works. The perception that invasive surveillance is confined only to a marginalized and deserving group of those "doing wrong"—the bad people—ensures that the majority acquiesces to the abuse of power or even cheers it on.

But that view radically misunderstands what goals drive all institutions of authority. "Doing something wrong," in the eyes of such institutions, encompasses far more than illegal acts, violent behavior, and terrorist plots. It typically extends to meaningful dissent and any genuine challenge. It is the nature of authority to equate dissent with wrongdoing, or at least with a threat.

The record is suffused with examples of groups and individuals being placed under government surveillance by virtue of their dissenting views and activism—Martin Luther King, the civil rights movement, antiwar activists, environmentalists. In the eyes of the government and J. Edgar Hoover's FBI, they were all "doing something wrong": political activity that threatened the prevailing order.

Nobody understood better than Hoover the power of surveillance to crush political dissent, confronted as he was with the challenge of how to prevent the exercise of First Amendment rights of speech and association when the state is barred from arresting people for expressing unpopular views. The 1960s ushered in a slew of Supreme Court cases that established rigorous protections for free speech, culminating in the unanimous 1969 decision in *Brandenburg v. Ohio*, which overturned the criminal conviction of a Ku Klux Klan leader who had threatened violence against political officials in a speech. The Court said that the First Amendment guarantees of free speech and free press are so strong that they "do not permit a State to forbid or proscribe advocacy of the use of force."

Given those guarantees, Hoover instituted a system to prevent dissent from developing in the first place.

The FBI's domestic counterintelligence program, COINTELPRO, was first exposed by a group of antiwar activists who had become convinced that the antiwar movement had been infiltrated, placed under surveillance, and targeted with all sorts of dirty tricks. Lacking documentary evidence to prove it and unsuccessful in convincing journalists to write about their suspicions, they broke into an FBI branch office in Pennsylvania in 1971 and carted off thousands of documents.

Files related to COINTELPRO showed how the FBI had targeted political groups and individuals it deemed subversive and dangerous, including the National Association for the Advancement of Colored

People, black nationalist movements, socialist and Communist organizations, antiwar protesters, and various right-wing groups. The bureau had infiltrated them with agents who, among other things, attempted to manipulate members into agreeing to commit criminal acts so that the FBI could arrest and prosecute them.

The FBI succeeded in convincing the *New York Times* to suppress the documents and even return them, but the *Washington Post* published a series of articles based on them. Those revelations led to the creation of the Senate Church Committee, which concluded:

> [Over the course of fifteen years] the Bureau conducted a sophisticated vigilate operation aimed squarely at preventing the exercise of First Amendment rights of speech and association, on the theory that preventing the growth of dangerous groups and the propagation of dangerous ideas would protect the national security and deter violence.
>
> Many of the techniques used woud be intolerable in a democratic society even if all of the targets had been involved in violent activity, but COINTELPRO went far beyond that. The unexpressed major premise of the programs was that a law enforcement agency has the duty to do whatever is necessary to combat perceived threats to the existing social and political order.

One key COINTELPRO memo explained that "paranoia" could be sown among antiwar activists by letting them believe there was "an F.B.I. agent behind every mailbox." In this way, dissidents, always convinced that they were being watched, would drown in fear and refrain from activism.

Unsurprisingly, the tactic worked. In a 2013 documentary entitled *1971*, several of the activists described how Hoover's FBI was "all over" the civil rights movement with infiltrators and surveillance, people who came to meetings and reported back. The monitoring impeded the movement's ability to organize and grow.

At the time, even the most entrenched institutions in Washington understood that the mere existence of government surveillance, no matter how it is used, stifles the ability to dissent. The *Washington Post*, in a

March 1975 editorial on the break-in, warned about precisely this oppressive dynamic:

> The FBI has never shown much sensitivity to the poisonous effect which
> its surveillance, and especially its reliance on faceless informers, has
> upon the democratic process and upon the practice of free speech. But
> it must be self-evident that discussion and controversy respecting gov-
> ernmental policies and programs are bound to be inhibited if it is known
> that Big Brother, under disguise, is listening to them and reporting them.

COINTELPRO was far from the only surveillance abuse found by
the Church Committee. Its final report declared that "millions of private
telegrams sent from, to, or through the United States were obtained by
the National Security Agency from 1947 to 1975 under a secret arrangement with three United States telegraph companies." Moreover, "some
300,000 individuals were indexed in a CIA computer system and separate files were created on approximately 7,200 Americans and over 100
domestic groups" during one CIA operation, CHAOS (1967–1973).

Additionally, "an estimated 100,000 Americans were the subjects of
United States Army intelligence files created between the mid-1960's and
1971" as well as some 11,000 individuals and groups who were investigated by the Internal Revenue Service "on the basis of political rather
than tax criteria." The bureau also used wiretapping to discover vulnerabilities, such as sexual activity, which were then deployed to "neutralize"
their targets.

These incidents were not aberrations of the era. During the Bush
years, for example, documents obtained by the ACLU revealed, as the
group put it in 2006, "new details of Pentagon surveillance of Americans opposed to the Iraq war, including Quakers and student groups."
The Pentagon was "keeping tabs on non-violent protestors by collecting information and storing it in a military anti-terrorism database." The
ACLU noted that one document, "labeled 'potential terrorist activity,'
lists events such as a 'Stop the War NOW!' rally in Akron, Ohio."

The evidence shows that assurances that surveillance is only targeted at those who "have done something wrong" should provide little

comfort, since a state will reflexively view any challenge to its power as wrongdoing.

The opportunity those in power have to characterize political opponents as "national security threats" or even "terrorists" has repeatedly proven irresistible. In the last decade, the government, in an echo of Hoover's FBI, has formally so designated environmental activists, broad swaths of antigovernment right-wing groups, antiwar activists, and associations organized around Palestinian rights. Some individuals within those broad categories may deserve the designation, but undoubtedly most do not, guilty only of holding opposing political views. Yet such groups are routinely targeted for surveillance by the NSA and its partners.

Indeed, after British authorities detained my partner, David Miranda, at Heathrow airport under an antiterrorism statute, the UK government expressly equated my surveillance reporting with terrorism on the ground that the release of the Snowden documents "is designed to influence a government and is made for the purposes of promoting a political or ideological cause. This therefore falls within the definition of terrorism." This is the clearest possible statement of linking a threat to the interests of power to terrorism.

None of this would come as any surprise to the American Muslim community, where the fear of surveillance on the grounds of terrorism is intense and pervasive, and for good reason. In 2012, Adam Goldman and Matt Apuzzo of the Associated Press exposed a joint CIA/New York Police Department scheme of subjecting entire Muslim communities in the United States to physical and electronic surveillance without the slightest whiff of any suggestion of wrongdoing. American Muslims routinely describe the effect of spying on their lives: each new person who shows up at a mosque is regarded with suspicion as an FBI informant; friends and family stifle their conversations for fear of being monitored and out of awareness that any expressed view deemed hostile to America can be used as a pretext for investigation or even prosecution.

One document from the Snowden files, dated October 3, 2012, chillingly underscores the point. It revealed that the agency has been monitoring the online activities of individuals it believes express "radical" ideas and who have a "radicalizing" influence on others. The memo discusses six individuals in particular, all Muslims, though it stresses that they are merely "exemplars."

The NSA explicitly states that none of the targeted individuals is a member of a terrorist organization or involved in any terror plots. Instead, their crime is the views they express, which are deemed "radical," a term that warrants pervasive surveillance and destructive campaigns to "exploit vulnerabilities."

Among the information collected about the individuals, at least one of whom is a "U.S. person," are details of their online sex activities and "online promiscuity"—the porn sites they visit and surreptitious sex chats with women who are not their wives. The agency discusses ways to exploit this information to destroy their reputations and credibility.

BACKGROUND (U)

(TS//SI//REL TO USA, FVEY) A previous SIGINT assessment report on radicalization indicated that radicalizers appear to be particularly vulnerable in the area of authority when their private and public behaviors are not consistent. (A) Some of the vulnerabilities, if exposed, would likely call into question a radicalizer's devotion to the jihadist cause, leading to the degradation or loss of his authority. Examples of some of these vulnerabilities include:

- Viewing sexually explicit material online or using sexually explicit persuasive language when communicating with inexperienced young girls;
- Using a portion of the donations they are receiving from the susceptible pool to defray their own personal expenses;
- Charging an exorbitant amount of money for their speaking fees and being singularly attracted by opportunities to increase their stature; or
- Being known to base their public messaging on questionable sources or using language that is contradictory in nature, leaving them open to credibility challenges.

(TS//SI//REL TO USA, FVEY) Issues of trust and reputation are important when considering the validity and appeal of the message. It stands to reason that exploiting vulnerabilities of character, credibility, or both, of the radicalizer and his message could be enhanced by an understanding of the vehicles he uses to disseminate his message to the susceptible pool of people and where he is vulnerable in terms of access.

As the ACLU's deputy legal director, Jameel Jaffer, observed, the NSA databases "store information about your political views, your medical history, your intimate relationships and your activities online." The agency claims this personal information won't be abused, "but these docu-

ments show that the NSA probably defines 'abuse' very narrowly." As
Jaffer pointed out, the NSA has historically, at a president's request, "used
the fruits of surveillance to discredit a political opponent, journalist, or
human rights activist." It would be "naive," he said, to think the agency
couldn't still "use its power that way."

Other documents describe the government's focus not only on
WikiLeaks and its founder, Julian Assange, but also on what the agency calls "the human network that supports WikiLeaks." In August 2010
the Obama administration urged several allies to file criminal charges
against Assange for the group's publication of the Afghanistan war logs.
The discussion around pressuring other nations to prosecute Assange
appears in an NSA file that the agency calls its "Manhunting Timeline."
It details, on a country-by-country basis, the efforts by the United States
and its allies to locate, prosecute, capture, and/or kill various individuals,
among them alleged terrorists, drug traffickers, and Palestinian leaders.
A timeline exists for each year between 2008 and 2012.

(U) Manhunting Timeline 2010

TOP SECRET//SI/TK//NOFORN

Jump to: navigation, search

Main article: Manhunting

See also: *Manhunting Timeline 2011*
See also: *Manhunting Timeline 2009*
See also: *Manhunting Timeline 2008*

(U) The following **manhunting operations took place in Calendar Year 2010**:

[edit] (U) November

Contents

[edit] (U) United States, Australia, Great Britain, Germany, Iceland

(U) The United States on 10 August urged other nations with forces in Afghanistan, including Australia, United
Kingdom, and Germany, to consider filing criminal charges against Julian Assange, founder of the rogue Wikileaks
Internet website and responsible for the unauthorized publication of over 70,000 classified documents covering the war
in Afghanistan. The documents may have been provided to Wikileaks by Army Private First Class Bradley Manning. The
appeal exemplifies the start of an international effort to focus the legal element of national power upon non-state actor
Assange, and the human network that supports Wikileaks.[16]

A separate document contains a summary of a July 2011 exchange
regarding whether WikiLeaks, as well as the file-sharing website Pirate

Bay, could be designated as "a 'malicious foreign actor' for the purposes of targeting." The designation would allow extensive electronic surveillance of those websites, including US users. The discussion appears in a running list of "Q&As" in which officials from the NTOC Oversight and Compliance office (NOC) and NSA's Office of General Counsel (OGC) provide answers to submitted questions.

[edit] (TS//SI//REL) Malicious foreign actor == disseminator of US data?

Can we treat a foreign server who stores, or potentially disseminates leaked or stolen US data on it's server as a 'malicious foreign actor' for the purpose of targeting with no defeats? Examples: WikiLeaks, thepiratebay.org, etc.

NOC/OGC RESPONSE: Let us get back to you. (Source #001)

One such exchange, from 2011, showed the NSA's indifference to breaking the surveillance rules. In the document, an operator says, "I screwed up," having targeted a US person instead of a foreigner. The response from the NSA's oversight office and general counsel is, "it's nothing to worry about."

[edit] (TS//SI//REL) Unknowingly targeting a US person

I screwed up...the selector had a strong indication of being foreign, but it turned out to be US...now what?

NOC/OGC RESPONSE: With all querying, if you discover it actually is US, then it must be submitted and go in the OGC quarterly report...'but it's nothing to worry about'. (Source #001)

The treatment of Anonymous, as well as the vague category of people known as "hacktivists," is especially troubling and extreme. That's because Anonymous is not actually a structured group but a loosely organized affiliation of people around an idea: someone becomes affiliated with Anonymous by virtue of the positions they hold. Worse still, the category "hacktivists" has no fixed meaning: it can mean the use of programming skills to undermine the security and functioning of the Internet but can also refer to anyone who uses online tools to promote political ideals. That the NSA targets such broad categories of people is tantamount to allowing it to spy on anyone anywhere, including in the United States, whose ideas the government finds threatening.

Gabriella Coleman, a specialist on Anonymous at McGill University, said that the group "is not a defined" entity but rather "an idea that mobilizes activists to take collective action and voice political discontent. It is a broad-based global social movement with no centralized or official organized leadership structure. Some have rallied around the name to engage in digital civil disobedience, but nothing remotely resembling terrorism." The majority who have embraced the idea have done so "primarily for ordinary political expression. Targeting Anonymous and hacktivists amounts to targeting citizens for expressing their political beliefs, resulting in the stifling of legitimate dissent," Coleman explained.

Yet Anonymous has been targeted by a unit of the GCHQ that employs some of the most controversial and radical tactics known to spycraft: "false flag operations," "honey-traps," viruses and other attacks, strategies of deception, and "info ops to damage reputations."

One PowerPoint slide presented by GCHQ surveillance officials at the 2012 SigDev conference describes two forms of attack: "information ops (influence or disruption)" and "technical disruption." GCHQ refers to these measures as "Online Covert Action," which is intended to achieve what the document calls "The 4 D's: Deny/Disrupt/Degrade/Deceive."

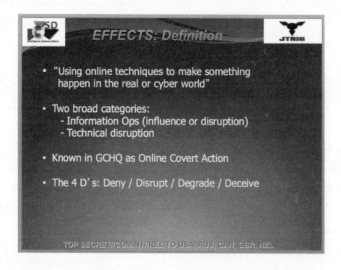

Another slide describes the tactics used to "discredit a target." These include "set up a honey-trap," "change their photos on social networking sites," "write a blog purporting to be one of their victims," and "email/text their colleagues, neighbors, friends, etc."

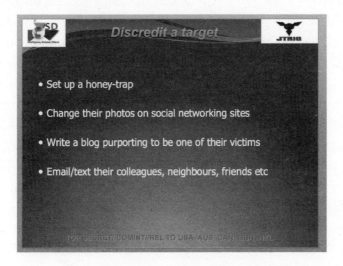

In accompanying notes, the GCHQ explains that the "honey trap"— an old Cold War tactic involving using attractive women to lure male targets into compromising, discrediting situations—has been updated for the digital age: now a target is lured to a compromising site or online encounter. The comment added: "a great option. Very successful when it works." Similarly, traditional methods of group infiltration are now accomplished online:

CK

Honey-trap; a great option. Very successful when it works.
 - Get someone to go somewhere on the internet, or a physical location to be met by a "friendly face".
 - JTRIG has the ability to "shape" the environment on occasions.

Photo change; you have been warned, "JTRIG is about!!"
Can take "paranoia" to a whole new level.

 Email/text:
  - Infiltration work.
  - Helps JTRIG acquire credibility with online groups etc.
  - Helps with bringing SIGINT/Effects together.

Another technique involves stopping "someone from communicating." To do that, the agency will "bombard their phone with text messages," "bombard their phone with calls," "delete their online presence," and "block up their fax machine."

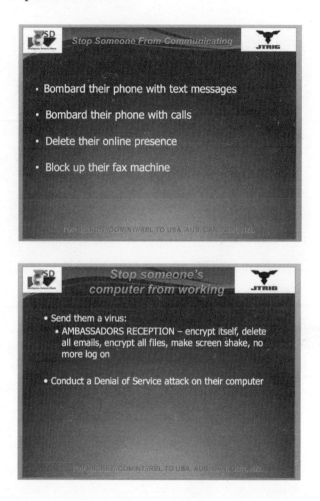

The GCHQ also likes to use "disruption" techniques in lieu of what it calls "traditional law enforcement" such as evidence-gathering, courts, and prosecutions. In a document entitled "Cyber Offensive Session: Pushing the Boundaries and Action Against Hacktivism," the GCHQ discusses its targeting of "hacktivists" with, ironically, "denial of service" attacks, a tactic commonly associated with hackers:

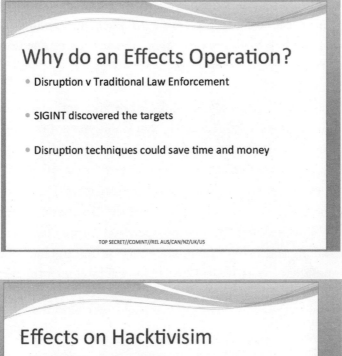

The British surveillance agency also uses a team of social scientists, including psychologists, to develop techniques of "online HUMINT" (human intelligence) and "strategic influence disruption." The document "The Art of Deception: Training for a New Generation of Online Covert Operations" is devoted to these tactics. Prepared by the agency's HSOC (Human Science Operation Cell), the paper claims to draw on sociology, psychology, anthropology, neuroscience, and biology, among other fields, to maximize the GCHQ's online deception skills.

One slide shows how to engage in "Dissimulation—Hide the Real," while propagating "Simulation—Show the False." It examines "the psychological building blocks of deception" and the "map of technologies" used to carry out the deceptions, including Facebook, Twitter, LinkedIn, and "Web Pages."

Emphasizing that "people make decisions for emotional reasons not rational ones," the GCHQ contends that online behavior is driven by "mirroring" ("people copy each other while in social interaction with them"), "accommodation," and "mimicry" ("adoption of specific social traits by the communicator from the other participant").

The document then lays out what it calls the "Disruption Operational Playbook." This includes "infiltration operation," "ruse operation," "false flag operation," and "sting operation." It vows a "full roll out" of the disruption program "by early 2013" as "150+ staff [are] fully trained."

SECRET//SI//REL TO USA, FVEY

DISRUPTION
Operational
Playbook

• Infiltration Operation
• Ruse Operation
• Set Piece Operation
• False Flag Operation
• False Rescue Operation
• Disruption Operation
• Sting Operation

Under the title "Magic Techniques & Experiment," the document references "Legitimisation of violence," "Constructing experience in mind of targets which should be accepted so they don't realize," and "Optimising deception channels."

Such government plans to monitor and influence Internet communications and disseminate false information online have long been a source of speculation. Harvard law professor Cass Sunstein, a close Obama adviser, the White House's former head of the Office of Information and Regulatory Affairs, and an appointee to the White House panel to review NSA activities, wrote a controversial paper in 2008 proposing that the US government employ teams of covert agents and pseudo-"independent" advocates for "cognitive infiltration" of online groups, chat rooms, social networks, and websites, as well as off-line activist groups.

These GCHQ documents show for the first time that these contro-versial techniques to deceive and harm reputations have moved from the proposal stage to implementation.

All of the evidence highlights the implicit bargain that is offered to citizens: pose no challenge and you have nothing to worry about. Mind your own business, and support or at least tolerate what we do, and you'll be fine. Put differently, you must refrain from provoking the authority that wields surveillance powers if you wish to be deemed free of wrongdoing. This is a deal that invites passivity, obedience, and conformity. The safest course, the way to ensure being "left alone," is to remain quiet, unthreatening, and compliant.

For many, the deal is an attractive one, persuading the majority that surveillance is benign or even beneficial. They are too boring to attract the government's attention, they reason. "I seriously doubt that the NSA is interested in me" is the sort of thing I've often heard. "If they want to listen to my boring life, then they're welcome." Or "the NSA isn't interested in your grandmother talking about her recipes or your dad planning his golf game."

These are people who have become convinced that they themselves are not going to be personally targeted—because they are unthreatening and compliant—and therefore either deny that it's happening, do not care, or are willing to support it outright.

Interviewing me soon after the NSA story broke, MSNBC host Lawrence O'Donnell mocked the notion of the NSA as "a big, scary surveillance monster." Summing up his view, he concluded:

> My feeling so far is . . . I'm not scared . . . the fact that the government is collecting [data] at such a gigantic, massive level means that it's even harder for the government to find me . . . and they have absolutely no incentive to find me. And so I, at this stage, feel completely unthreatened by this.

The *New Yorker*'s Hendrik Hertzberg also asserted similarly dismissive views of the dangers of surveillance. Conceding that there "are reasons to be concerned about intelligence-agency overreach, excessive secrecy, and lack of transparency," he wrote that "there are also reasons to remain calm," in particular, that the threat posed "to civil liberties, such as it is, is abstract, conjectural, unspecified." And the *Washington Post*'s columnist Ruth Marcus, belittling concern over NSA powers, announced—absurdly—"my metadata almost certainly hasn't been scrutinized."

In one important sense, O'Donnell, Hertzberg, and Marcus are right. It is the case that the US government "has absolutely no incentive" to target people like them, for whom the threat from a surveillance state is little more than "abstract, conjectural, unspecified." That's because journalists who devote their careers to venerating the country's most powerful official—the president, who is the NSA's commander-in-chief—and defending his political party rarely, if ever, risk alienating those in power.

Of course, dutiful, loyal supporters of the president and his policies, good citizens who do nothing to attract negative attention from the powerful, have no reason to fear the surveillance state. This is the case in every society: those who pose no challenge are rarely targeted by oppressive measures, and from their perspective, they can then convince themselves that oppression does not really exist. But the true measure of a society's freedom is how it treats its dissidents and other marginalized groups, not how it treats good loyalists. Even in the world's worst tyrannies, dutiful supporters are immunized from abuses of state power. In Mubarak's Egypt, it was those who took to the street to agitate for his overthrow who were arrested, tortured, gunned down; Mubarak's supporters and people who quietly stayed at home were not. In the United States, it was NAACP leaders, Communists, and civil rights and anti-war activists who were targeted with Hoover's surveillance, not well-behaved citizens who stayed mute about social injustice.

We shouldn't have to be faithful loyalists of the powerful to feel safe from state surveillance. Nor should the price of immunity be refraining from controversial or provocative dissent. We shouldn't want a society where the message is conveyed that you will be left alone only if you mimic the accommodating behavior and conventional wisdom of an establishment columnist.

Beyond that, the sense of immunity felt by a particular group currently in power is bound to be illusory. That is made clear when we look at how partisan affiliation shapes people's sense of the dangers of state surveillance. What emerges is that yesterday's cheerleaders can quickly become today's dissenters.

At the time of the 2005 NSA warrantless eavesdropping controversy, liberals and Democrats overwhelmingly viewed the agency's surveillance program as menacing. Part of this, of course, was typical partisan hackery: George W. Bush was president and Democrats saw an opportunity to inflict political harm on him and his party. But a significant part of their fear was genuine: because they considered Bush malicious and dangerous, they perceived that state surveillance under his control was therefore threatening and that they in particular were endangered as political opponents. Accordingly, Republicans had a more benign or supportive view of the NSA's actions. In December 2013, by contrast, Democrats and progressives had converted to the leading NSA defenders.

Ample polling data reflected this shift. At the end of July 2013, the Pew Research Center released a poll showing that the majority of Americans disbelieved the defenses offered for the NSA's actions. In particular, "a majority of Americans—56%—say that federal courts fail to provide adequate limits on the telephone and Internet data the government is collecting as part of its anti-terrorism efforts." And "an even larger percentage (70%) believes that the government uses this data for purposes other than investigating terrorism." Moreover, "63% think the government is also gathering information about the content of communications."

Most remarkably, Americans now considered the danger of surveillance of greater concern than the danger of terrorism:

> Overall, 47% say their greater concern about government anti-terrorism policies is that they have gone too far in restricting the average person's civil liberties, while 35% say they are more concerned that policies have not gone far enough to protect the country. This is the first time in Pew Research polling that more have expressed concern over civil liberties than protection from terrorism since the question was first asked in 2004.

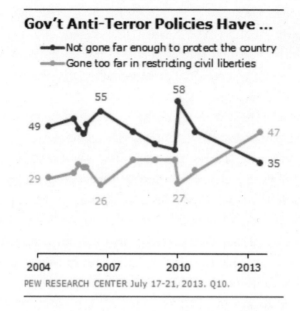

Gov't Anti-Terror Policies Have ...

—●—Not gone far enough to protect the country
—●—Gone too far in restricting civil liberties

PEW RESEARCH CENTER July 17-21, 2013. Q10.

That polling data was good news for anyone alarmed by use of excessive government power and the chronic exaggeration of the threat of terrorism. But it highlighted a telling inversion: Republicans, who had been defenders of the NSA under Bush, had been supplanted by Democrats once the surveillance system had come under the control of President Obama, one of their own. "Nationwide, there is more support for the government's data-collection program among Democrats (57% approve) than among Republicans (44%)."

Similar polling data from the *Washington Post* revealed that conservatives were far more concerned about NSA spying than liberals. When asked, "How concerned are you, if at all, about the collection and use of your personal information by the National Security Agency?" 48 percent of conservatives were "very concerned" compared to only 26 percent of liberals. As law professor Orin Kerr noted, this represented a fundamental change: "It's an interesting reversal from 2006, when the President was a Republican instead of a Democrat. Back then, a Pew poll found 75% of Republicans approved of NSA surveillance but only 37% of Democrats approved."

A Pew chart makes the shift clear:

Partisan Shifts in Views of NSA Surveillance Programs

Views of NSA surveillance programs
(See previous table for differences in question wording)

| | January 2006 | | June 2013 | |
	Accept-able %	Un-acceptable %	Accept-able %	Un-acceptable %
Total	51	47	56	41
Republican	75	23	52	47
Democrat	37	61	64	34
Independent	44	55	53	44

PEW RESEARCH CENTER June 6-9, 2013. Figures read across. Don't know/Refused responses not shown.

The arguments for and against surveillance brazenly rotate, based on which party in power. The NSA's collection of bulk metadata was vehemently denounced by one senator on *The Early Show* in 2006 in this way:

> I don't have to listen to your phone calls to know what you're doing. If I know every single phone call that you made, I am able to determine every single person you talked to. I can get a pattern about your life that is very, very intrusive. . . . And the real question here is: What do they do with this information that they collect that does not have anything to do with Al Qaeda? . . . And we're going to trust the president and the vice president of the United States that they're doing the right thing? Don't count me in on that.

The senator so harshly attacking metadata collection was Joe Biden, who subsequently, as vice president, became part of a Democratic administration that advanced precisely the same arguments he once derided.

The relevant point here is not merely that many partisan loyalists are unprincipled hypocrites with no real convictions other than a quest for power, although that is certainly true. More important is what such statements reveal about the nature of how one regards state surveillance. As with so many injustices, people are willing to dismiss fear of government overreach when they believe that those who happen to be in control are benevolent and trustworthy. They consider surveillance dangerous or worth caring about only when they perceive that they themselves are threatened by it.

Radical expansions of power are often introduced in this way, by persuading people that they affect just a specific, discrete group. Governments have long convinced populations to turn a blind eye to oppressive conduct by leading citizens to believe, rightly or wrongly, that only certain marginalized people are targeted, and everyone else can acquiesce to or even support that oppression without fear that it will be applied to them. Leaving aside the obvious moral shortcomings of this position— we do not dismiss racism because it is directed at a minority, or shrug off hunger on the grounds that we enjoy a plentiful supply of food—it is almost always misguided on pragmatic grounds.

The indifference or support of those who think themselves exempt invariably allows for the misuse of power to spread far beyond its original application, until the abuse becomes impossible to control—as it inevitably will. There are too many examples to count, but perhaps the most recent and potent one is the exploitation of the Patriot Act. A near-unanimous Congress approved a massive increase in surveillance and detention powers after 9/11, convinced by the argument that doing so would detect and prevent future attacks.

The implicit assumption was that the powers would be used principally against Muslims in relation to terrorism—a classic expansion of power confined to a particular group engaged in a particular kind of act—which is one reason why the measure received overwhelming backing. But what happened was very different: the Patriot Act has been applied well beyond its ostensible purpose. In fact, since its enactment, it has been used overwhelmingly in cases having nothing at all to do with terrorism or national security. *New York* magazine revealed that from 2006 to 2009, the "sneak and peek" provision of the act (license to execute a search warrant without immediately informing the target) was used in 1,618 drug-related cases, 122 cases connected with fraud, and just 15 that involved terrorism.

But once the citizenry acquiesces to a new power, believing that it does not affect them, it becomes institutionalized and legitimized and objection becomes impossible. Indeed, the central lesson learned by Frank Church in 1975 was the extent of the danger posed by mass surveillance. In an interview on *Meet the Press*, he said:

> That capability at any time could be turned around on the American people and no American would have any privacy left, such is the capability to monitor everything—telephone conversations, telegrams, it doesn't matter. There would be no place to hide. If this government ever became a tyrant . . . the technological capacity that the intelligence community has given the government could enable it to impose total tyranny, and there would be no way to fight back because the most careful effort to combine together in resistance . . . is within the reach of the government to know. Such is the capacity of this technology.

Writing in the *New York Times* in 2005, James Bamford observed that the threat from state surveillance is far more dire today than it was in the 1970s: "With people expressing their innermost thoughts in e-mail messages, exposing their medical and financial records to the Internet, and chatting constantly on cellphones, the agency virtually has the ability to get inside a person's mind."

Church's concern, that any surveillance ability "could be turned around on the American people," is precisely what the NSA has done post-9/11. Despite operating under the Foreign Intelligence Surveillance Act, and despite the prohibition on domestic spying embedded in the agency's mission from the start, many of its surveillance activities are now focused on US citizens on US soil.

Even absent abuse, and even if one is not personally targeted, a surveillance state that collects it all harms society and political freedom in general. Progress both in the United States and other nations was only ever achieved through the ability to challenge power and orthodoxies and to pioneer new ways of thinking and living. Everyone, even those who do not engage in dissenting advocacy or political activism, suffers when that freedom is stifled by the fear of being watched. Hendrik

Hertzberg, who downplayed concerns about the NSA programs, none-theless acknowledged that "harm has been done. The harm is civic. The harm is collective. The harm is to the architecture of trust and account-ability that supports an open society and a democratic polity."

Surveillance cheerleaders essentially offer only one argument in defense of mass surveillance: it is only carried out to stop terrorism and keep people safe. Indeed, invoking an external threat is a historical tactic of choice to keep the population submissive to government powers. The US government has heralded the danger of terrorism for more than a decade to justify a host of radical acts, from renditions and torture to assassina-tions and the invasion of Iraq. Ever since the 9/11 attack, US officials reflexively produce the word "terrorism." It is far more of a slogan and tactic than an actual argument or persuasive justification for action. And in the case of surveillance, overwhelming evidence shows how dubious a justification it is.

To begin with, much of the data collection conducted by the NSA has manifestly nothing to do with terrorism or national security. Intercept-ing the communications of the Brazilian oil giant Petrobras or spying on negotiation sessions at an economic summit or targeting the demo-cratically elected leaders of allied states or collecting all Americans' com-munications records has no relationship to terrorism. Given the actual surveillance the NSA does, stopping terror is clearly a pretext.

Moreover, the argument that mass surveillance has prevented ter-ror plots—a claim made by President Obama and a range of national security figures—has been proved false. As the *Washington Post* noted in December 2013, in an article headlined "Officials' Defenses of NSA Phone Program May Be Unraveling," a federal judge declared the phone metadata collection program "almost certainly" unconstitutional, in the process saying that the Justice Department failed to "cite a single case in which analysis of the NSA's bulk metadata collection actually stopped an imminent terrorist attack."

That same month, Obama's hand-picked advisory panel (composed of, among others, a former CIA deputy director and a former White

House aide, and convened to study the NSA program through access to classified information) concluded that the metadata program "was not essential to preventing attacks and could readily have been obtained in a timely manner using conventional [court] orders."

Quoting the *Post* again: "In congressional testimony, [Keith] Alexander has credited the program with helping to detect dozens of plots both in the United States and overseas" but the advisory panel's report "cut deeply into the credibility of those claims."

Additionally, as Democratic senators Ron Wyden, Mark Udall, and Martin Heinrich—all members of the Intelligence Committee—baldly stated in the *New York Times*, the mass collection of telephone records has not enhanced Americans' protection from the threat of terrorism.

> The usefulness of the bulk collection program has been greatly exaggerated. We have yet to see any proof that it provides real, unique value in protecting national security. In spite of our repeated requests, the N.S.A. has not provided evidence of any instance when the agency used this program to review phone records that could not have been obtained using a regular court order or emergency authorization.

A study by the centrist New America Foundation testing the veracity of official justifications for the bulk metadata collection concurred that the program "has had no discernible impact on preventing acts of terrorism." Instead, as the *Washington Post* noted, in most cases where plots were disrupted the study found that "traditional law enforcement and investigative methods provided the tip or evidence to initiate the case."

The record is indeed quite poor. The collect-it-all system did nothing to detect, let alone disrupt, the 2012 Boston Marathon bombing. It did not detect the attempted Christmas-day bombing of a jetliner over Detroit, or the plan to blow up Times Square, or the plot to attack the New York City subway system—all of which were stopped by alert bystanders or traditional police powers. It certainly did nothing to stop the string of mass shootings from Aurora to Newtown. Major international attacks from London to Mumbai to Madrid proceeded without detection, despite involving at least dozens of operatives.

And despite exploitative claims from the NSA, bulk surveillance would not have given the intelligence services better tools to prevent the attack on 9/11. Keith Alexander, speaking to a House intelligence committee, said, "I would much rather be here today debating" the program "than trying to explain how we failed to prevent another 9/11." (The same argument, verbatim, appeared in talking points the NSA gave its employees to use to fend off questions.)

The implication is rank fearmongering and deceitful in the extreme. As CNN security analyst Peter Bergen has shown, the CIA had multiple reports about an al-Qaeda plot and "quite a bit of information about two of the hijackers and their presence in the United States," which "the agency didn't share with other government agencies until it was too late to do anything about it."

Lawrence Wright, the New Yorker's al-Qaeda expert, also debunked the NSA's proposition that metadata collection could have stopped 9/11, explaining that the CIA "withheld crucial intelligence from the FBI, which has the ultimate authority to investigate terrorism in the U.S. and attacks on Americans abroad." The FBI could have stopped 9/11, he argued.

> It had a warrant to establish surveillance of everyone connected to Al Qaeda in America. It could follow them, tap their phones, clone their computers, read their e-mails, and subpoena their medical, bank, and credit-card records. It had the right to demand records from telephone companies of any calls they had made. There was no need for a metadata-collection program. What was needed was cooperation with other federal agencies, but for reasons both petty and obscure those agencies chose to hide vital clues from the investigators most likely to avert the attacks.

The government was in possession of the necessary intelligence but had failed to understand or act on it. The solution that it then embarked on—to collect everything, en masse—has done nothing to fix that failure.

Over and over, from multiple corners, the invocation of the terrorism threat to justify surveillance was exposed as a sham.

In fact, mass surveillance has had quite the opposite effect: it makes detecting and stopping terror more difficult. Democratic Congressman Rush Holt, a physicist and one of the few scientists in Congress, has made the point that collecting everything about everyone's communications only obscures actual plots being discussed by actual terrorists. Directed rather than indiscriminate surveillance would yield more specific and useful information. The current approach swamps the intelligence agencies with so much data that they cannot possibly sort through it effectively.

Beyond providing too much information, NSA surveillance schemes end up increasing the country's vulnerability: the agency's efforts to override the encryption methods protecting common Internet transactions—such as banking, medical records, and commerce—have left these systems open to infiltration by hackers and other hostile entities.

Security expert Bruce Schneier, writing in the *Atlantic* in January 2014, pointed out:

> Not only is ubiquitous surveillance ineffective, it is extraordinarily costly. . . . It breaks our technical systems, as the very protocols of the Internet become untrusted. . . . It's not just domestic abuse we have to worry about; it's the rest of the world, too. The more we choose to eavesdrop on the Internet and other communications technologies, the less we are secure from eavesdropping by others. Our choice isn't between a digital world where the NSA can eavesdrop and one where the NSA is prevented from eavesdropping; it's between a digital world that is vulnerable to all attackers, and one that is secure for all users.

What is perhaps most remarkable about the bottomless exploitation of the threat of terrorism is that it is so plainly exaggerated. The risk of any American dying in a terrorist attack is infinitesimal, considerably less than the chance of being struck by lightning. John Mueller, an Ohio State University professor who has written extensively about the balance between threat and expenditures in fighting terrorism, explained in 2011: "The number of people worldwide who are killed by Muslim-type terrorists, Al Qaeda wannabes, is maybe a few hundred outside of war zones. It's basically the same number of people who die drowning in the bathtub each year."

More American citizens have "undoubtedly" died "overseas from traffic accidents or intestinal illnesses," the news agency McClatchy reported, "than from terrorism."

The idea that we should dismantle the core protections of our political system to erect a ubiquitous surveillance state for the sake of this risk is the height of irrationality. Yet exaggeration of the threat is repeated over and over. Shortly before the 2012 Olympics in London, controversy erupted over a supposed lack of security. The company contracted to provide security had failed to appoint the number of guards required by its contract, and shrill voices from around the globe insisted that the games were therefore vulnerable to a terrorist attack.

After the trouble-free Olympics, Stephen Walt noted in *Foreign Policy* that the outcry was driven, as usual, by severe exaggeration of the threat. He cited an essay by John Mueller and Mark G. Stewart in *International Security* for which the authors had analyzed fifty cases of purported "Islamic terrorist plots" against the United States, only to conclude that "virtually all of the perpetrators were 'incompetent, ineffective, unintelligent, idiotic, ignorant, unorganized, misguided, muddled, amateurish, dopey, unrealistic, moronic, irrational, and foolish.'" Mueller and Stewart quoted from Glenn Carle, former deputy national intelligence officer for transnational threats, who said, "We must see jihadists for the small, lethal, disjointed and miserable opponents that they are," and they noted that al-Qaeda's "capabilities are far inferior to its desires."

The problem, though, is that there are far too many power factions with a vested interest in the fear of terrorism: the government, seeking justification for its actions; the surveillance and weapons industries, drowning in public funding; and the permanent power factions in Washington, committed to setting their priorities without real challenge. Stephen Walt made this point:

> Mueller and Stewart estimate that expenditures on domestic homeland security (i.e., not counting the wars in Iraq or Afghanistan) have increased by more than $1 trillion since 9/11, even though the annual risk of dying in a domestic terrorist attack is about 1 in 3.5 million. Using conservative assumptions and conventional risk-assessment methodol-

ogy, they estimate that for these expenditures to be cost-effective "they would have had to deter, prevent, foil or protect against 333 very large attacks that would otherwise have been successful every year." Finally, they worry that this exaggerated sense of danger has now been "internalized": even when politicians and "terrorism experts" aren't hyping the danger, the public still sees the threat as large and imminent.

As the fear of terrorism has been manipulated, the proven dangers of allowing the state to operate a massive secret surveillance system have been seriously understated.

Even if the threat of terrorism were at the level claimed by the government, that would still not justify the NSA's surveillance programs. Values other than physical safety are at least as if not more important. This recognition was embedded in US political culture from the nation's inception, and is no less crucial for other countries.

Nations and individuals constantly make choices that place the values of privacy and, implicitly, freedom above other objectives, such as physical safety. Indeed, the very purpose of the Fourth Amendment in the US Constitution is to prohibit certain police actions, even though they might reduce crime. If the police were able to barge into any home without a warrant, murderers, rapists, and kidnappers might be more easily apprehended. If the state were permitted to place monitors in our homes, crime would probably fall significantly (this is certainly true of house burglaries, yet most people would recoil in revulsion at the prospect). If the FBI were permitted to listen to our conversations and seize our communications, a wide array of crime could conceivably be prevented and solved.

But the Constitution was written to prevent such suspicionless invasions by the state. By drawing the line at such actions, we knowingly allow for the probability of greater criminality. Yet we draw that line anyway, exposing ourselves to a higher degree of danger, because pursuing absolute physical safety has never been our single overarching societal priority.

Above even our physical well-being, a central value is keeping the state out of the private realm—our "persons, houses, papers, and effects," as the Fourth Amendment puts it. We do so precisely because that realm is the crucible of so many of the attributes typically associated with the quality of life—creativity, exploration, intimacy.

Forgoing privacy in a quest for absolute safety is as harmful to a healthy psyche and life of an individual as it is to a healthy political culture. For the individual, safety first means a life of paralysis and fear, never entering a car or airplane, never engaging in an activity that entails risk, never weighing quality of life over quantity, and paying any price to avoid danger.

Fearmongering is a favored tactic by authorities precisely because fear so persuasively rationalizes an expansion of power and curtailment of rights. Since the beginning of the War on Terror, Americans have frequently been told that they must relinquish their core political rights if they are to have any hope of avoiding catastrophe. From Senate Intelligence chair Pat Roberts, for example: "I am a strong supporter of the First Amendment, the Fourth Amendment and civil liberties. But you have no civil liberties if you are dead." And GOP senator John Cornyn, who ran for reelection in Texas with a video of himself as a tough guy in a cowboy hat, issued a cowardly paean to the benefit of giving up rights: "None of your civil liberties matter much after you're dead."

Talk radio host Rush Limbaugh piled on, displaying historical ignorance by asking his large audience: "When is the last time you heard a president declare war on the basis that we gotta go protect our civil liberties? I can't think of one. . . . Our civil liberties are worthless if we are dead! If you are dead and pushing up daisies, if you're sucking dirt inside a casket, do you know what your civil liberties are worth? Zilch, zero, nada."

A population, a country that venerates physical safety above all other values will ultimately give up its liberty and sanction any power seized by authority in exchange for the promise, no matter how illusory, of total security. However, absolute safety is itself chimeric, pursued but never obtained. The pursuit degrades those who engage in it as well as any nation that comes to be defined by it.

The danger posed by the state operating a massive secret surveillance system is far more ominous now than at any point in history. While the government, via surveillance, knows more and more about what its citizens are doing, its citizens know less and less about what their government is doing, shielded as it is by a wall of secrecy.

It is hard to overstate how radically this situation reverses the defining dynamic of a healthy society or how fundamentally it shifts the balance of power toward the state. Bentham's Panopticon, designed to vest unchallengeable power in the hands of authorities, was based on exactly this reversal: "The essence of it," he wrote, rests in "the centrality of the inspector's situation" combined with the "most effectual contrivances for seeing without being seen."

In a healthy democracy, the opposite is true. Democracy requires accountability and consent of the governed, which is only possible if citizens know what is being done in their name. The presumption is that, with rare exception, they will know everything their political officials are doing, which is why they are called public servants, working in the public sector, in public service, for public agencies. Conversely, the presumption is that the government, with rare exception, will not know anything that law-abiding citizens are doing. That is why we are called private individuals, functioning in our private capacity. Transparency is for those who carry out public duties and exercise public power. Privacy is for everyone else.

5

THE FOURTH ESTATE

One of the principal institutions ostensibly devoted to monitoring and checking abuse of state power is the political media. The theory of a "fourth estate" is to ensure government transparency and provide a check on overreach, of which the secret surveillance of entire populations is surely among the most radical examples. But that check is only effective if journalists act adversarially to those who wield political power. Instead, the US media has frequently abdicated this role, being subservient to the government's interests, even amplifying, rather than scrutinizing, its messages and carrying out its dirty work.

In this context, I knew that media hostility toward my reporting on Snowden's disclosures was inevitable. On June 6, the day after the first NSA article ran in the *Guardian*, the *New York Times* introduced the possibility of a criminal investigation. "After writing intensely, even obsessively, for years about government surveillance and prosecution of journalists, Glenn Greenwald has suddenly put himself directly at the intersection of those two issues, and perhaps in the crosshairs of federal prosecutors," the paper proclaimed in a profile of me. My NSA reporting, it added, "is expected to attract an investigation from the Justice Department, which has aggressively pursued leakers." The profile quoted the neoconservative Gabriel Schoenfeld of the Hudson Institute, who has long advocated the prosecution of journalists for publishing secret information, calling me "a highly professional apologist for any kind of anti-Americanism no matter how extreme."

The most revealing evidence of the *Times*'s intentions came from the journalist Andrew Sullivan, who was quoted in the same profile saying, "Once you get into a debate with [Greenwald], it can be hard to get the last word," and "I think he has little grip on what it actually means to govern a country or run a war." Disturbed by the use of his comments out of context, Andrew later sent me his full exchange with the *Times* reporter Leslie Kaufman, which included praise for my work that the paper had notably chosen to omit. What was more telling, however, were the original questions Kaufman had sent him:

- "He obviously had strong opinions, but how is he as a journalist? Reliable? Honest? Quotes you accurately? Accurately describes your positions? Or is more advocate than journalist?"
- "He says you are a friend, is this so? I get the sense that he is something of a loner and has the kind of uncompromising opinions that makes it hard to keep friends, but could be wrong."

The second question—that I'm "something of a loner" who has trouble keeping friends—was, in some sense, even more significant than the first. Discrediting the messenger as a misfit to discredit the message is an old ploy when it comes to whistle-blowing, and it often works.

The effort to discredit me personally was fully brought home when I received an email from a reporter for the *New York Daily News*. He said he was investigating various aspects of my past, including debts, tax liability, and partnership in an adult video distribution company by a private corporation in which I had owned shares eight years earlier. Because the *Daily News* is a tabloid often trafficking in personal sleaze, I decided not to respond: there was no reason to bring more attention to the issues it had raised.

But that same day, I received an email from a *Times* reporter, Michael Schmidt, also interested in writing about my past tax debt. How the two newspapers had simultaneously learned of such obscure details was a mystery, but the *Times* had evidently decided that my prior debt was newsworthy—even as it refused to provide any rationale for why that was the case.

These issues were plainly trivial and intended to smear. The *Times* ended up not running the story, unlike the *Daily News*, which even included details of a conflict I had in my apartment building ten years earlier over a claim that my dog exceeded the weight limit allowed by the condominium bylaws.

While the smear campaign was predictable, the effort to deny my status as a journalist was not, and it had potentially drastic ramifications. Again, this campaign was kicked off by the *New York Times*, also in its June 6 profile. In the headline the paper went out of its way to assign me some non-journalistic title: "Blogger, with Focus on Surveillance, Is at Center of a Debate." As bad as the headline was, the online original was even worse: "Anti-Surveillance Activist Is at Center of a New Leak."

The paper's public editor, Margaret Sullivan, criticized the headline, saying she found it "dismissive." She added: "There's nothing wrong with being a blogger, of course—I am one myself. But when the media establishment uses the term, it somehow seems to say, 'You're not quite one of us.'"

The article went on repeatedly to cast me as something other than a "journalist" or "reporter." I was, it declared, a "lawyer and longtime blogger" (I have not practiced law for six years, and had worked for years as a columnist at major news venues, in addition to having published four books). To the extent I ever acted "as a journalist," it said, my experience was "unusual," not because of my "clear opinions" but because I had "rarely reported to an editor."

The media in full then got into a debate about whether I was in fact a "journalist" as opposed to something else. The most commonly offered alternative was "activist." Nobody bothered to define any of these words, relying instead on ill-defined clichés, as the media tends to do, particularly when the goal is demonization. Thereafter, the empty, vapid label was routinely applied.

The designation had real significance on several levels. For one, removing the label of "journalist" diminishes the legitimacy of the reporting. Moreover, turning me into an "activist" could have legal—that is, criminal—consequences. There are both formal and unwritten legal protections offered to journalists that are unavailable to anyone else. While it is considered generally legitimate for a journalist to publish government secrets, for example, that's not the case for someone acting in any other capacity.

Intentionally or not, those pushing the idea that I was not a journalist—despite the fact that I was writing for one of the oldest and largest newspapers in the Western world—were making it easier for the government to criminalize my reporting. After the *New York Times* proclaimed me an "activist," Sullivan, the public editor, acknowledged that "these matters have taken on more significance in the current climate, and could be crucial for Mr. Greenwald."

The allusion to "the current climate" was shorthand for two major controversies that had engulfed Washington involving the administration's treatment of journalists. The first was the DOJ's secret acquisition of emails and telephone records of Associated Press reporters and editors to find out their source for a story.

The second, more extreme incident involved the DOJ's effort to learn the identity of another source who had leaked secret information. To do so, the department filed an affidavit in federal court seeking a warrant to read the emails of Fox News Washington bureau chief James Rosen.

In the application for the warrant, government lawyers branded Rosen a "co-conspirator" in the source's felonies by virtue of the fact that he had obtained classified material. The affidavit was shocking because, as the *New York Times* put it, "no American journalist has ever been prosecuted for gathering and publishing classified information, so the language raised the prospect that the Obama administration was taking its leak crackdown to a new level."

The behavior cited by the DOJ to justify Rosen's designation as "co-conspirator"—working with his source to obtain documents, establishing a "covert communication plan" to speak without detection, and "employing flattery and playing to [his source's] vanity and ego" to persuade him to leak—were all things investigative journalists routinely do.

As veteran Washington reporter Olivier Knox put it, the DOJ had "accused Rosen of breaking anti-espionage law with behavior that—as described in the agent's own affidavit—falls well inside the bounds of traditional news reporting." To view Rosen's conduct as a felony was to criminalize journalism itself.

This move was perhaps less surprising than it might have been, given the larger context of the Obama administration's attacks on whistle-blowers and sources. In 2011, the *New York Times* revealed that the DOJ, attempting to find the source for a book written by James Risen, had "obtained extensive records about his phone calls, finances and travel history," including "his 'credit card and bank records and certain records of his airline travel' and three credit reports listing his financial accounts."

The DOJ was also trying to force Risen to reveal his source's identity, with the likely prospect of prison if he refused to do so. Journalists around the country were dismayed by Risen's treatment: if one of the most accomplished and institutionally protected investigative reporters could be subject to such an aggressive attack, then so could any journalist.

Many in the press responded with alarm. One typical article, from *USA Today*, noted that "President Obama finds himself battling charges that his administration has effectively launched a war on journalists," and quoted former *Los Angeles Times* national security reporter Josh Meyer saying: "There's a red line that no other administration has crossed before that the Obama administration has blown right past." Jane Mayer, the widely admired investigative reporter for the *New Yorker*, warned in the *New Republic* that the Obama DOJ's targeting of whistle-blowers was operating as an attack on journalism itself: "It's a huge impediment to reporting, and so chilling isn't quite strong enough, it's more like freezing the whole process into a standstill."

The Committee to Protect Journalists—an international organization that monitors attacks on press freedoms by the state—was moved by the situation to issue its first-ever report about the United States. Written by Leonard Downie Jr., past executive editor of the *Washington Post*, the report, issued in October 2013, concluded:

> The administration's war on leaks and other efforts to control information are the most aggressive . . . since the Nixon administration.

. . . The 30 experienced Washington journalists at a variety of news
organizations . . . interviewed for this report could not remember any
precedent.

The dynamic extended beyond national security to encompass, as one
bureau chief said, an effort "to thwart accountability reporting about
government *agencies*."

US journalists, for years overwhelmingly enamored of Barack Obama,
were now commonly speaking of him in these terms: as some sort of
grave menace to press freedoms, the most repressive leader in this regard
since Richard Nixon. That was quite a remarkable turn for a politician
who was ushered into power vowing "the most transparent administration in US history."

To tamp down the growing scandal, Obama ordered Attorney General Eric Holder to meet with representatives of the media and review the
rules governing the DOJ's treatment of journalists. Obama claimed to be
"troubled by the possibility that leak investigations may chill the investigative journalism that holds government accountable"—as though he
hadn't presided over five years of precisely those sorts of assaults on the
news-gathering process.

Holder vowed in a Senate hearing on June 6, 2013 (the day after the
Guardian's first NSA story) that the DOJ would never prosecute "any
reporter for doing his or her job." The DOJ's goal, he added, is merely
"to identify and prosecute government officials who jeopardize national
security by violating their oaths, not to target members of the press or
discourage them from carrying out their vital work."

On some level, this was a welcome development: the administration
had evidently felt sufficient backlash to create at least the appearance of
addressing press freedom. But there was a huge, gaping hole in Holder's vow: the DOJ had determined, in the case of Fox News's Rosen, that
working with one's source to "steal" classified information was beyond
the scope of the "reporter's job." Thus Holder's guarantee depended on
the DOJ's view of what journalism is and what exceeds the boundaries of
legitimate reporting.

Against that background, the effort by some media figures to cast me out of "journalism"—to insist that what I was doing was "activism," not reporting, and therefore criminal—was potentially dangerous.

The first explicit call to prosecute me came from New York Republican congressman Peter King, who had served as chairman of the House Subcommittee on Terrorism and had convened McCarthyite hearings on the terror threat posed "from within" by the American Muslim community (ironically, King was a longtime supporter of the IRA). King confirmed to CNN's Anderson Cooper that reporters working on the NSA stories should be prosecuted "if they willingly knew that this was classified information . . . especially on something of this magnitude." He added, "There is an obligation both moral but also legal, I believe, against a reporter disclosing something that would so severely compromise national security."

King later clarified on Fox News that he was speaking specifically of me:

> I'm talking about Greenwald . . . not only did he disclose this information, he has said that he has names of CIA agents and assets around the world, and they're threatening to disclose that. The last time that was done in this country, we saw a CIA station chief murdered in Greece. . . .
> I think [prosecution of journalists] should be very targeted, very selective and certainly a very rare exception. But, in this case, when you have someone who discloses secrets like this and threatens to release more, yes, there has to be—legal action taken against him.

That I had threatened to release the names of CIA agents and assets was a complete fabrication. Nonetheless, his remarks opened the floodgates and commentators piled on. The *Washington Post*'s Marc Thiessen, a former Bush speechwriter who wrote a book justifying the US torture program, defended King under the headline, "Yes, Publishing NSA Secrets Is a Crime." Accusing me of "violating 18 USC 798, which makes it a criminal act to publish classified information revealing government cryptography or communications intelligence," he added, "Greenwald clearly violated this law (as did the *Post*, for that matter, when it published classified details of the NSA's PRISM program)."

Alan Dershowitz went on CNN and pronounced: "Greenwald—in my view—clearly has committed a felony." A known defender of civil liberties and press freedoms, Dershowitz nonetheless said that my reporting "doesn't border on criminality—it's right in the heartland of criminality."

The growing chorus was joined by General Michael Hayden, who led both the NSA and then the CIA under George Bush, and implemented the agency's illegal warrantless eavesdropping program. "Edward Snowden," he wrote on CNN.com, "will likely prove to be the most costly leaker of American secrets in the history of the Republic," and then added that "Glenn Greenwald" is "far more deserving of the Justice Department's characterization of a co-conspirator than Fox's James Rosen ever was."

At first largely confined to right-wing figures who could be expected to view journalism as a crime, the chorus of voices raising the question of prosecution grew during a now-infamous appearance on *Meet the Press*.

The White House itself has praised *Meet the Press* as a comfortable venue for DC political figures and other elites to deliver their message without much challenge. The weekly NBC program was hailed by Catherine Martin, former vice president Dick Cheney's communications director, as "our best format" because Cheney was able to "control the message." Putting the vice president on *Meet the Press* was, she said, a "tactic we often used." Indeed, a video of the show's host, David Gregory, onstage at the White House Correspondents' Dinner, dancing awkwardly but enthusiastically behind a rapping Karl Rove, went viral because it so vividly symbolized what the show is: a place where political power goes to be amplified and flattered, where only the most staid conventional wisdom is heard, where only the narrowest range of views is permitted.

I was invited to appear on the program at the last minute and only out of necessity. Hours earlier, the news broke that Snowden had left Hong Kong and was on a plane to Moscow, a dramatic turn of events that would inevitably dominate the news cycle. *Meet the Press* had no choice but to lead with the story, and, as one of the very few people in contact with Snowden, I was asked to be on the show as the lead guest.

I had harshly criticized Gregory over the years and anticipated an adversarial interview. But I did not expect this question from him: "To the extent that you have aided and abetted Snowden, even in his current movements, why shouldn't you, Mr. Greenwald, be charged with a crime?" There were so many things wrong with the question that it took a minute to process that he had actually asked it.

The most glaring problem was the number of baseless assumptions embedded in the question. The statement "To the extent" that I had "aided and abetted Snowden, even in his current movements" is no different than saying "To the extent that Mr. Gregory has murdered his neighbors . . ." This was nothing but a striking example of the "When did you stop beating your wife?" formulation.

But beyond the rhetorical fallacy, a TV journalist had just given credence to the notion that other journalists could and should be prosecuted for doing journalism, an extraordinary assertion. Gregory's question implied that every investigative reporter in the United States who works with sources and receives classified information is a criminal. It was precisely this theory and climate that had made investigative reporting so precarious.

Predictably, Gregory repeatedly depicted me as something other than a "journalist." He prefaced one question by proclaiming: "You are a polemicist here, you have a point of view, you are a columnist." And he announced: "The question of who's a journalist may be up to a debate with regard to what you're doing."

But Gregory wasn't the only one making these arguments. Not one of the *Meet the Press* panel, convened to discuss my exchange with Gregory, objected to the notion that a journalist could be prosecuted for working with a source. NBC's Chuck Todd bolstered that theory by ominously raising "questions" about what he called my "role" in "the plot":

> Glenn Greenwald . . . how much was he involved in the plot? . . . did he have a role beyond simply being a receiver of this information? And is he going to have to answer those questions? You know, there is—there is—there is a point of law.

One CNN show, *Reliable Sources*, debated the question while a graphic remained on the screen that read, "Should Glenn Greenwald be prosecuted?"

The *Washington Post*'s Walter Pincus—who spied on US students abroad on behalf of the CIA in the 1960s—wrote a column strongly suggesting that Laura, Snowden, and I were all operating as part of a plot secretly masterminded by WikiLeaks founder Julian Assange. The column was filled with so many factual errors (ones I documented in an open letter to Pincus) that the *Post* was forced to append an unusually large, three-paragraph, two-hundred-word correction acknowledging multiple mistakes.

On his own CNBC show, *New York Times* financial columnist Andrew Ross Sorkin said:

> I feel like, A, we've screwed this up, even letting [Snowden] get to Russia. B, clearly the Chinese hate us to even let him out of the country. . . . I would arrest him, and now I would almost arrest Glenn Greenwald, who's the journalist who seems to want to help him get to Ecuador.

That a reporter for the *Times*, which had fought all the way to the US Supreme Court in order to publish the Pentagon Papers, would advocate my arrest was a potent sign of the devotion of many establishment journalists to the US government: after all, criminalizing investigative journalism would have a grave impact on that paper and its employees. Sorkin did later apologize to me, but his remarks demonstrated the speed and ease with which such assertions gain traction.

Fortunately, this view was far from unanimous among the American press corps. Indeed, the specter of criminalization prompted many journalists to rally in support of my work, and on various mainstream television programs the hosts were more interested in the substance of the revelations than in demonizing those involved. Much condemnation of Gregory's question was voiced during the week following his interview. From the *Huffington Post*: "We still can't quite believe what David Gregory asked Glenn Greenwald just now." Toby Harnden, the Washington bureau chief of the UK's *Sunday Times*, tweeted: "I was jailed by Mugabe's Zimbabwe for 'practicing journalism.' Is David Gregory saying Obama's America should do the same?" Numerous reporters and columnists at the *New York Times*, the *Post*, and other places defended me both publicly and privately. But no amount of support could counter the fact that the reporters themselves had sanctioned the prospect of legal jeopardy.

Lawyers and other advisers agreed that there was a real risk of arrest should I return to the United States. I tried to find one person whose judgment I trusted to tell me that the risk was nonexistent, that it was inconceivable that the DOJ would prosecute me. No one said that. The general view was that the DOJ would not move against me explicitly for my reporting, wanting to avoid the appearance of going after journalists. The concern was rather that the government would concoct a theory that the supposed crimes I had committed were outside of the realm of journalism. Unlike the *Washington Post*'s Barton Gellman, I had traveled to Hong Kong to meet Snowden before publishing the stories; I had spoken to him regularly once he arrived in Russia and had published stories about the NSA on a freelance basis with newspapers around the world. The DOJ could try to claim that I had "aided and abetted" Snowden in his leaks or had helped a "fugitive" flee justice, or that my work with foreign newspapers constituted some type of espionage.

Moreover, my commentary about the NSA and the US government had deliberately been aggressive and defiant. The government was no doubt desperate to punish someone for what had been called the most damaging leak in the country's history, if not to alleviate institutional rage, then at least as a deterrent to others. Since the head most wanted on a pike was safely residing under the shield of political asylum in Moscow, Laura and I were a desirable second choice.

For months, several lawyers with high-level contacts in the Justice Department attempted to obtain informal assurances that I would not be prosecuted. In October, five months after the first story ran, Congressman Alan Grayson wrote to Attorney General Holder, noting that prominent political figures had called for my arrest and that I had had to decline an invitation to testify before Congress about the NSA due to concerns about possible prosecution. He concluded the letter saying:

I regard this as regrettable because (1) the commission of journalism is not a crime; (2) on the contrary, it is protected explicitly under the First Amendment; (3) Mr. Greenwald's reports regarding these subjects have, in fact, informed me, other members of Congress, and the general public of serious, pervasive violations of law and constitutional rights committed by agents of the government.

The letter asked whether the Department of Justice intended to bring charges against me and whether, should I seek to enter the United States, "the Department of Justice, the Department of Homeland Security, or any other office of the federal government intends to detain, question, arrest or prosecute" me. But as Grayson's hometown paper, the *Orlando Sentinel*, reported in December, Grayson never received a response to his letter.

At the end of 2013 and into the beginning of 2014, the threat of prosecution only increased as government officials kept up a clearly coordinated attack designed to criminalize my work. In late October, NSA chief Keith Alexander, in an obvious reference to my freelance reporting around the world, complained "that newspaper reporters have all these documents, the 50,000—whatever they have and are selling," and he chillingly demanded that "we"—the government—"ought to come up with a way of stopping it." House Intelligence Committee chairman Mike Rogers, at a hearing in January, repeatedly told FBI director James Comey that some of the journalists were "selling stolen property," making them "fences" or "thieves," and he then specified that he was talking about me. When I began reporting on Canadian spying with the Canadian Broadcasting Corporation, the parliamentary spokesman for Stephen Harper's right-wing government denounced me as a "porno-spy" and accused the CBC of buying stolen documents from me. In the United States, Director of National Intelligence James Clapper started using the criminal term "accomplices" to refer to journalists covering the NSA.

I believed that the probability of arrest upon my return to the United States was less than 50 percent, if only for reasons of image and worldwide controversy. The potential stain on Obama's legacy, as the first president to prosecute a journalist for doing journalism, was, I assumed, sufficient constraint. But if the recent past proved anything, it was that the US government was willing to do all sorts of reprehensible things under the guise of national security, without regard to how the rest of the world perceived them. The consequences of guessing wrong—ending up in handcuffs and charged under espionage laws, to be adjudicated by a federal judiciary that had proved itself shamelessly deferential to Washington in such matters—were too significant to blithely dismiss. I was determined to return to the United States, but only once I had a clearer understanding of the risk. Meanwhile, my family, friends, and all sorts of important opportunities to talk in the United States about the work I was doing were out of reach.

That lawyers and a congressman considered the risk real was itself extraordinary, a powerful measure of the erosion of press freedom. And that journalists had joined the call to treat my reporting as a felony was a remarkable triumph of propaganda for the powers of government, which could rely on trained professionals to do their work for them and equate adversarial investigative journalism with a crime.

The attacks on Snowden were of course far more virulent. They were also bizarrely identical in theme. Leading commentators who knew nothing at all about Snowden instantly adopted the same script of clichés to demean him. Within hours of learning his name, they marched in lockstep to malign his character and motives. He was driven, they intoned, not by any actual conviction but by "fame-seeking narcissism."

CBS News host Bob Schieffer denounced Snowden as a "narcissistic young man" who thinks "he is smarter than the rest of us." The *New Yorker*'s Jeffrey Toobin diagnosed him as "a grandiose narcissist who deserves to be in prison." The *Washington Post*'s Richard Cohen pronounced that Snowden "is not paranoiac; he is merely narcissistic," referring to the report that Snowden covered himself with a blanket to prevent his passwords being captured by overhead cameras. Cohen added, bizarrely, that Snowden "will go down as a cross-dressing Little Red Riding Hood" and that his supposed desire for fame will be thwarted."

These characterizations were patently ridiculous. Snowden was determined to disappear from sight, as he said, to do no interviews. He understood that the media love to personalize every story, and he wanted to keep the focus on NSA surveillance, not on him. True to his word, Snowden refused all media invitations. On a daily basis, for many months, I received calls and emails from almost every US television program, TV news personality, and famous journalist, pleading for a chance to talk with Snowden. *Today* show host Matt Lauer called several times to make his pitch; *60 Minutes* was so relentless in their requests that I stopped taking their calls; Brian Williams dispatched several different representatives to make his case. Snowden could have spent all day and night on the most influential television shows, with the world watching him, had he wanted to do that.

But he was unmovable. I conveyed the requests and he declined them, to avoid taking attention away from the revelations. Strange behavior for a fame-seeking narcissist.

Other denunciations of Snowden's personality followed. *New York Times* columnist David Brooks mocked him on the grounds that "he could not successfully work his way through community college." Snowden is, Brooks decreed, "the ultimate unmediated man," symbolic of "the rising tide of distrust, the corrosive spread of cynicism, the fraying of the social fabric and the rise of people who are so individualistic in their outlook that they have no real understanding of how to knit others together and look after the common good."

To *Politico*'s Roger Simon, Snowden was "a loser" because he "dropped out of high school." Democratic congresswoman Debbie Wasserman Schultz, who also serves as chair of the Democratic National Committee, condemned Snowden, who had just ruined his life to make the NSA disclosures, as "a coward."

Inevitably, Snowden's patriotism was called into question. Because he had gone to Hong Kong, assertions were made that he was likely working as a spy for the Chinese government. It's "not hard to image that Snowden has been a Chinese double agent and will soon defect," announced veteran GOP campaign consultant Matt Mackowiak.

But when Snowden left Hong Kong to travel to Latin America via Russia, the accusation seamlessly switched from Chinese to Russian spy. People like Congressman Mike Rogers made this charge with no evidence at all, and despite the obvious fact that Snowden was only in Russia because the United States had revoked his passport and then bullied countries such as Cuba into rescinding their promise of safe passage. Moreover, what kind of Russian spy would go to Hong Kong, or work with journalists and identify himself publicly, rather than passing on his stash to his bosses in Moscow? The claim never made any sense and was based on not a particle of fact, but that was no deterrent to it spreading.

Among the most reckless and baseless innuendos spread against Snowden came from the *New York Times*, which claimed that he had been allowed to leave Hong Kong by the Chinese government, not Hong Kong authorities, and then added a rank and damaging speculation: "Two Western intelligence experts, who worked for major government spy agencies, said they believed that the Chinese government had managed to drain the contents of the four laptops that Mr. Snowden said he brought to Hong Kong."

The *New York Times* had no evidence at all that the Chinese government had been able to obtain Snowden's NSA data. The paper simply led readers to conclude that it had, based on two anonymous "experts" who "believed" it may have happened.

At the time this story ran, Snowden was stuck at the Moscow airport and unable to go online. As soon as he resurfaced, he vehemently denied, via an article I published in the *Guardian*, that he had passed any data to China or Russia. "I never gave any information to either government, and they never took anything from my laptops," he said.

The day after Snowden's denial ran, Margaret Sullivan criticized the *Times* for its article. She interviewed Joseph Kahn, the paper's foreign editor, who said that "it's important to see this passage in the story for what it is: an exploration of what might have happened, based on experts who did not claim to have direct knowledge." Sullivan commented that "two sentences in the middle of a *Times* article on such a sensitive subject—though they may be off the central point—have the power to sway the discussion or damage a reputation." She concluded by agreeing with a reader who had complained about the story, saying: "I read the *Times* for the truth. I can read publication of speculation almost anywhere."

Via Janine Gibson, *Times* executive editor Jill Abramson—at a meeting to convince the *Guardian* to collaborate on certain NSA stories—sent a message: "Please tell Glenn Greenwald personally that I agree with him completely about the fact that we should never have run that claim about China 'draining' Snowden's laptops. It was irresponsible."

Gibson seemed to expect that I would be pleased, though I was anything but: How could an executive editor of a newspaper conclude that an obviously damaging article was irresponsible and should not have been published, and then not retract it or at least run an editor's note?

Aside from the lack of evidence, the claim that Snowden's laptops had been "drained" made no sense on its own terms. People haven't used laptops to transport large amounts of data in years. Even before laptops became common, quantities of documents would have been stored on discs; now on thumb drives. It is true that Snowden had four laptops with him in Hong Kong, each one serving a different security purpose, but these had no relation to the quantity of documents he carried. They were on thumb drives, which were encrypted through sophisticated cryptographic methods. Having worked as an NSA hacker, Snowden knew that they could not be cracked by the NSA, let alone by Chinese or Russian intelligence agencies.

Touting the number of Snowden's laptops was a deeply misleading way to play on people's ignorance and fears—*he took so many documents, he needed four laptops to store them all!* And had the Chinese somehow drained their contents, they would have obtained nothing of value.

Equally nonsensical was the notion that Snowden would try to save himself by giving away surveillance secrets. He had dismantled his life and risked a future in prison to tell the world about a clandestine surveillance system he believed must be stopped. That he would reverse himself by helping China or Russia to improve their surveillance capabilities, all to avoid prison, was just inane.

The claim might have been nonsense, but the damage was as substantial as it was predictable. Any TV discussion of the NSA invariably involved someone asserting, with no contradiction, that China was now in possession, via Snowden, of the United States' most sensitive secrets. Under the headline "Why China Let Snowden Go," the *New Yorker* told its readers, "His usefulness was almost exhausted. Intelligence experts cited by the *Times* believed that the Chinese government 'had managed to drain the contents of the four laptops that Mr. Snowden said he brought to Hong Kong.'"

Demonizing the personality of anyone who challenges political power has been a long-standing tactic used by Washington, including by the media. One of the first and perhaps most glaring examples of that tactic was the Nixon administration's treatment of Pentagon Papers whistle-blower Daniel Ellsberg, which included breaking into the office of Ellsberg's psychoanalyst to steal Ellsberg's files and pry into his sexual history. As nonsensical as the tactic might seem—why would exposure of embarrassing personal information counter evidence of government deceit?—Ellsberg understood it clearly: people do not want to be associated with someone who has been discredited or publicly humiliated.

The same tactic was used to damage Julian Assange's reputation well before he was accused of sex crimes by two women in Sweden. Notably, the attacks on Assange were carried out by the same newspapers that had worked with him and had benefited from Chelsea Manning's disclosures, which Assange and WikiLeaks had enabled.

When the *New York Times* published what it called "The Iraq War Logs," thousands of classified documents detailing atrocities and other abuses during the war by the US military and its Iraqi allies, the paper featured a front-page article—as prominently as the disclosures themselves—by pro-war reporter John Burns that had no purpose other than to depict Assange as bizarre and paranoid, with little grip on reality.

The article described how Assange "checks into hotels under false names, dyes his hair, sleeps on sofas and floors, and uses cash instead of credit cards, often borrowed from friends." It noted what it called his "erratic and imperious behavior" and "delusional grandeur," and said his detractors "accuse him of pursuing a vendetta against the United States." And it added this psychological diagnosis from a disgruntled WikiLeaks volunteer: "He is not in his right mind."

Casting Assange as crazy and delusional became a staple of US political discourse generally and the *New York Times*'s tactics specifically. In one article, Bill Keller quoted a *Times* reporter who described Assange as "disheveled, like a bag lady walking in off the street, wearing a dingy, light-colored sport coat and cargo pants, dirty white shirt, beat-up sneakers and filthy white socks that collapsed around his ankles. He smelled as if he hadn't bathed in days."

The *Times* also led the way on the Manning coverage, insisting that what drove Manning to become a massive whistle-blower was not conviction or conscience but personality disorders and psychological instability. Numerous articles speculated, with no basis, that everything from gender struggles to anti-gay bullying in the army to conflicts with Manning's father were the prime motives in the decision to disclose such important documents.

Attributing dissent to personality disorders is hardly an American invention. Soviet dissidents were routinely institutionalized in psychological hospitals, and Chinese dissidents are still often forcibly treated for mental illness. There are obvious reasons for launching personal attacks on critics of the status quo. As noted, one is to render the critic less effective: few people want to align themselves with someone crazy or weird. Another is deterrence: when dissidents are cast out of society and demeaned as emotionally imbalanced, others are given a strong incentive not to become one.

But the key motive is logical necessity. For guardians of the status quo, there is nothing genuinely or fundamentally wrong with the prevailing order and its dominant institutions, which are viewed as just. Therefore, anyone claiming otherwise—especially someone sufficiently motivated by that belief to take radical action—must, by definition, be emotionally unstable and psychologically disabled.

Put another way, there are, broadly speaking, two choices: obedience to institutional authority or radical dissent from it. The first is a sane and valid choice only if the second is crazy and illegitimate. For defenders of the status quo, mere *correlation* between mental illness and radical opposition to prevailing orthodoxy is insufficient. Radical dissent is evidence, even proof, of a severe personality disorder.

At the heart of this formulation is an essential deceit: that dissent from institutional authority involves a moral or ideological choice, while obedience does not. With that false premise in place, society pays great attention to the motives of dissenters, but none to those who submit to our institutions, either by ensuring that their actions remain concealed or by using any other means. Obedience to authority is implicitly deemed the natural state.

In fact, both observing and breaking the rules involve moral choices, and both courses of action reveal something important about the individual involved. Contrary to the accepted premise—that radical dissent demonstrates a personality disorder—the opposite could be true: in the face of severe injustice, a refusal to dissent is the sign of a character flaw or moral failure.

Philosophy professor Peter Ludlow, writing in the *New York Times* about what he calls "the leaking, whistle-blowing and hacktivism that has vexed the United States military and the private and government intelligence communities"—activities associated with a group he calls "Generation W," with Snowden and Manning as leading examples—makes exactly this point:

> The media's desire to psychoanalyze members of generation W is natural enough. They want to know why these people are acting in a way that they, members of the corporate media, would not. But sauce for the goose is sauce for the gander; if there are psychological motivations for whistleblowing, leaking and hacktivism, there are likewise psychological motivations for closing ranks with the power structure within a system—in this case a system in which corporate media plays an important role.
>
> Similarly it is possible that the system itself is sick, even though the actors within the organization are behaving in accord with organizational etiquette and respecting the internal bonds of trust.

That discussion is one the institutional authorities are most eager to avoid. This reflexive demonization of whistle-blowers is one way that the establishment media in the United States protects the interests of those who wield power. So profound is this subservience that many of the rules of journalism are crafted, or at least applied, so as to promote the government's message.

Take, for instance, the notion that leaking classified information is some sort of malicious or criminal act. In fact, the Washington journalists who applied that view to Snowden or to me do not deplore all disclosures of secret information, only those disclosures that displease or undermine the government.

The reality is that Washington is always drowning in leaks. The most celebrated and revered DC reporters, such as Bob Woodward, have secured their position by routinely receiving classified information from high-level sources and then publishing it. Obama officials have repeatedly gone to the *New York Times* to dish out classified information about topics like drone killings and Osama bin Laden's assassination. Former secretary of defense Leon Panetta and CIA officials fed secret information to the director of *Zero Dark Thirty*, hoping the film would trumpet Obama's greatest political triumph. (At the same time Justice Department lawyers told federal courts that, to protect national security, they could not release information about the bin Laden raid.)

No establishment journalist would propose prosecution for any of the officials responsible for those leaks or for the reporters who received and then wrote about them. They would laugh at the suggestion that Bob Woodward, who has been spilling top secrets for years, and his high-level government sources are criminals.

That is because those leaks are sanctioned by Washington and serve the interests of the US government, and are thus considered appropriate and acceptable. The only leaks that the Washington media condemns are those that contain information officials would prefer to hide.

Consider what happened just moments before David Gregory suggested on *Meet the Press* that I be arrested for my reporting on the NSA. At the start of the interview, I referred to a top secret judicial ruling issued in 2011 by the FISA court that deemed substantial parts of the NSA's domestic surveillance program unconstitutional and in violation of statutes regulating spying. I only knew about the ruling because I had read about it in the NSA documents Snowden had given me. On *Meet the Press*, I had called for its release to the public.

However, Gregory sought to argue that the FISA opinion had decided differently:

With regard to that specific FISA opinion, isn't it the case, based on people that I've talked to, that the FISA opinion based on the government's request is that they said, "well, you can get this but you can't get that. That would actually go beyond the scope of what you're allowed to do"—which means that the request was changed or denied, which is the whole point the government makes, which is that there is actual judicial review here and not abuse.

The point here is not the specifics of the FISA court opinion (although when it was released, eight weeks later, it became clear that the ruling did indeed conclude that the NSA had acted illegally). More important is that Gregory claimed that he knew about the ruling because his sources had told him about it, and he then broadcast the information to the world.

Thus moments before Gregory raised the specter of arrest for my reporting, he himself leaked what he thought was top secret information from government sources. But nobody would ever suggest that Gregory's work should be criminalized. Applying the same rationale to the host of *Meet the Press* and his source would be considered ludicrous.

Indeed, Gregory would likely be incapable of understanding that his disclosure and mine were even comparable, since his came at the behest of a government seeking to defend and justify its actions, while mine was done adversarially, against the wishes of officialdom.

This, of course, is precisely the opposite of what press freedoms were supposed to achieve. The idea of a "fourth estate" is that those who exercise the greatest power need to be challenged by adversarial pushback and an insistence on transparency; the job of the press is to disprove the falsehoods that power invariably disseminates to protect itself. Without that type of journalism, abuse is inevitable. Nobody needed the US Constitution to guarantee press freedom so that journalists could befriend, amplify, and glorify political leaders; the guarantee was necessary so that journalists could do the opposite.

The double standard applied to publishing classified information is even more pronounced when it comes to the unwritten requirement of "journalistic objectivity." It was the supposed violation of this rule that made me an "activist" rather than a "journalist." As we are told endlessly, journalists do not express opinions; they simply report the facts.

This is an obvious pretense, a conceit of the profession. The perceptions and pronouncements of human beings are inherently subjective. Every news article is the product of all sorts of highly subjective cultural, nationalistic, and political assumptions. And all journalism serves one faction's interest or another's.

The relevant distinction is not between journalists who have opinions and those who have none, a category that does not exist. It is between journalists who candidly reveal their opinions and those who conceal them, pretending they have none.

The very idea that reporters should be free of opinions is far from some time-honored requirement of the profession; in fact, it is a relatively new concoction that has the effect, if not the intent, to neuter journalism.

This recent American view reflects, as Jack Shafer, Reuters's media columnist, observed, a "sad devotion to the corporatist ideal of what journalism" should be, as well as "a painful lack of historical understanding." From the United States' founding, the best and most consequential journalism frequently involved crusading reporters, advocacy, and devotion to battling injustice. The opinion-less, color-less, soul-less template of corporate journalism has drained the practice of its most worthy attributes, rendering establishment media inconsequential: a threat to nobody powerful, exactly as intended.

But aside from the inherent fallacy of objective reporting, the rule is almost never consistently applied by those who claim to believe it. Establishment journalists constantly express their opinions on a whole range of controversial issues without being denied their professional status. But if the opinions they offer are sanctioned by Washington officialdom, they are thus perceived as legitimate.

Throughout the controversy over the NSA, *Face the Nation* host Bob Schieffer denounced Snowden and defended NSA surveillance, as did Jeffrey Toobin, legal correspondent for the *New Yorker* and CNN. John Burns, the *New York Times*'s correspondent who covered the Iraq War, admitted after the fact that he supported the invasion, even describing the US troops as "my liberators" and "ministering angels." CNN's Christiane Amanpour spent the summer of 2013 advocating for the use of American military force in Syria. Yet these positions were not condemned as "activism" because, for all the reverence of objectivity, there is in fact no prohibition on journalists having opinions.

Just like the supposed rule against leaking, the "rule" of objectivity is no rule at all but rather a means of promoting the interests of the dominant political class. Hence, "NSA surveillance is legal and necessary" or "the Iraq War is right" or "the United States should invade that country" are acceptable opinions for journalists to express, and they do so all the time.

"Objectivity" means nothing more than reflecting the biases and serving the interests of entrenched Washington. Opinions are problematic only when they deviate from the acceptable range of Washington orthodoxy.

The hostility toward Snowden was not hard to explain. The hostility toward the reporter breaking the story—myself—is perhaps more complex. Part competitiveness and part payback for the years of professional criticism I had directed at US media stars, there was, I believe, also anger and even shame over the truth that adversarial journalism had exposed: reporting that angers the government reveals the real role of so many mainstream journalists, which is to amplify power.

But far and away, the most significant reason for the hostility was that establishment media figures have accepted the rule of dutiful spokespeople for political officials, especially where national security is concerned. It follows, then, that like the officials themselves, they are contemptuous of those who challenge or undermine Washington's centers of power.

The iconic reporter of the past was the definitive outsider. Many who entered the profession were inclined to oppose rather than serve power, not just by ideology but by personality and disposition. Choosing a career in journalism virtually ensured outsider status: reporters made little money, had little institutional prestige, and were typically obscure.

That has now changed. With the acquisition of media companies by the world's largest corporations, most media stars are highly paid employees of conglomerates, no different than other such employees. Instead of selling banking services or financial instruments, they peddle media products to the public on behalf of that corporation. Their career path is determined by the same metrics that amount to success in such an environment: the extent to which they please their corporate bosses and advance the company's interests.

Those who thrive within the structure of large corporations tend to be adept at pleasing rather than subverting institutional power. It follows that those who succeed in corporate journalism are suited to accommodate power. They identify with institutional authority and are skilled at serving, not combating it.

The evidence is abundant. We know about the *New York Times*'s willingness to suppress, at the White House's behest, James Risen's discovery of the NSA's illegal wiretapping program in 2004; the paper's public editor at the time described the paper's excuses for suppression as "woefully inadequate." In a similar incident at the *Los Angeles Times*, editor Dean Baquet killed a story in 2006 by his reporters about a secret collaboration between AT&T and the NSA, based on information given by whistle-blower Mark Klein. He had come forward with reams of documents to reveal AT&T's construction of a secret room in its San Francisco office, where the NSA was able to install splitters to divert telephone and Internet traffic from the telecom's customers into agency repositories.

As Klein put it, the documents showed that the NSA was "trolling through the personal lives of millions of innocent Americans." But Baquet blocked publication of the story, Klein recounted to *ABC News* in 2007, "at the request of then-Director of National Intelligence John Negroponte and then-director of the NSA Gen. Michael Hayden." Shortly thereafter, Baquet became Washington chief for the *New York Times* and was then promoted to the position of that paper's managing editor.

That the *Times* would advance so willing a servant of government interests should come as no surprise. Its public editor, Margaret Sullivan, noted that the *Times* might want to take a look in the mirror if its editors

wanted to understand why sources revealing major national security stories, like Chelsea Manning and Edward Snowden, did not feel safe or motivated to bring them their information. It is true that the *New York Times*
published large troves of documents in partnership with WikiLeaks, but
soon after, former executive editor Bill Keller took pains to distance the
paper from its partner: he publicly contrasted the Obama administration's anger toward WikiLeaks with its appreciation of the *Times* and its
"responsible" reporting.

Keller proudly trumpeted his paper's relationship with Washington
on other occasions, too. During a 2010 appearance on the BBC discussing telegrams obtained by WikiLeaks, Keller explained that the *Times*
takes direction from the US government about what it should and
shouldn't publish. The BBC host asked incredulously, "Are you saying
that you sort of go to the government in advance and say: 'What about
this, that and the other, is it all right to do this and all right to do that,' and
you get clearance, then?" The other guest, former British diplomat Carne
Ross, said that Keller's comments made him think one shouldn't go to
the *New York Times* for these telegrams. It's extraordinary that the *New
York Times* is clearing what it says about this with the U.S. Government."

But there's nothing extraordinary about this kind of media collaboration with Washington. It is routine, for example, for reporters to
adopt the official US position in disputes with foreign adversaries and
to make editorial decisions based on what best promotes "US interests"
as defined by the government. Bush DOJ lawyer Jack Goldsmith hailed
what he called "an underappreciated phenomenon: the patriotism of the
American press," meaning that the domestic media tend to show loyalty
to their government's agenda. He quoted Bush CIA and NSA director
Michael Hayden, who noted that American journalists display "a willingness to work with us," but with the foreign press, he added, "it's very,
very difficult."

This identification of the establishment media with the government is
cemented by various factors, one of them being socioeconomic. Many of
the influential journalists in the United States are now multimillionaires.
They live in the same neighborhoods as the political figures and financial elites over which they ostensibly serve as watchdogs. They attend the

same functions, they have the same circles of friends and associates, their children go to the same elite private schools.

This is one reason why journalists and government officials can switch jobs so seamlessly. The revolving door moves the media figures into high-level Washington jobs, just as government officials often leave office to the reward of a lucrative media contract. *Time* magazine's Jay Carney and Richard Stengel are now in government while Obama aides David Axelrod and Robert Gibbs are commentators on MSNBC. These are lateral transfers far more than career changes: the switch is so stream-lined precisely because the personnel still serve the same interests.

US establishment journalism is anything but an outsider force. It is wholly integrated into the nation's dominant political power. Culturally, emotionally, and socioeconomically, they are one and the same. Rich, famous, insider journalists do not want to subvert the status quo that so lavishly rewards them. Like all courtiers, they are eager to defend the system that vests them with their privileges and contemptuous of anyone who challenges that system.

It is but a short step to full identification with the needs of political officials. Hence, transparency is bad; adversarial journalism is malignant, possibly even criminal. Political leaders must be permitted to exercise power in the dark.

In September 2013, these points were powerfully made by Seymour Hersh, the Pulitzer Prize–winning reporter who uncovered both the My Lai massacre and the Abu Ghraib scandal. In an interview with the *Guardian*, Hersh railed against what he called "the timidity of journalists in America, their failure to challenge the White House and be an un-popular messenger of truth." He said the *New York Times* spends so much time "carrying water for Obama." The administration lies systematically, he argued, "yet none of the leviathans of American media, the TV networks or big print titles" pose a challenge.

Hersh's proposal "on how to fix journalism" was to "close down the news bureaus of NBC and ABC, sack 90 percent of editors in publishing and get back to the fundamental job of journalists," which is to be an out-sider. "Start promoting editors that you can't control," Hersh advocated. "The troublemakers don't get promoted," he said. Instead, "chickenshit editors" and journalists are ruining the profession because the overarching mentality is not to dare to be an outsider.

Once reporters are branded as activists, once their work is tainted by the accusation of criminal activity and they are cast out of the circle of protections for journalists, they are vulnerable to criminal treatment. This was made clear to me very quickly after the NSA story broke.

Within minutes of my return home to Rio after my stay in Hong Kong, David told me that his laptop had vanished. Suspecting that its disappearance was connected to a conversation we had while I was away, he reminded me that I had called him on Skype to talk about a large encrypted file of documents I intended to send electronically. Once it arrived, I'd said, he should put the file somewhere safe. Snowden had considered it vital that someone I trusted without question should have a complete set of the documents, in case my own archive was lost, damaged, or stolen.

"I may not be available for much longer," he said. "And you never know how your working relationship with Laura will proceed. Someone should have a set so that you'll always have access, no matter what happens."

The obvious choice was David. But I never did send the file. It was one of the things I lacked the time to do while in Hong Kong.

"Less than forty-eight hours after you told me that," David said, "my laptop was stolen from the house."

I resisted the idea that the theft of the laptop was connected to our Skype conversation. I told David I was determined that we not become those paranoid people who attribute every unexplained event in their lives to the CIA. Maybe the laptop was lost or someone visiting the house had taken it, or maybe it had been stolen in an unconnected robbery.

David shot down my theories one by one: he never took that laptop out of the house; he had turned the place upside down and it was nowhere to be found; nothing else had been taken or disturbed. I was being irrational, he felt, by refusing to entertain what seemed like the only explanation.

By this point, a number of reporters had noted that the NSA had virtually no idea what Snowden had taken or given me, not just the specific documents but also the quantity. It made sense that the US government (or perhaps even other governments) would be desperate to learn what I had. If taking David's computer would give up the information, why wouldn't they steal it?

By then, I also knew that a conversation with David via Skype was anything but secure, as vulnerable to NSA monitoring as any other form of communication. So the government had the ability to hear that I planned to send the documents to David, which gave them a strong motive to get hold of his laptop.

I learned from David Schultz, the *Guardian*'s media lawyer, that there was reason to believe David's theory of the theft. Contacts in the US intelligence community had let him know that the CIA's presence was more robust in Rio than almost anywhere else in the world and that the Rio station chief was "notoriously aggressive." Based on that, Schultz told me, "You should pretty much assume that everything you say, everything you do, and everywhere you go are being closely monitored."

I accepted that my ability to communicate would now be severely restricted. I refrained from using the telephone for anything but the vaguest and most trivial conversations. I sent and received emails only through cumbersome encryption systems. I confined my discussions with Laura, Snowden, and various sources to encrypted online chat programs. I was able to work on articles with *Guardian* editors and other journalists only by having them travel to Rio to meet face-to-face. I even exercised caution speaking to David in our home or car. The theft of the laptop had made clear the possibility that even those most intimate spaces might be under surveillance.

If I needed more evidence of the threatening climate in which I was now working, it came in the form of a report about a conversation overheard by Steve Clemons, a well-connected and regarded DC policy analyst and editor at large for the *Atlantic*.

On June 8, Clemons had been in Dulles airport in the United Airlines lounge and recounted that he overheard four US intelligence officials saying loudly that the leaker and reporter on the NSA stuff should be "disappeared." He said that he recorded a bit of the conversation on his phone. Clemons thought the talk seemed like just "bravado" but decided to publish the conversation nonetheless.

I didn't take the report too seriously, although Clemons is quite credible. But just the fact of such idle public chitchat among establishment types about "disappearing" Snowden—and the journalists with whom he was working—was alarming.

In the months that followed, the possible criminalization of the NSA reporting shifted from an abstract idea to reality. This drastic change was driven by the British government.

I first heard from Janine Gibson, via encrypted chat, about a remarkable event that had taken place at the *Guardian's* London office in mid-July. She described what she called a "radical change" in the tenor of the conversations between the *Guardian* and the GCHQ that had occurred in the past few weeks. What had originally been "very civilized conversations" about the paper's reporting had degenerated into a series of increasingly bellicose demands and then outright threats from the British spying agency.

Then, more or less suddenly, Gibson told me, the GCHQ announced that it would no longer "permit" the paper to keep publishing stories based on top secret documents. They demanded that the *Guardian* in London hand over all copies of the files received from Snowden. If the *Guardian* refused, a court order would prohibit any further reporting.

That threat was not idle. The UK has no constitutional guarantee of press freedoms. British courts are so deferential to government demands of "prior restraint" that the media can be barred in advance from reporting anything claimed to threaten national security.

Indeed, in the 1970s, the reporter who first uncovered and then reported on the existence of the GCHQ, Duncan Campbell, was arrested and prosecuted. In the UK the courts could shut the *Guardian* down at any point and seize all its material and equipment. "No judge would say no if they were asked," Janine said. "We know that and they know we know it."

The documents the *Guardian* possessed were a fraction of the full archive Snowden had passed on in Hong Kong. He had felt strongly that reporting relating specifically to the GCHQ should be done by British journalists, and on one of the last days in Hong Kong, he gave a copy of those documents to Ewen MacAskill.

On our call, Janine told me that she and editor Alan Rusbridger, along with other staffers, had been on a retreat the previous weekend in a remote area outside of London. They suddenly heard that GCHQ officials were on their way to the *Guardian* newsroom in London where they intended to seize the hard drives on which the documents were stored. "You've had your fun," they told Rusbridger, as he later recounted, "now we want the stuff back." The group had been in the country for only two and a half hours before they heard from the GCHQ. "We had to drive straight back to London to defend the building. It was very hairy," Janine said.

The GCHQ demanded that the *Guardian* turn over all copies of the archive. Had the paper complied, the government would have learned what Snowden had passed on and his legal standing could have been further jeopardized. Instead, the *Guardian* agreed to destroy all the relevant hard drives with GCHQ officials overseeing the process to make sure that the destruction was done to their satisfaction. What occurred was, in Janine's words, "a very elaborate dance of stalling, diplomacy, smuggling, and then cooperative 'demonstrable destruction.'"

The term "demonstrable destruction" was newly invented by the GCHQ to describe what took place. The officials accompanied *Guardian* staff, including the editor in chief, to the basement of the newsroom and watched as they smashed the hard drives to pieces, even demanding that they break particular parts further "just to be sure there was nothing in the mangled bits of metal that could possibly be of any interest to passing Chinese agents," Rusbridger recounted. "We can call off the black helicopters," he recalled a security expert joking, as *Guardian* staff "swept up the remains of a MacBook Pro."

The image of a government sending agents into a newspaper to force destruction of its computers is inherently shocking, the sort of thing Westerners are told to believe happens only in places like China, Iran, and Russia. But it is also stunning that a revered newspaper would voluntarily, meekly, submit to such orders.

If the government was threatening to shut down the paper, why not call its bluff and force the threat out into the daylight? As Snowden said when he heard the about the threat, "the only right answer is, go ahead, shut us down!" Voluntarily complying in secret is to enable the government to conceal its true character from the world: a state that thuggishly stops journalists from reporting on one of the most significant stories in the public interest.

Worse, the act of destroying the materials that a source had risked his liberty and even life to reveal was utterly antithetical to the purpose of journalism.

Aside from the need to expose such despotic behavior, it is unquestionably newsworthy when a government marches into a newsroom and forces a paper to destroy its information. But the *Guardian* apparently intended to remain silent, powerfully underscoring how precarious any freedom of the press is in the UK.

In any case, Gibson assured me that the *Guardian* still had a copy of the archive in its New York office. Then she told me some startling news: another set of those documents was now with the *New York Times*, given by Alan Rusbridger to executive editor Jill Abramson, to ensure that the paper would still have access to the files even if a British court tried to force the *Guardian* US to destroy its copy.

This, too, was not good news. Not only had the *Guardian* agreed, in secret, to destroy its own documents but, without consulting or even advising Snowden or me, it had given them to the very newspaper Snowden had excluded because he did not trust its close and subservient relationship to the US government.

From the *Guardian*'s perspective, it could not afford to be cavalier in the face of UK government threats, given the absence of constitutional protection and hundreds of employees and a century-old paper to protect. And destroying the computers was better than handing GCHQ the archive. But I was nonetheless disturbed by their compliance with the government's demands and, more so, their evident decision not to report it.

Still, both before the destruction of its hard drives and after, the *Guardian* remained aggressive and intrepid in how it published

Snowden's revelations—more, I believe, than any other paper comparable in size and stature would have been. Despite the authorities' intimidation tactics, which only intensified, the editors continued to publish one NSA and GCHQ story after the next, and they deserve much credit for doing so.

But Laura and Snowden were both quite angry—that the *Guardian* would submit to such government bullying and that they would then keep quiet about what had happened. Snowden was particularly furious that the GCHQ archive had ended up with the *New York Times*. He felt that this was a breach of his agreement with the *Guardian* and of his wish that only British journalists would work on the British documents, and especially that the *New York Times* would not be given documents. As it turned out, Laura's reaction eventually led to dramatic consequences.

From the beginning of our reporting, Laura's relationship with the *Guardian* was uneasy and now the tension broke out into the open. While working together for a week in Rio, Laura and I discovered that part of one of the NSA archives Snowden had given me on the day he went into hiding in Hong Kong (but hadn't had the chance to give to Laura) was corrupted. Laura was unable to fix it in Rio but thought she might be able to do so when back in Berlin.

A week later, after she returned to Berlin, Laura let me know that the archive was ready to return to me. We arranged for a *Guardian* employee to fly to Berlin, pick up the archive, and then bring it to me in Rio. But clearly in a state of fear after the GCHQ drama, the *Guardian* employee then told Laura that instead of giving the archive to him personally, she should FedEx it to me.

This made Laura as agitated and furious as I had ever seen her. "Don't you see what they're doing?" she asked me. "They want to be able to say, 'We had nothing to do with transporting these documents, it was Glenn and Laura who passed them back and forth.'" She added that using FedEx to send top secret documents across the world—and to send them from her in Berlin to me in Rio, a neon sign to interested parties—was as severe a breach of operational security as she could imagine.

"I will never trust them again," she declared.

But I still needed that archive. It contained vital documents related to stories I was working on, as well as many others still to be published.

Janine insisted that the problem was a misunderstanding, that the staffer had misinterpreted comments by his supervisor, that some managers in London were now skittish about carrying documents between Laura and me. There was no problem, she said. Someone from the *Guardian* would fly to Berlin to pick up the archive that same day.

It was too late. "I will never, ever give these documents to the *Guardian*," Laura said. "I just don't trust them now."

The size and sensitivity of the archive made Laura unwilling to send it electronically. It had to be delivered personally, by someone she trusted. That someone was David, who, when he heard about the problem, immediately volunteered to go to Berlin. We both saw that this was the perfect solution. David understood every part of the story, Laura knew and trusted him, and he had been planning to visit her anyway to talk about potential new projects. Janine happily signed on to the idea and agreed that the *Guardian* would cover the cost of David's trip.

The *Guardian*'s travel office booked David's flights on British Airways and then emailed him the itinerary. The notion that he would have any problem traveling never occurred to us. *Guardian* journalists who had written stories about the Snowden archives, as well as staffers who had couriered documents back and forth, had flown in and out of Heathrow Airport multiple times without incident. Laura herself had flown to London only a few weeks earlier. Why would anyone think that David—a far more peripheral figure—would be at risk?

David left for Berlin on Sunday, August 11, due to return a week later with the archive from Laura. But on the morning of his expected arrival, I was woken up early by a call. The voice on the line, speaking with a thick British accent, identified himself as a "security agent at Heathrow Airport" and asked whether I knew David Miranda. "We're calling to inform you," he went on, "that we've detained Mr. Miranda under the Terrorism Act of 2000, Schedule 7."

The word "terrorism" did not sink in right away—I was more confused than anything else. The first question I asked was how long he had been detained at that point, and when I heard that it had been three hours already, I knew that this was no standard immigration screening. The man explained that the UK had the "legal right" to hold him for a total of nine hours, at which point a court could extend the time. Or they could arrest him. "We don't yet know what we intend to do," the security agent said.

Both the United States and the United Kingdom have made clear that there are no limits—ethical, legal, or political—that they will observe when they claim to be acting in the name of "terrorism." Now David was in custody, being held under a terrorism law. He hadn't even tried to enter the UK: he was passing through the airport in transit. The UK authorities had reached out into what is technically not even British territory and nabbed him, and had invoked the most chilling and murky grounds to do so.

Guardian lawyers and Brazilian diplomats got to work, immediately attempting to secure David's release. I wasn't worried about how David would handle the detention. An unimaginably difficult life growing up orphaned in one of the poorest favelas in Rio de Janeiro had made him extremely strong, willful, and street smart. I knew he would understand exactly what was happening and why, and I had no doubt that he was giving his interrogators at least as hard a time as they were giving him. Still, the *Guardian* lawyers noted how rare it was for anyone to be held this long.

Researching the Terrorism Act, I learned that only three out of every thousand people are stopped and most interrogations, over 97 percent, last under an hour. Only 0.06 percent are held for more than six hours. There seemed to be a substantial chance that David would be arrested once the nine-hour mark arrived.

The stated purpose of the Terrorism Act, as the name suggests, is to question people about ties to terrorism. The detention power, the UK government claims, is used "to determine whether that person is or has been involved in the commission, preparation or instigation of acts of terrorism." There was no remote justification for detaining David under such a law, unless my reporting was now being equated with terrorism, which appeared to be the case.

With each hour that went by, the situation seemed increasingly grim. All I knew was that Brazilian diplomats, as well as the *Guardian*'s lawyers, were trying to locate David at the airport and get access to him, all without success. But at two minutes shy of the nine-hour mark, an email message from Janine gave me the news I needed to hear, in one word: "RELEASED."

David's shocking detention was instantly condemned around the world as a thuggish attempt at intimidation. A report from Reuters confirmed that this was indeed the British government's intention: "One U.S. security official told Reuters that one of the main purposes of the . . . detention and questioning of Miranda was to send a message to recipients of Snowden's materials, including the *Guardian*, that the British government was serious about trying to shut down the leaks."

But as I told the horde of journalists who gathered at the Rio airport, waiting for David's return, the UK's bullying tactics would not impede my reporting. If anything, I was even more emboldened. The UK authorities had shown themselves to be abusive in the extreme; the only proper response, in my view, was to exert more pressure and demand greater transparency and accountability. That is a primary function of journalism. When asked how I thought the episode would be perceived, I said I thought the UK government would come to regret what they had done because it would make them look repressive and abusive.

A crew from Reuters wildly distorted and mistranslated my comments—which were made in Portuguese—to mean that in response to what they had done to David, I would now publish documents about the UK I had previously decided to withhold. As a wire service item, this distortion was quickly transmitted worldwide.

For the next two days, the media angrily reported that I had vowed to carry out "revenge journalism." It was an absurd misrepresentation: my point was that the UK's abusive behavior had only made me more determined to continue my work. But as I had learned many times over, claiming that your comments have been reported out of context does nothing to halt the media machine.

Misreported or not, the reaction to my comments was telling: the United Kingdom and the United States had for years behaved as bullies, responding to any challenge with threats and worse. The British authorities had only recently forced the *Guardian* to destroy its computers and had just detained my partner under a terrorism law. Whistle-blowers had been prosecuted and journalists threatened with prison. Yet even the perception of a forceful response to such aggression is met with great indignation from the state's loyalists and apologists: *My God! He talked of revenge!* Meek submission to intimidation by officialdom is viewed as an obligation; defiance is condemned as an act of insubordination.

Once David and I finally escaped the cameras, we were able to talk. He told me that he had been defiant throughout the entire nine hours, but he admitted that he was scared.

He had clearly been targeted: the passengers on his flight were instructed to show their passports to agents waiting outside the plane. When they saw his, he was detained under the terrorism law and "threatened from the first second until the last," David said, that he would go to prison if he did not "cooperate fully." They took all of his electronic equipment, including his cell phone containing personal photographs, his contacts, and his chats with friends, forcing him to give up the password to his cell phone upon threat of arrest. "I feel like they invaded my whole life, like I'm naked," he said.

David had kept thinking about what the United States and the United Kingdom had done under the cover of fighting terrorism over the last decade. "They kidnap people, imprison them without charges or a lawyer, disappear them, put them in Guantanamo, they kill them," David said. "There's really nothing scarier than being told by those two governments that you're a terrorist," he told me—something that would not occur to most American or British citizens. "You realize they can do anything to you."

The controversy over David's detention went on for weeks. It led the news in Brazil for days, and the Brazilian population was almost uniformly outraged. British politicians called for reform of the Terrorism Act. Of course it was gratifying that people recognized the UK's act for the abuse that it was. At the same time, though, the law had been a scandal for years—but mostly used against Muslims, so few people had cared. It shouldn't have needed the detention of the spouse of a high-profile, white, Western journalist to bring attention to the abuse, but it did.

Unsurprisingly, it was revealed that the British government had spoken with Washington in advance of David's detention. When asked in a press conference, a White House spokesman said, "There was a heads-up . . . so this was something we had an indication was likely to occur." The White House refused to condemn the detention and acknowledged that it had taken no steps to stop or even discourage it.

Most journalists understood how dangerous this step was. "Journalism is not terrorism," declared an indignant Rachel Maddow on her MS-NBC show, cutting to the heart of the matter. But not everyone felt the same way. Jeffrey Toobin praised the UK government on prime-time television, equating David's conduct to that of a "drug mule." Toobin added that David should be grateful he hadn't been arrested and prosecuted.

That specter seemed a little more plausible when the British government announced that it formally commenced a criminal investigation into the documents David had been carrying. (David himself had initiated a lawsuit against the UK authorities, alleging that his detention was unlawful because it had nothing to do with the sole purpose of the law under which he was held: to investigate a person's ties to terrorism.) It is hardly surprising that authorities would be so emboldened when the most prominent of journalists likens crucial reporting in the public interest to the rank illegality of drug traffickers.

Shortly before he died in 2005, the heralded Vietnam war correspondent David Halberstam gave a speech to students at the Columbia Journalism School. The proudest moment of his career, he told them, was when US generals in Vietnam threatened to demand that his editors at the *New York Times* remove him from covering the war. He had, Halberstam said, "enraged Washington and Saigon by filing pessimistic dispatches on the war." The generals considered him "the enemy" since he had also interrupted their press conferences to accuse them of lying.

For Halberstam, infuriating the government was a source of pride,

the true purpose and calling of journalism. He knew that being a journalist meant taking risks, confronting rather than submitting to abuses
of power.

Today, for many in the profession, praise from the government for
"responsible" reporting—for taking its direction about what should and
should not be published—is a badge of honor. That this is the case is the
true measure of how far adversarial journalism in the United States has
fallen.

EPILOGUE

In the very first online conversation I had with Edward Snowden, he told me he had only one fear about coming forward: that his revelations might be greeted with apathy and indifference, which would mean he had unraveled his life and risked imprisonment for nothing. To say that this fear has gone unrealized is to dramatically understate the case.

Indeed, the effects of this unfolding story have been far greater, more enduring, and more wide-ranging than we ever dreamed possible. It focused the world's attention on the dangers of ubiquitous state surveillance and pervasive government secrecy. It triggered the first global debate about the value of individual privacy in the digital age and prompted challenges to America's hegemonic control over the Internet. It changed the way people around the world viewed the reliability of any statements made by US officials and transformed relations between countries. It radically altered views about the proper role of journalism in relation to government power. And within the United States, it gave rise to an ideologically diverse, trans-partisan coalition pushing for meaningful reform of the surveillance state.

One episode in particular underscored the profound shifts brought about by Snowden's revelations. Just a few weeks after my first Snowden-based article for the *Guardian* exposed the NSA's bulk metadata collection, two members of Congress jointly introduced a bill to defund that NSA program. Remarkably, the bill's two cosponsors were John Conyers, a Detroit liberal serving his twentieth term in the House, and Justin Amash, a conservative Tea Party member in only his second House term. It is hard to imagine two more different members of Congress, yet here they were, united in opposition to the NSA's domestic spying. And their proposal quickly gained dozens of cosponsors across the entire ideological spectrum, from the most liberal to the most conservative and everything in between—a truly rare event in Washington.

When the bill came up for a vote, the debate was televised on C-SPAN, and I watched it while chatting online with Snowden, who was also watching C-SPAN on his computer in Moscow. We were both amazed at what we saw. It was, I believe, the first time he truly appreciated the magnitude of what he had accomplished. One House member after another stood up to vehemently denounce the NSA program, scoffing at the idea that collecting data on the calls of every single American is necessary to stop terrorism. It was by far the most aggressive challenge to the national security state to emerge from Congress since the 9/11 attacks.

Until the Snowden revelations, it was simply inconceivable that any bill designed to gut a major national security program could receive more than a handful of votes. But the final vote tally on the Conyers-Amash bill shocked official Washington: it failed by just a tiny margin, 205–217. Support for it was wholly bipartisan, with 111 Democrats joining 94 Republicans to vote for the bill. This discarding of traditional party-line divisions was as exciting to Snowden and me as the substantial support for reining in the NSA. Official Washington depends upon blind tribalism engendered by rigid partisan warfare. If the red versus blue framework can be eroded, and then transcended, there is much more hope for policy making based on the actual interests of the citizenry.

Over the following months, as more and more NSA stories were published around the world, many pundits predicted that the public would lose interest in the subject. But, in fact, interest in the surveillance discussion only intensified, not just domestically but internationally. The events of a single week in December 2013—more than six months after my first report appeared in the *Guardian*—illustrate just how much Snowden's disclosures continue to resonate and just how untenable the NSA's position has become.

The week began with the dramatic opinion issued by US federal judge Richard Leon that the NSA metadata collection was likely to be found in violation of the Fourth Amendment to the US Constitution, denouncing it as "almost Orwellian" in scope. As noted, the Bush-appointed jurist pointedly added that the government had not cited a single instance "in which analysis of the NSA's bulk metadata collection" had stopped a terrorist attack. Just two days later, President Obama's advisory panel, formed when the NSA scandal first broke, issued its 308-page report. That report, too, decisively rejected the NSA's claims about the vital importance of its spying. "Our review suggests that the information contributed to terrorist investigations by the use of [the Patriot Act's] section 215 telephony meta-data was not essential to preventing attacks," the panel wrote, confirming that in not a single instance would the outcome have been different "without the section 215 telephony meta-data program."

Meanwhile, outside the United States the NSA's week was going no better. The UN general assembly unanimously voted in favor of a resolution—introduced by Germany and Brazil—affirming that online privacy is a fundamental human right, which one expert characterized as "a strong message to the United States that it's time to reverse course and end NSA dragnet surveillance." And on the same day, Brazil announced that it would not award a long-expected $4.5 billion contract for fighter jets to US-based Boeing but instead would purchase planes from the Swedish company Saab. Brazil's outrage over the NSA's spying on its leaders, its companies, and its citizenry was clearly a key factor in the surprise decision. "The NSA problem ruined it for the Americans," a Brazilian government source told Reuters.

None of this is to say that the battle has been won. The security state is incredibly powerful, probably even more so than our highest elected officials, and it boasts a wide array of influential loyalists ready to defend it at all costs. So it is not surprising that it, too, has scored some victories. Two weeks after Judge Leon's ruling, another federal judge, exploiting the memory of 9/11, declared the NSA program constitutional in a different case. European allies have backed away from their initial displays of anger, falling meekly in line with the United States, as they so often do. Support from the American public has also been inconstant: polls show that a majority of Americans, though they oppose the NSA programs that Snowden exposed, nonetheless want to see him prosecuted for those exposures. And top US officials have even begun arguing that not only Snowden himself but also some of the journalists with whom he worked, including me, deserve prosecution and imprisonment.

Yet the supporters of the NSA have clearly been set back on their heels, and their arguments against reform have been increasingly flimsy. Defenders of suspicionless mass surveillance often insist, for example, that some spying is always necessary. But this is a straw man proposition; nobody disagrees with that. The alternative to mass surveillance is not the complete elimination of surveillance. It is, instead, targeted surveillance, aimed only at those for whom there is substantial evidence to believe they are engaged in real wrongdoing. Such targeted surveillance is far more likely to stop terrorist plots than the current "collect it all" approach, which drowns intelligence agencies in so much data that analysts cannot sift it effectively. And unlike indiscriminate mass surveillance, it is consistent with American constitutional values and basic precepts of Western justice.

Indeed, in the aftermath of the surveillance abuse scandals uncovered by the Church Committee in the 1970s, it was precisely this principle— that the government must provide some evidence of probable wrongdoing or status as a foreign agent before it can listen in on a person's conversations—which led to the establishment of the FISA court. Unfortunately, that court has been made into a mere rubber stamp, providing no meaningful judicial review to the government's surveillance requests. But the essential idea is sound nonetheless, and shows a way forward. Converting the FISA court into a real judicial system, rather than the one-sided current setup in which only the government gets to state its case, would be a positive reform.

Such domestic legislative changes by themselves are unlikely to be sufficient for solving the surveillance problem because the national security state so often co-opts the entities meant to provide oversight. (As we have seen, for instance, the congressional intelligence committees have by now been thoroughly captured.) But these sorts of legislative changes can at least bolster the principle that indiscriminate mass surveillance has no place in a democracy ostensibly guided by constitutional guarantees of privacy.

Other steps, too, can be taken to reclaim online privacy and limit state surveillance. International efforts—currently being led by Germany and Brazil—to build new Internet infrastructure so that most network traffic no longer has to transit the United States could go a long way toward loosening the American grip on the Internet. And individuals also have a role to play in reclaiming their own online privacy. Refusing to use the services of tech companies that collaborate with the NSA and its allies will put pressure on those companies to stop such collaboration and will spur their competitors to devote themselves to privacy protections. Already, a number of European tech companies are promoting their email and chat services as a superior alternative to offerings from Google and Facebook, trumpeting the fact that they do not—and will not—provide user data to the NSA.

Additionally, to prevent governments from intruding into personal communications and Internet use, all users should be adopting encryption and browsing-anonymity tools. This is particularly important for people working in sensitive areas, such as journalists, lawyers, and human rights activists. And the technology community should continue developing more effective and user-friendly anonymity and encryption programs.

On all of these fronts, there is a great deal of work still to be done. But less than a year after I first met Snowden in Hong Kong, there is no question that his disclosures have already brought about fundamental, irreversible changes in many countries and many realms. And beyond the specifics of NSA reform, Snowden's acts have also profoundly advanced the cause of government transparency and reform in general. He has created a model to inspire others, and future activists will likely follow in his footsteps, perfecting the methods he embraced.

The Obama administration, which has brought more prosecutions against leakers than all prior presidencies combined, has sought to create a climate of fear that would stifle any attempts at whistle-blowing. But Snowden has destroyed that template. He has managed to remain free, outside the grasp of the United States; what's more, he has refused to remain in hiding but proudly came forward and identified himself. As a result, the public image of him is not a convict in orange jumpsuit and shackles but an independent, articulate figure who can speak for himself, explaining what he did and why. It is no longer possible for the US government to distract from the message simply by demonizing the messenger. There is a powerful lesson here for future whistle-blowers: speaking the truth does not have to destroy your life.

And for the rest of us, Snowden's inspirational effect is no less profound. Quite simply, he has reminded everyone about the extraordinary ability of any human being to change the world. An ordinary person in all outward respects—raised by parents without particular wealth or power, lacking even a high school diploma, working as an obscure employee of a giant corporation—he has, through a single act of conscience, literally altered the course of history.

Even the most committed activists are often tempted to succumb to defeatism. The prevailing institutions seem too powerful to challenge; orthodoxies feel too entrenched to uproot; there are always many parties with a vested interest in maintaining the status quo. But it is human beings collectively, not a small number of elites working in secret, who can decide what kind of world we want to live in. Promoting the human capacity to reason and make decisions: that is the purpose of whistle-blowing, of activism, of political journalism. And that's what is happening now, thanks to the revelations brought about by Edward Snowden.

A NOTE ON SOURCES

The endnotes and index for this book can be found at www.glenngreenwald.net.

ACKNOWLEDGMENTS

In recent years, the efforts of Western governments to conceal their most consequential actions from their own citizens have been repeatedly thwarted by a series of remarkable disclosures from courageous whistleblowers. Time after time, people who worked inside government agencies or the military establishment of the United States and its allies have decided that they could not remain silent when they discovered serious wrongdoing. Instead, they came forward and made official misdeeds public, sometimes consciously breaking the law to do so, and always at great personal cost: risking their careers, their personal relationships, and their freedom. Everyone living in a democracy, everyone who values transparency and accountability, owes these whistleblowers a huge debt of gratitude.

The long line of predecessors who inspired Edward Snowden begins with Pentagon Papers leaker Daniel Ellsberg, one of my long-time personal heroes and now my friend and colleague, whose example I try to follow in all of the work I do. Other courageous whistle-blowers who have endured persecution to bring vital truths to the world include Chelsea Manning, Jesselyn Radack, and Thomas Tamm, as well as former NSA officials Thomas Drake and Bill Binney. They played a critical role in inspiring Snowden as well.

Bringing to light the ubiquitous system of suspicionless surveillance being secretly constructed by the United States and its allies was Snowden's own self-sacrificing act of conscience. To watch an otherwise ordinary 29-year-old knowingly risk life in prison for the sake of a principle, acting in defense of basic human rights, was simply stunning. Snowden's fearlessness and unbreakable tranquility—grounded in the conviction that he was doing the right thing—drove all the reporting I did on this story, and will profoundly influence me for the rest of my life.

The impact this story had would have been impossible without my incomparably brave and brilliant journalistic partner and friend, Laura Poitras. Despite years of harassment at the hands of the US government for the films she made, she never once hesitated in pursuing this story aggressively. Her insistence on personal privacy, her aversion to the public spotlight, has sometimes obscured how indispensable she has been to all of the reporting we were able to do. But her expertise, her strategic genius, her judgment, and her courage were at the heart and soul of all the work we did. We spoke almost every day and made every big decision collaboratively. I could not have asked for a more perfect partnership or a more emboldening and inspiring friendship.

As Laura and I knew it would be, Snowden's courage ended up being contagious. Numerous journalists pursued this story intrepidly, including *Guardian* editors Janine Gibson, Stuart Millar, and Alan Rusbridger, along with several of the paper's reporters, led by Ewen MacAskill. Snowden was able to remain free and thus able to participate in the debate he helped trigger because of the daring, indispensable support given by WikiLeaks and its official, Sarah Harrison, who helped him leave Hong Kong and then remained with him for months in Moscow at the expense of her ability to safely return to the United Kingdom, her own country.

Numerous friends and colleagues provided me very wise counsel and support in many difficult situations, including the ACLU's Ben Wizner and Jameel Jaffer; my lifelong best friend, Norman Fleisher; one of the world's best and bravest investigative journalists, Jeremy Scahill; the strong and resourceful Brazilian reporter Sonia Bridi of Globo; and Freedom of the Press Foundation Executive Director Trevor Timm. Family members, who often worried about what was happening (as only family members can), nonetheless remained steadfastly supportive (as only family members can), including my parents, my brother Mark, and my sister-in-law Christine.

This was not an easy book to write, particularly under the circumstances, which is why I'm truly grateful to Metropolitan Books: to Connor Guy for his efficient management; to Grigory Tovbis for his insightful editorial contributions and technical proficiency; and especially to Riva Hocherman, whose intelligence and high standards have made her the best possible editor for this book. This is the second consecutive book I've published with Sara Bershtel and her remarkably wise and creative mind, and I cannot imagine ever wanting to write one without her. My literary agent, Dan Conaway, was once again a steady and wise voice throughout the process. Deep thanks as well to Taylor Barnes for her critical help in putting this book together; her research talents and intellectual energy leave no doubt that a stellar journalistic career lies ahead.

As always, at the center of everything I do is my life partner, my husband of nine years, my soul mate David Miranda. The ordeal to which he was subjected as part of the reporting we did was infuriating and grotesque, but the benefit was that the world got to see what an extraordinary human being he is. Every step of the way, he injected me with fearlessness, bolstered my resolve, guided my choices, offered insights that made things clear, and stood right by me, unflinching, with unconditional support and love. A partnership like that is incomparably valuable, as it extinguishes fear, destroys limits, and makes everything possible.

WITHDRAWN FROM STOCK

she's up the duff, again!!